PROMOTIONAL
FEATS

PROMOTIONAL FEATS

FEATS

The Role of Planned
Events in the
Marketing
Communications Mix

ERIC J. SOARES

QUORUM BOOKS

NEW YORK • WESTPORT, CONNECTICUT • LONDON

Library of Congress Cataloging-in-Publication Data

Soares, Eric J.
   Promotional feats : the role of planned events in the marketing
communications mix / Eric J. Soares.
     p.   cm.
   Includes bibliographical references and index.
   ISBN 0–89930–515–6 (lib. bdg.)
    1. Sales promotion. 2. Promotion of special events. I. Title.
HF5438.5.S64 1991
658.8'2—dc20   91–7809

British Library Cataloguing in Publication Data is available.

Library of Congress Catalog Card Number: 91–7809
ISBN: 0–89930–515–6

First published in 1991

Quorum Books, 88 Post Road West, Westport, CT 06881
An imprint of Greenwood Publishing Group, Inc.

Printed in the United States of America

The paper used in this book complies with the
Permanent Paper Standard issued by the National
Information Standards Organization (Z39.48–1984).

10 9 8 7 6 5 4 3 2 1

This book is dedicated to Ben Franklin,
the icon of America,
father of American advertising,
inventor, diplomat, and philanthropist.

Contents

Preface

This is a book of stories that chronicle promotional feats—excellent promotional activities that exceed goals and make headlines. Promotional feats are the first, best, or most powerful advertisements, sales promotions, publicity stunts, sales activities, or displays. Even a product or service can achieve promotional feat status by compelling consumers to buy though its inherent communication.

In this work, which is intended for practicing or aspiring promotion executives, marketing managers, and entrepreneurs, I focus on excellent consumer-based promotion activities. Most promotion events described are for products, although I intend the word *product* to include services, persons, events, information, entertainment—anything that is marketed.

Most companies mentioned are large manufacturers because they spend the most on promotion and make the news the most. By *company* I mean all organizations—big, small, service, retail, international, profit, nonprofit.

As an aware consumer and by selling for 32 years, I have gained experience and insight into promotions. I began my selling career at age five by harvesting and marketing digger pine nuts, mistletoe, and blackberries. Now, as president of Tsunami Products, I sell small boats. I am also an associate professor of marketing at California State University in Hayward, where I teach promotion, business communication, sales training, and marketing research. I help small businesses in the San Francisco Bay area with cost-effective promotions and marketing research.

Most of the stories you will read here were gleaned from other sources—mostly books, magazines, and newspapers. For the past two years, I searched through every page of my local newspaper, the *San Francisco Chronicle*, and *Newsweek*. I try to give credit when due, but I may have missed someone. I apologize in advance.

Also, because most information came from published sources, I have no way of verifying all the facts. In other words, I didn't see many of these feats, I only read about them, so what actually occurred may differ from my portrayal. So I ask that you view these stories as illustrative and motivational.

I think you will find these feats—from military, athletic, and entertainment feats to advertising and sales promotion feats—to be entertaining and inspiring. If you read just one story that moves you to create and execute excellent promotions, then this book will have served its purpose. Have fun!

PROMOTIONAL
FEATS

Promotional Feats:
A Marketing
Communication Function

*"The entire marketing mix—promotion *and* product, price, and place—must be coordinated for greatest communication impact."*
—Kotler & Armstrong

MARKETING IS COMMUNICATION! That got your attention, even though the statement is not entirely true. I estimate that about 90 percent of marketing involves communicating, usually from sender (your organization) to receiver (consumers and relevant publics). The 10 percent residual comprises the remainder of the marketing function.

In this chapter, I will demonstrate that marketing is primarily communication. I further show that marketing communications (management of advertising, promotions, and publicity), to be effective, must cut through the clutter of messages to impact consumers. To effectively reach and persuade your target audience, I describe and advocate the strategic and tactical use of promotional feats (superlative advertising, promotions or publicity efforts), the subject of this book. To showcase the pervasiveness and importance of communication in marketing, let us first examine the state of the world in the near future.

THE MARKETING ENVIRONMENT OF THE 1990S

We know that for an organization to fulfill its specific mission to help humans meet their needs or desires, its leaders must assess its strengths and weaknesses (and those of its competition) and develop programs to reach target consumers. These marketing programs are executed by manipulating the marketing mix within the ever-changing marketing environment.

And what will the general marketing environment look like as we enter the final decade before the year 2000? We will see an international free market featuring a reunified Germany and products from Eastern Europe. The Soviet Union will undoubtedly begin to compete in the world market. Mainland China will get its act together and join a Pacific Rim common market, led by Japan and California. A short time ago, no one would have foreseen any of this. But thanks to great people willing to take big risks, good timing, and worldwide mediated communication (satellite television and telephone), all this is possible, even likely. Marketers must be ready to take advantage of new international challenges and opportunities.

And there's more. We will see companies within industries working together to propel us into the twenty-first century. By 1999, we'll be flying and shipping goods on the space plane, thanks to joint effort. It's probable that sea and space will be used for commerce more than ever before imagined. We may see the advent of airports and resort hotels located not on oceanfront property, but on the ocean itself—or in space.

Marketing opportunities and responsibilities will stem from consumers' concern for the environment. The blossoming industries of bioengineering, recycling, and toxic waste cleanup will provide many jobs. There will be plenty of competition and room for marketers in environmentalism, according to a *Forbes* cover story (Morgenson and Eisenstodt 1990), if we would let "the free market reconcile the industrial revolution with the age of environmentalism" (p. 100).

Auto manufacturers will scramble to produce hydrogen- or electric-powered cars. GM may lead the way. Where will we get the electricity needed to run these automobiles? Big Oil. Yes, the oil companies will take advantage of their research on solar and wind power to market "energy" stations to replace gas stations. Believe me, the oil industry is just as disgusted as the general public with all these oil spills. They are looking for alternatives. Do people really do this kind of thing? Yes—just ask Chevron.

Speaking of electricity, we'll commute in electromagnetically levitated trains—and later our cars will run on electromagnetic "streets." All this is courtesy of the burgeoning superconductor manufacturing and support industries. Think of the jobs that will be created in the construction trades as cities gear up for new modes of transportation.

Megamemory personal computers that run tomorrow's electronic homes and businesses, along with cellular phones and videophones, will be affordable. Computers and robotic devices will do a lot of work and make our lives easier. It's hard to believe that in 1980 most food stores did not have UPC scanners, banks had no automated tellers, and fax machines were unknown to the general public. Now, not only are we aware of these services, but we need and prefer them, thanks to good marketing communication efforts to educate and persuade us. Do you think the world is ready for yet more efficient, convenient, and satisfying products and services? Who will develop and market all these great new things? Smart people.

But you ain't seen nothin' yet. The arts, sports, travel, human potential, entertainment, and recreation industries will flourish in the 1990s as more people worldwide have more disposable income and more leisure time. There's lots of room for good marketing people here.

How can I make these predictions? I am not clairvoyant, I just read a lot. And there's a lot to read—more than ever. We get information from all kinds of print media, television and radio, movies, and computerized information retrieval networks. We are exposed to much more data chaff than we can possibly absorb. However, if we select only useful information, cogitate and then extrapolate, we can predict the future. That's no secret. We live in the midst of the information age and the communication age. There are few limits to obtaining information and many ways to communicate it. Knowing and using the best ways to communicate will serve marketers well in the nineties. More on that later.

Public Image

Communication will help marketers keep abreast of and participate in economic and political changes and governmental regulations and policies. Corporations big and small will have to consider their public image in the coming years, for public interest groups are lobbying government and boldly communicating their message to the entire globe. Their message is simple: Take care of the world. They want human rights and liberty for all. They want to heal and preserve the planet. In short, they want a truly higher standard of living. The question is, can we as marketers satisfy our customers?

Some countries have not polished their act recently and their public images have turned sour. South Africa, China, and Colombia serve as examples. But they will change when they tire of world censure.

During the past few years, some companies have befouled their public images. Let's take the case of Nestlé, the Swiss multinational conglomerate. They make chocolate, the very best, they claim. Nestlé also makes infant formula to replace or supplement breast milk. Sales were big after World War II but declined with the birth rate in developed countries. Nestlé looked for a new market to increase sales, found it in third world countries, aggressively marketed their formula, and achieved market share dominance in a billion-dollar industry. So what is wrong with this tale? You remember, because you read about it somewhere. During the late 1970s and mid–1980s, hundreds of articles were written about Nestlé.

According to Hartley (1986: 47–61), Nestlé used several promotional strategies that would have been appropriate with a different population but harmed third world consumers. Specifically, it employed missionary sales agents under the guise of "milk nurses" to give away samples and discourage breast feeding. Nestlé also promoted heavily through physicians. In addition to their marketing practices, Nestlé was criticized for bad quality control and for not ensuring that customers knew how to properly use the formula. Many infant illnesses and deaths resulted. This triggered responses from health agencies and concerned citizens around the world. The media blasted Nestlé. Consumer boycotts of Nestlé products were organized—with notable success. A worldwide boycott started in 1977 and was in full swing by 1981 when the World Health Organization came down on infant formula advertising.

What did Nestlé do? Nothing, at first. But the negative publicity worsened. They hired public relations firms to help them, but they were not successful with mailings to clergy. Nestlé had taken an adversarial approach to criticism and it failed. Finally, Nestlé agreed to be monitored by a special committee. By 1984, most consumer groups loosened their grips on Nestlé's throat, and the situation improved. Today, most Americans buy as many Nestlé products as they ever did. But some people don't; the ordeal left a bad taste in their mouths.

The boycott and subsequent loss of face was a bitter pill for Nestlé to swallow. Hartley reported that Nestlé estimated a profit loss of $40 million. The company learned its lesson and vowed to work with public leaders in the future should problems arise.

Hartley observed that organizations, especially giant corporations, should remember that their public image is vulnerable. Hostile press coverage can be very powerful and not necessarily objective, a bad image can last a long time, and a last-ditch public relations effort is often too little, too late. He recommended that companies devote a good deal of energy to creating and communicating a positive public image that fits the company's mission. He believes that this needs to be done on all levels, from physical facilities to dealers to prices to advertising and public relations.

I agree with Hartley and want to add one more thing. The public image must be congruent with the company's actual practices. Carefully crafted Machiavellian duplicity will eventually fail in today's communication age. Nowadays, enquiring minds want to know what's going on behind the scenes. Just ask the Watergate burglars, John DeLorean, Gary Hart, the savings and loan senators, Manuel Noriega, and Drexel Burnham Lambert. Public figures and organizations are scrutinized and held accountable by the media. A hundred years ago businesses could do whatever they wanted, and oftentimes, only local media (newspapers) would investigate and report anything wrong. That was before television could expose a story to 2.5 billion people at once, as it does today. As former President Ronald Reagan used to say, "You can run, but you can't hide."

Sometimes, even when a company is just going about its business, things go awry. This is what happened to Exxon on March 24, 1989, when the tanker *Exxon Valdez* struck a reef in Alaska and spewed 11 million gallons of crude oil into Prince William Sound. The accident's size caused the press and public to go after Exxon, even though many other spills had occurred before. According to Sims (1989: 40), in the 12 years before the Exxon accident, Prince William Sound suffered "40 lesser spills and leakages." In the year following the Exxon spill, there were a number of smaller oil accidents in the Gulf of Mexico, San Francisco Bay, Los Angeles, Washington, and Alaska again, not to mention spills elsewhere in the world. But the focus has remained on Exxon.

Exxon lost its cargo and spent almost $2 billion on the cleanup. Although this is a lot of money, remember that Exxon enjoyed sales of $79.6 billion in 1988. Exxon bought full page ads in major newspapers across the country to report its progress on the cleanup efforts. The company will likely pay hundreds of millions or even billions in fines and lawsuits before the debacle ends.

The public is angry at Exxon not just because of the circumstances involving the worst oil spill in United States history, but because of the perception that its response to the accident was cavalier. It appeared to be making excuses for being slow in cleaning up (Postman 1989), and it seemed that Exxon was arrogant in dealing with the Coast Guard and other officials. They came across as defensive in their dealings with reporters. Their ads touting their progress were viewed as hype. In court, they blamed the Coast Guard for part of the accident.

As of the writing, I don't know what Exxon should do to clean up its image. Perhaps time and nature herself will turn the tide of negative public sentiment and Exxon will emerge tarnished, but alive, unlike the hundreds of thousands of unfortunate sea animals who paid the ultimate price for Exxon's error. *National Geographic* articles on the spill (Lee 1989, Hodgson 1990) treated Exxon fairly, even kindly. A well-respected magazine such as *National Geographic*, with a circulation over 10 million, can do much to soften public opinion.

Exxon did not benefit from the Nestlé experience, probably because Exxon was caught off guard and just did the best it could under the circumstances. But rest assured that competing oil companies learned from Exxon's experience. British Petroleum launched its new chain of BP gas stations in 1989 and featured an ecologically positive color of bright, healthy green on its signs—no copycat red, white, and blue like Exxon, Chevron, Arco, or Mobil. More importantly, when a BP tanker leaked 280,000 gallons of Alaskan crude off Los Angeles in February 1990, BP jumped to clean up the mess and let everyone know how socially responsible they were. According to an article in the *San Francisco Chronicle* (Nolte 1990: A14), a BP spokesman said: "Price is not our primary concern. As long as oil is on the water, you have an environmental threat. . . . We won't be satisfied until the water is back to normal." That's what the public wants to hear—genuine concern, not hubris.

On the same day that BP made their promise, all Perrier mineral water in the U.S. was recalled because benzene traces were found in samples. Perrier president Ronald V. Davis said that there was no significant health risk but added, "we're trying to act aggressively and responsibly in the interests of the public" (*Washington Post* 1990).

Because Perrier's success depends upon product purity, the benzene scare could be difficult to overcome. This will take time and patience for Perrier. Meanwhile, according to *Newsweek* (Miller, et al. 1990a: 53), rivals such as Evian, Pepsi (H20h!), and Coors "Rocky Mountain Sparkling Water" are scrambling to fill the empty cup left by Perrier. The $2.2 billion bottled water market is spilling over with competitors. By mid–1990, Perrier had sprung back with soft, new advertising showing cavemen enjoying Perrier water. Perrier showed that they were still floating.

AT&T went beyond communicating "we'll do the right thing" and came through with action when a glitch in their highly publicized, infallible supercomputer caused massive service breakdowns in January 1990. AT&T officials were momentarily stunned, then promised customers reduced rates for a day to compensate for the inconvenience. Sure enough, they delivered as promised—on Valentine's Day. What a present. Customers responded by placing 13 percent more calls than normal. So, AT&T received a Valentine also, "a bonanza in free, mostly favorable publicity" (Hall 1990: C1).

Societal Marketing

We see that BP, Perrier, and AT&T communicated a responsible, consumer-conscious public image. As marketers, if we go one step farther in creating a responsible public image, we might embrace what Kotler and Armstrong (1990: 14) call the "societal marketing concept," which argues that an organization should not only compete more effectively than rival organizations in satisfying customers, but should do it in a manner "that maintains or improves the consumer's and the society's well-being."

Well-being may be difficult to operationalize, but a recent example may suffice. When the "Great California Earthquake" hit the San Francisco Bay area in October 1989, potable water was difficult to find in some areas of San Francisco. (I know because I was there.) While some stores were jacking up prices for bottled water to exploit the disaster, Safeway gave bottled water away for free. This was definitely the neighborly thing to do. This benevolent deed created goodwill locally for Safeway and made national news when the "Osgood Report" on CBS News Radio and *Newsweek* gave Safeway kudos for the virtuous act.

What did Safeway communicate by this gesture? They communicated, "Since we're neighbors, let's help each other." Safeway also prints charitable messages on its paper food sacks (e.g., Second Harvest National Food Bank Network).

Here is a recent and perfect example of a societal marketing company and its communication relationship with consumers. Many people believe that cosmetics are capricious products, things we do not need. But we all use them and contribute to the multibillion dollar industry. Most cosmetics manufacturers and retailers advertise and promote a lot and this garners attention from consumers. One cosmetics company, The Body Shop, communicates differently. According to Clifton (1990: 65–66), the British-based half-billion-a-year cosmetics organization is an environmentally concerned, socially responsible company that uses natural ingredients like carrots and cucumbers (no animal testing) in its creams. Its biodegradable plastic bottles are labeled in simple black and white, nothing fancy. The Body Shop's founder, Anita Roddick, establishes factories in areas of high unemployment. She has her employees do two hours of social work each week—at company cost. Society, and The Body Shop, reap the dividends.

She set up a factory and very successful franchise in Berkeley, California. The store decor is simple, not glitzy. Her prices are not cheap but reflect the perceived value of quality cosmetics at reasonable prices. She makes no spurious claims but states: "We don't mention the word 'beauty,' we don't make promises of any kind, other than to say that our stuff will clean and protect your hair and skin, amen" (Clifton p. 66).

Her target market appreciates her company's honesty and rewards The Body Shop with repeat business and the best form of advertising: word of mouth. The Body Shop uses no other mode of paid promotion, as it would be difficult to compete with Revlon in advertising. However, The Body Shop does receive favorable publicity, as Clifton's article in *Newsweek* attests. The Body Shop is just entering the U.S. market. Roddick has only 14 stores on the East Coast, but they brought in $8 million in sales in 1989. Not bad.

Marketers, entrepreneurs, and venture capitalists take note. Environmentalism and social responsibility will be hallmarks of successful businesses in this decade. We'll find that many baby boom consumers will favor companies that do the right thing for the environment. They'll purchase cosmetics and other products that do not use fluoride, red dye no. 3, cfc packaging, msg, asbestos, or anything else that may hurt trees or people.

As we see from the Safeway and Body Shop examples, societal marketing is not difficult. It's a good turn here, a true word there, and it all adds up—as will profits. Don't take my word for it, but listen to patriot, diplomat, inventor, printer, and successful businessman Benjamin Franklin (1955: 111), who at age 79 wrote: "Nothing so likely to make a man's fortune as virtue."

What do Confucius, film director Spike Lee, and Procter & Gamble's statement of purpose have in common? They all say: Do the right thing.

Master Your Marketing Mission

Some marketing strategists rationalize that their company basically does the right thing, with a little fudging here and there. That may be so, but there is no time like the present to make a quick, honest assessment of company policies and practices. Then plan and implement changes in company mission, products, and marketing activities so your organization is socially responsible. Communicate these changes to all employees, from the top down. Concentrate and focus especially on marketing, advertising, and sales personnel, as these are the people who communicate the company mission to the world.

It is essential that your marketing people believe that your organization genuinely, not speciously, cares about consumers. When marketers know that their company ethic is authentic, they sleep well at night, are free from doubt and guilt, are infused with enthusiasm, and are eager to use the marketing communications mix to create promotional feats to astound the public and sell your company's products. When coming up with promotional ideas or dealing with unexpected image crises, they automatically think of society's well-being and do the right thing.

In turn, customers and other publics learn to perceive your company's public communication as authentic and develop respect for your company and the image it projects. Even if consumers do not buy your products, if they respect you they are more likely to give you slack—or even help out if an accident occurs, such as an oil spill.

The time to rethink your marketing mission is *now*. Don't wait until the Pentagon looks over your shoulder to mull over ideas about social responsibility. General Dynamics, which purposefully overbilled the Defense Department, was forced to create and adhere to a comprehensive ethics policy. This should have been unnecessary, but they waited until they were caught before doing the right thing.

Not only must you do the right thing, but you must do the right thing well—no, excellently. Robert Townsend, in his popular book *Up the Organization* (1970: 40), exhorted all executives: "If you don't do it excellently, don't do it at all. Because if it's not excellent it won't be profitable or fun, and if you're not in business for fun or profit, what the hell are you doing here?"

Advertising superagent David Ogilvy (1963, 1988: 17) adds this: 'The pursuit of excellence is less profitable than the pursuit of bigness, but it can be more satisfying."

In their book *In Search of Excellence* (which broke all sales records in the business category), Peters and Waterman (1982) advocated excellence in all areas, and this includes marketing communication. I hope the book's enormous sales reflect an equally high regard for what the authors were trying to communicate: be excellent. As a marketer, you will need to be excellent to create promotional feats.

COMMUNICATION ASPECTS OF THE MARKETING MIX

Over the past two years, I've asked hundreds of people from varied backgrounds what *marketing* means to them. Invariably, they respond with "selling," "promoting," or both. I tell them they are correct; selling and promoting is job one for marketers, be they chief executives, brand managers, or sales clerks. Selling and promoting are primarily communicative activities: selling involves interpersonal or group communication, and promoting is usually public or mass communication in nature. Public relations and publicity fall under the same umbrella as promoting and selling, as they also involve direct communication with the public. These four activities comprise the promotions mix, which will be discussed later in this chapter.

It's no surprise that managing and executing the promotions mix variables is not the sole function of a marketer. Marketing professor extraordinaire Philip Kotler and his writing cohort Gary Armstrong (1990: 4) state that selling is often not the most important part of marketing. "If the marketer does a good job of identifying consumer needs, developing good products, and pricing, distributing and promoting them effectively, these goods will sell very easily."

Management guru Peter Drucker (1973: 64–65) would agree. He believes "The aim of marketing is to make selling superfluous. The aim is to know and understand the customer so well that the product or service fits him and sells itself."

We know that even a new, improved, perfect product (or service or idea) can't sell itself if people don't know about it. But Drucker, Kotler, and Armstrong have a good point. Selling and promoting are a big part of marketing, but only one part of four in the marketing mix. According to Kotler and Armstrong (pp. 43–44), the marketing mix is "the set of controllable marketing variables that the firm blends to produce the response it wants in the target market."

These elements—the four P's— of the marketing mix are product, price, place, and promotion. Let's discuss each of these and center on the communication aspects of each.

Product refers to goods and services a company offers to its potential customers. Product can be further subdivided into several elements. One of these is position, the place the product occupies in the consumer's mind. Position is determined by marketing strategists and then communicated to the public by advertising slogans such as "We do chicken right"; "We try harder"; "The right choice"; and the like. Other product attributes complement and reinforce positioning. Positioning is of paramount importance to differentiate your products from competitors'.

Basic product ingredients, quality, options, warranties, service and repair policies—all harmonize to communicate a unified, congruent message to consumers. Chrysler's air bags and "7 year, 70,000-mile warranty" support its positioning message of "the best-built, best-backed American cars."

Brand names and brand marks communicate in words and symbols and complement other product attributes. For example, BankAmericard was just another credit card, but when it became Visa it communicated that it was a passport that would enable customers to buy just about anything, anywhere. Visa's slogan: It's everywhere you want to be. Thus, without distinctive branding, your product may be indistinguishable from a generic product. Instead of occupying a dedicated niche in consumers' minds, it will fall into the heap of clutter, ignored by everyone.

Product design is a major nonverbal communication variable that marketers must take full advantage of. Auto manufacturers have exploited this for years, placing different car bodies on the same chassis to create different models. Classic cars with distinctive designs are now worth much more than when they were manufactured. (So much for planned obsolescence.) Product design includes shape, size, and most important, form with function. A form/function congruence communicates on more than one level and is usually more effective than "style" alone. Color choices also communicate: "You can have any color, as long as it's black."

Packaging is yet another product variable, offering a perfect opportunity for marketers to communicate their message in a way that favorably impacts consumers. Packaging and product design are similar, in that functional form is best in both instances. One of my favorite packages is the plastic catsup bottle; I won't buy catsup in glass. (I only wish someone would make salsa in plastic containers that chips could be dipped into.) Labels are a cost-effective way to enhance a package and communicate the product position to consumers.

Product attributes are such important communication devices that I devote all of Chapter 4 to outstanding product features. Price and place are also important communication devices, especially when integrated with properly promoted product attributes.

Price can be determined in a number of ways. When introducing new products, marketers must decide to either skim (high prices) or penetrate (low prices) the market. The dream is to achieve market penetration with high prices. To skim or penetrate, or later to initiate price changes or respond to others' actions, requires a good deal of strategizing. The same is true when planning discounts and allowances, credit terms and payment periods, and all price-related activities.

Some manufacturers mistakenly base their prices on economics rather than on perceived value. If a product's (or product line's) marketing mix variables are working in harmony, then price will be easy to determine. Psychological pricing is the only way to set prices. Simply price the product in congruence with your communicated value of the product. Consumers should receive a price message which fits into their mindset of your product compared with others. A problem arises when manufacturers think a product is premium and price it as such, but retailers and/or customers view it differently. Judicious use of marketing research can nip this problem in the bud. More on that later.

To illustrate what I mean about psychological pricing according to a product's attributes, let me describe one promotional pricing feat. Kotler and Armstrong (1990: 311) report Heublein's clever pricing coup. Heublein's Smirnoff vodka (the market leader) was assaulted by Wolfschmidt vodka, which was touted as high quality but priced a dollar lower than Smirnoff. What should Heublein do: Nothing? Start a price war? Increase promotional efforts? None of these. Heublein increased Smirnoff's price by a dollar, positioning it as a premium vodka. Heublein covered their flanks and blunted Wolfschmidt's attack by introducing two more vodkas to compete with Wolfschmidt—Relska, priced the same as Wolfschmidt, and Popov, priced a dollar less than Wolfschmidt.

According to Kotler and Armstrong, the strategy worked: "Heublein's clever strategy produced a large increase in its overall profits." The punchline is that all three Heublein vodkas were basically the same. They used price alone to communicate value. What a feat.

Place, or distribution, refers to channels that move goods and services from manufacturer to consumer. On the surface, this may not seem much of a communication activity (at least not from organization to consumers), but it is. Let's look at shipping companies, for instance. Federal Express advertises it always knows where your package is—

especially if you absolutely, positively want to know. UPS underscores its reliability with this credo: The tightest ship in the shipping industry.

Multilevel marketing systems such as Amway communicate a close, interpersonal relationship with each person in the sales/buyer network. Direct marketers such as L. L. Bean communicate convenience and quality through their mail catalog.

Retailers, often the final distribution point for many products, complement a product's overall message. L'Eggs hosiery, packaged in plastic eggs, was sold through food stores, an innovative idea that worked. Macy's stopped retailing Levi's jeans when Levi Strauss started selling through J. C. Penney. Macy's refused to lower its high-brow status by selling products available in lower-class department stores (Morgenson 1989: 41–42). Different retail outlets communicate different messages to consumers. Specialty stores portray a dramatically contrasting image to hypermarkets. Both are successful.

Most service organizations have no channels to worry about; they market to their publics directly. Some manufacturers emulate service organizations by taking control of distribution and retailing. They may offer their own retail outlets (e.g., Esprit), or franchise. Franchising allows a manufacturer to take advantage of its unique products, brand names, and service methods to directly and uniformly manage all forms of communication to the consumer, including distribution variables. Because franchising gives manufacturers such control over communication, it will enjoy success in the future.

The key in distribution is to put the customer's needs foremost and then tell them about it. Pearson (1981: 17–23) argues that distribution suffers when the focus is put on the product rather than on the consumer.

In all the marketing mix variables discussed (product, price, and place), I've emphasized coordinating communication efforts to ensure a consistent message to consumers. The communication message must say, "We always give you best product and service *value* for your money." Making products of true value (quality) and communicating it via the "4 P's" is the best way to serve your customers and your organization. Kotler and Armstrong (1990: 233) say it best:

> Companies must do more than simply build quality into their products; they must also communicate product quality. The product's look and feel should communicate its quality level. Quality is also communicated through other elements of the marketing mix. A high price usually signals a premium-quality product. The product's brand name, packaging, distribution and promotion also announce its quality. All of these elements must work together to communicate and support the brand's image.

Promotion, the fourth variable, ties together the subtle communication efforts of the other three variables in an overt way. So marketing management (i.e., analysis, planning, implementation, and control of the marketing mix to reach target market objectives) consists largely of coordinating people, resources, and budgets to communicate to relevant publics about an organization's products and services. Promotion, as the fourth P and the coordinating function that integrates and unites the other three P's, is the heart of marketing.

PROMOTION MANAGEMENT

A promotion manager is a marketing manager responsible for an organization's marketing communication and promotional efforts. Marketing communication is any and all communication involved in the marketing mix, as described above. Marketing communication is sometimes accidental, but should always be intentional to ensure consistent congruence in manufacturers', retailers', and consumers' minds.

The promotion manager, in addition to ensuring marketing communications congruence, is in charge of all overt efforts to promote a product. This includes advertising, sales promotion, public relations and publicity, personal selling, display, and anything new. These tools comprise the promotional mix.

To maximize understanding, here are brief definitions of these tools. *Advertising* is paid, nonpersonal mass communication or direct marketing tools such as flyers, brochures, catalogs, and the like. *Sales promotions* are marketing events which stimulate purchasing. These include sweepstakes, contests, grand openings, coupons, premiums, samples, price packs, and rebates. *Publicity* is free, nonpersonal (but sometimes personal) mass communication. It is composed of press releases and publicity stunts that attract media attention and subsequent coverage in news stories and editorials. *Public relations* encompasses publicity and also includes personal and nonpersonal communication by company speakers through newsletters, lobbying, and contact with media and citizens. *Personal selling* is personal communication with a sales agent persuading consumers to buy products and services. *Display* refers to point-of-purchase items such as posters, signs, and other in-store media that direct consumers to buy a particular product.

These six promotional mix factors sometimes run independently yet concurrently, which is fine if that is the intention. In an ideal promotion marketing scenario, all six factors would operate in concert, like the Philadelphia Orchestra. Our promotional maestro would conduct a symphonic masterpiece that would astound the world for centuries. The horns (advertising) and woodwinds (personal selling) would blow, percussion (display) and drums (sales promotions) would crash and boom, the strings (public relations) would mesmerize, and our featured pianist (publicity stunt) would command a standing ovation night after night. We'd headline the news for months. Our house would always be packed. We'd serve the community in a significant way and—most importantly— have fun. And earn a profit. Why not?

The symphony analogy shows that conducting an orchestra excellently is quite an accomplishment. But an orchestra must sound excellent. Who listens to a mediocre orchestra if given a choice? Unfortunately for many organizations (profit and nonprofit, big and small), instead of being coordinated, promotional efforts occur haphazardly, like one band warming up on stage while another is playing. Or worse, promotion happens out of habit rather than brilliance. Who wants to hear uninspired musicians play the same tired tunes in the same muted manner?

The point is, not many big companies have well-coordinated promotion management. The public relations department is not affiliated with the publicity staff, who aren't told what's happening at the advertising agency, which is against the idea of sales promotions. All these people are competent; that is not at issue. Like solo musicians, many play well, even excellently.

Promotion Managers Must Be Generalists

Big and small organizations may successfully operate a small, efficient yet effective promotion team, a jazz ensemble. But this also requires great skill. Managing marketing communications and the promotional mix is a big job, one that must be performed excellently.

This requires a marketing and promotions generalist, a person well acquainted with the total organizational and communications picture. Regrettably, many people in the promotion business are specialists. They often take either the marketing or communication education and experience path, but seldom both. Early in their careers, they let themselves be funneled into sales or copywriting; later, they become sales managers or art directors; finally, they achieve vice president of sales or advertising. The depth acquired by specializing is desirable, but breadth is also needed to effectively coordinate an organization's communication program so it promotes with minimum expense and maximum impact.

Buckminster Fuller (1969: 14) provides a clear and appropriate example of why humans should strive to be generalists instead of specialists. Fuller believes:

> Mind apprehends and comprehends the general principles governing flight and deep sea diving, and man puts on his wings or his lungs, then takes them off when not using them. The

specialist bird is greatly impeded by its wings when trying to walk. The fish cannot come out of the sea and walk upon land, for birds and fish are specialists.

By analogy, we see that a superlative promotions manager, a generalist, can, through education and experience, master general business and marketing as well as the six promotional mix communication methods.

Promotions Must Cut Through Clutter

Earlier in this chapter, I listed opportunities and challenges for marketers in the next few years. Whereas I see a clear need and trend for marketers in general to be savvy about social responsibility, we must also discover, create, and then execute innovative campaigns that pierce the cacophony of promotional clutter that surrounds the minds of everyone.

Clutter is so pervasive that the problem made the front page of the *San Francisco Chronicle*. Williams (1990: A1) reported that social scientists are starting to think that Americans have so many choices in the marketplace that consumers "are becoming overwhelmed, even paralyzed by all these choices. . . . "

Williams says the bottom line is so many choices make people anxious and decisions more difficult. The choice dilemma has reached pandemic proportions and is spreading. Williams notes, "Americans can choose from more than 25,000 items on their supermarket shelves, tune in as many as 53 television stations, buy any of 11,092 magazines or periodicals and be solicited by tens of thousands of special-interest and public-interest groups" (p. A1).

What's that spell? T-R-O-U-B-L-E, with a capital T. What are we promotion managers going to do about it? We can't go on singing the same old song. What we can do is judiciously conduct marketing research to gather information about target consumers, such as their media preferences, demographics, and psychographics. (See Soares 1988: *Cost-Effective Marketing Research*.) In short, we need to discover what motivates people now. We must find out what it takes to capture their attention, develop and keep their interest, and secure their commitment to purchase our products.

We need competitive intelligence (CI) to determine what exactly our competitors are doing, so we can do it better, or at least differently (never the same). Read Vella and McGonagle's *Improved Business Planning Using Competitive Intelligence* (1987), for more on the benefits of CI. Sadly, some promotion people believe marketing research is anathema to creative copywriting, but this is simply not true. Research permits us to aim our promotions in the light—perhaps only a dim flash, but preferable to a shot in the dark.

Once we know what motivates people and how key competitors attempt to do so, we still must figure a way to cut through clutter with our communication (short of spending billions on a massive advertising war). We need promotion so entertaining, so compelling, that target consumers go out of their way to seek us out, not just for our products but even for the promotion itself. Here's an example.

During this year's Super Bowl, my 12-year-old daughter watched with keen interest. I was happy that she had finally learned to appreciate football and told her so. "No way," she said. "I'm watching to see the new commercials." Now that's compelling entertainment.

I'm convinced and will prove to you that we need to create entertaining events, daring deeds, and scintillating stunts to penetrate clutter, enthrall target consumers, and position a positive product image in their minds. We need to create *promotional feats*!

PROMOTIONAL FEATS

I'm committing promotional blasphemy. I am suggesting that we *entertain* people, not just sell them. Ogilvy supports me, even though he wrote in 1983 (p. 161) that ad memorability has nothing to do with effectiveness and ad recall "is for the birds." On that same page he wrote, "When I want a high recall score, all I have to do is show a gorilla in a jock strap." Right! For Bike (which makes jock straps), that idea might be great, though outrageous.

In 1963, in his classic *Confessions of an Advertising Man*, Ogilvy declared: "The purpose of a commercial is not to *entertain* the viewer, but to *sell* him . . . there is no correlation between people *liking* commercials and being *sold* by them" (p. 129). In his 1988 update of the same book, he amended that statement in the preface: "Recent research at the Ogilvy Center for Research and Development has revealed that commercials which people like sell more than commercials they don't like" (p. ix).

In his updated book he also wrote "You cannot *bore* people into buying your product; you can only *interest* them in buying it." But he cautions against "the temptation to entertain instead of selling . . . " (p xvii), and he rails against advertisers who have never sold but "regard advertising as an avant-garde art form" (p. xv). He believes these artsy advertising agents "At best are mere entertainers, and rather feeble ones at that (pp. xv–xvi).

To address Ogilvy and other critics of entertainment in promotion, I say I agree. Entertainment without persuasion is wasteful. I also agree and insist that we stop boring people and start interesting them in our products. We must create promotional feats.

Traditional ways to promote don't always work: innovation is needed. Consider this. Ten percent or less of news releases are published by editors (Schafer 1969). Free samples and price discounts are expensive—and then customers go back to their old brands right after the sales promotion. With "zipping and zapping" occurring in TV, over 50 stations to choose from, and viewership of major network stations declining, it costs an average of $176,000 to create a national ad for television (Walley 1989), and between $100,000 and $200,000 or more for 30 seconds of advertising on prime-time TV (Kotler & Armstrong 1990: 411). It costs $550,000 to place one ad during the Super Bowl. The ad had better be good.

And with all the clutter, "today's advertising messages must be better planned, more imaginative, more entertaining, and more rewarding to consumers." (Kotler and Armstrong 1990: 411). I rest the argument portion of my case. I present the evidence to support my contention throughout the book.

What Is a Promotional Feat?

A promotional feat is a marketing communication event or system that promotes products in a way that surpasses normal marketing objectives. A promotional feat is excellent advertising, sales promotions, displays, publicity, public relations, and personal selling. It entails excellent use of the communicative aspects of the marketing mix. *Excellent* means that marketing objectives are met in an outstanding way. This does not mean that the promotional feat is necessarily expensive or artsy, but that it efficiently and very effectively meets marketing objectives.

Operationalizing a promotional feat is tricky. I could examine sales figures, market share, or product recall—and that would be good, except these are not often readily available or directly attributable to the promotional effort alone. So, for this book, I operationalize promotional feat to be an event (or series of events) that received "positive" mention in any medium germane to the sponsoring organization.

If I do not see or hear it, I don't know about it. I do not use content microanalysis, which involves counting lines of copy or seconds of air time devoted to the promotional event. I simply look for stories about effective ads, great publicity stunts, and the like. For example, if an ad wins a CLIO award and a photo about that appears in every major newspaper in the country, that would be a promotional feat, even if the ad was a little too artsy and failed to sell its product well. Hopefully, the media attention would give the promotional effort a little more mileage than it might have gotten on its own, and that may indeed be the feat.

A simple press release is no promotional feat. However, if a press release triggers television news coverage and a *Newsweek* cover story, such as Steve Job's 1988 announcement of his NeXT computer unveiling, that constitutes a promotional feat. If several press releases published over time increase an organization's public awareness and approval level (such as AT&T's numerous "product innovation" releases), then that constitutes a promotional feat.

Promotional Feat Categories

Promotional feats are classified into six broad categories: sponsor type, duration, scope, originality, degree of planning, and marketing mix variables (which includes promotional mix elements). Each of these rubrics can be broken into subcategories. Let's look at each.

Sponsor type refers to key identifying characteristics of the sponsoring organization that performed or benefited from the promotional feat. An organization could be some combination of profit/nonprofit, industrial/consumer, big/small, product/service, manufacturer/retailer, and so forth. Salient attributes of the sponsoring organization are mentioned when describing its promotional feats, if that organization is not already well-known.

Duration denotes the feat's time length. That is, was the promotional feat a one-shot affair like a publicity stunt, or was it a series of ads that lasted years and that's the feat?

Scope means number of people targeted for the feat. In other words, was it a local media event (perfect for a small business), or regional, national, or international (appropriate for a multinational corporation)?

Originality is also described. Was the feat the first ever done of its type? Or was it a classic promotional vehicle executed in an outstanding way?

Degree of planning refers to how much control the sponsoring organization had over the feat. Was the feat strategically planned and executed, or was it serendipity that accounted for its success? Was the sponsor proacting or reacting? For example, when Coca-Cola announced its new formula, it expected a positive reaction from Coke drinkers and hoped that Pepsi drinkers would try Coke's sweeter taste and switch. The "new, improved" product announcement was planned. The uproar from Coke loyalists was unplanned. The major networks covered the fiasco for weeks. Coca-Cola finally appeased its loyal fans (most couldn't tell Coke from Pepsi in a blind taste test) by reintroducing its old formula under the name "Classic Coke." (See Gelman, et al. 1985.)

Marketing mix variables includes communicative aspects of the marketing mix, such as product features, price, and place feats. Naturally, the promotional mix variables described earlier are discussed.

PLAN OF THE BOOK

This chapter showed that much of marketing involves communicating with the public, a public which demands social responsibility from manufacturers. I argued that a marketing or promotions manager who is a generalist, and therefore able to adapt well to changing situations and new challenges, should use all promotional forms appropriately to cut through clutter and create excellent promotion campaigns that best meet organizational objectives. In short, I advocate conscious planning and execution of *promotional feats*.

In Chapter 2, I examine historical feats which can serve as models for modern promotional feats. The military marketing model is critiqued and pertinent military and political communication feats (propaganda) are described. Marketing warfare will be cast in a new spotlight. This chapter also highlights famous adventures and physical stunts from the wide and varied world of sports.

In Chapter 3 I explicate and advocate the entertainment model of marketing. Numerous examples of ballyhoo and publicity stunts from the arts are detailed. (Ordinary business promotions will appear dull in comparison.) Media events from the movie industry—where entertainment is the sole product—are showcased.

Part two of the book centers on promotional feats in business. Chapter 4 covers promotions targeted on marketing mix aspects of a product. Outstanding product designs, brands, and slogans are featured in this chapter.

Chapters 5 and 6 zoom in on feats from advertising and sales promotions, respectively. I present tips from experts on how to make your ads and sales promotions excellent.

In Chapter 7, company icons, spokespersons, and super sales agents are highlighted. We'll look at the public relations coups of Lee Iacocca and meet Cal Worthington and his dog Spot.

In Chapter 8, management of marketing communications is discussed. Planning, budgeting, and evaluating communication programs receive special emphasis. Marketing communication systems and feats of AT&T, gigantic Warner Communications, and my small company, Tsunami Products, are compared and contrasted. Ideas and developments for the future of promotional feats are presented.

Is everyone seated? Lights! Camera! *Action*!

2

Famous Feats Throughout History

"The influence of words over men is astounding."
—Napoleon

"You furnish the pictures, I'll furnish the war."
—William Randolph Hearst

MARKETING IS WAR! As the whole world gears for peace (e.g., the fall of the Berlin wall, Mandela's release from prison in South Africa, democratic elections in Nicaragua, U.S. and Soviet missile cuts and troop reductions), marketers and other business people talk in terms of war. We see battle words everywhere in business: Japan bashing, corporate raiders, hostile takeovers, cola wars.

It seems ordinary business executives fancy themselves as warriors, valiantly defending market share, aggressively attacking weak companies' territories. Billionaire Donald Trump's lawyer calls himself a killer in the courtroom. "I can rip skin off a body," he boasted. (Garchik 1990: A10)

Hip marketing managers quote ancient war and attack strategies of Musashi, Sun Tzu, and Von Clausewitz. Captains of industry line their shelves with the latest best-selling military marketing books. Some of the popular ones include *Battling for Profits* (Hendon 1986), *Winning the Marketing War* (Michaelson 1987), *Guerrilla Marketing Attack* (Levinson 1989), *Streetfighting* (Slutsky 1984), and *Leadership Secrets of Attila the Hun* (Roberts 1985). Probably the most popular book of this type is Ries and Trout's *Marketing Warfare* (1986).

Ries and Trout (p. 13) write: "So William assigned 20 Norman knights to break through the Saxon lines and get Harold. (Today we would send 20 lawyers armed with 5-year contracts.)" They were attempting humor, yet there is still an "ain't we great generals" tone to this statement that seeps out in books such as this.

There's nothing wrong with quixotic dreams of marketing conquest, but we must remember that war is carnage. Real battles leave dead and mutilated bodies. Military warriors face real physical danger. Marketing warriors and paunchy, "skin-ripping" lawyers face no danger whatsoever, except to their pocketbooks and egos. Although I am a businessman and academician, as a Navy veteran, martial artist, and professional daredevil, I respect the reality of physical danger.

In the docudrama film *The Right Stuff*, a story about military test pilots and Mercury astronauts, three test pilot wives discuss the danger their husbands face. Mrs. Gordo Cooper says:

> When I went back East to our reunion and all my friends could talk about was their husbands' work, how dog-eat-dog and cut-throat it was on Madison Avenue and places like that—[the other women laugh]—Cutthroat? I wondered how they would've felt, if each time their husband went in to make a deal, there was a one in four chance he wouldn't come out of that meeting.

This illustrates that though business executives may have the right stuff, they are not strapped into an X–1 rocket and told to break the sound barrier. Marketing strategists fight enemies (competitors) on the battle-field of the mind, a much safer reality.

MILITARY FEATS

Despite the false illusion of equating marketing with actual warfare, these books contain worthwhile principles that help marketers compete more effectively. First let's look at some of these principles and military examples used to illustrate them. Then I will present other military and diplomatic principles, just as powerful and compelling, which show that even in real warfare, the true battlefield is the mind and the weapon is words.

Principles of War

Principles of war have existed for thousands of years. Principles of modern marketing have been around for about a hundred years, al-though commerce has coexisted with war throughout history. *Competition* is the central theme in marketing warfare books. Marketing warfare advocates such as Michaelson believe that business competition is social

Darwinian "survival of the fittest." Ries and Trout (p. 8) say "Free enterprise is marketing warfare. If you want to play in the free enterprise game, it seems to make sense to learn the principles first."

And what are these principles? Ries and Trout believe that the "customer is king" paradigm that has ruled marketing practice since World War II is outmoded. It seems that everyone is customer-oriented, so it's time to focus on besting the competition. Principles of warfare are most appropriate for this end, they claim. Military strategy and tactics should be applied.

Ries and Trout offer four strategies for fighting a marketing war: defensive, offensive, flanking, and guerrilla. Defensive principles are for market leaders; they include self-attack to maintain the edge and blocking competitors.

Offensive strategy is for strong competitors of the market leader. The key principle is to concentrate resources on a narrow front or weakness in the leader's strength. Flanking strategy is touted as "the most innovative way to fight a marketing war" (Ries & Trout, p. 83). In a flanking maneuver, a company must make a decisive, surprise move to occupy an uncontested market segment. Further, the flanker must pursue the advantage to secure a strong niche.

The guerrilla strategy involves finding a small, defensible position and becoming the leader of it. A guerrilla should not challenge the overall market leader and should be prepared to "bug out at a moment's notice."

Michaelson (1987) looks at defense, offense, flanking, and guerrilla strategies a bit differently. His emphasis is on maneuvering. He includes the four strategies just described, and adds the blitz, where one goes around resistance and zooms into the target. He also lists encirclement, Fabian (refusing battle), relocation of the battle (finding a new war), and retreat.

There are several principles of war that most military marketing authors address in one way or another. Here are the top ten:

1. The force with absolute or relative *superiority* wins. (Big beats small.)

2. The force with the stronger *position* wins. (Well-defended high ground is difficult to attack.)

3. The force with *information* about the enemy has the advantage. (Know your enemy, yourself, and the battlefield.)

4. *Concentrate resources* at the decisive place and time.

5. *Maneuver* (flank, blitz, etc.) to keep the enemy unbalanced and to achieve good positioning for attack.

6. Apply *economy* of force. (Don't waste resources.)

7. Exploit the *initiative*. (Keep attacking; pursue.)

8. Maintain the *objective* (strategically and tactically).

9. Use resourceful and charismatic *leaders* to command troops.

10. Use *surprise* to catch the enemy off guard.

Now let's examine military and marketing examples that illustrate the ten principles.

Military and Marketing Examples

The first principle, *superiority of numbers*, has many examples throughout military history which show that the numerically superior force usually wins. Von Clausewitz (1966: 192) said that superior numbers, in tactics and strategy, is "the most general principle of victory." In examining European wars, he found few major incidents where the smaller force beat the larger army. He noted that Frederick the Great "beat 80,000 Austrians at Leuthen with about 30,000 men" (p. 194), but for the most part, the superior force brought together at the decisive point wins. (Later in this chapter I provide examples of soldiers overcoming odds of 2-to-1 or greater. But since none are European battles, Clausewitz excluded them.)

We need only look at corporate giants such as General Motors, Procter & Gamble, and IBM to see that the big stay on top. I cannot think of any examples where a numerically inferior marketing force went head to head in a frontal assault on a big company and won. However, in war, there are many instances where armies of *relative* superiority prevailed, especially if they made good use of surprise, strategem, and propaganda. But more on that later.

As for *position*, fortified positions on high ground (or the best geographic position) are difficult to assail. We can take almost any example of siege and see that offensive forces won only with great losses in men, resources, and time. It took Alexander the Great seven months to penetrate the island fortress of Tyre. Cortez took the Aztec capitol of Tenochtitlan in three months, with heavy losses on both sides, especially the Aztecs, who lost 12,000 on one day, 40,000 on another, and 15,000 on the last day of the assault. (See Innes 1969: 192–193.)

Of course, there are ways to besiege other than direct assault. One can blockade a city and wait for the defenders to starve. Conversely, one can catapult bread over the walls as El Cid did, and thus win the hearts of the people through strategic kindness. And then there's always the Trojan horse technique to gain entry. How about bribing the gatekeeper to open the city? If that doesn't work, try constant bombardment until there is no city left to occupy (Dresden and Tokyo during World War II, Beirut today).

The point is, novel ways must be used to overcome heavily fortified positions. Clausewitz believed that defense is inherently stronger than offense. This may be true. But new weapons, applied decisively, can break through an entrenched defense, regardless of superiority in numbers. A case in point: in World War I, when the Germans first used poison gas in the trenches, Allied soldiers were routed in panic.

In marketing, we look at attacks on the big guys. There is no way that a competitor would starve, bomb, or gas GM. However, it could introduce a small car such as the Volkswagen Beetle or Japanese compacts and subcompacts (when Volkswagen got confused and could no longer compete with cheap cars).

The third principle of marketing warfare concerns *intelligence*. Hendon (1986) stresses the importance of espionage. Michaelson (1987) places the organization of intelligence first in developing a plan. Ries and Trout (1986) denigrate standard marketing research, which is customer oriented, and opt for developing dossiers on the activities of the competition.

There are numerous war examples which show the importance of timely intelligence. Attila the Hun lost one battle only, and this was because he didn't know what the Romans would do. His enemy Aetius knew what the Huns would do, prepared for it, and blasted Attila and his horde. Attila lost 162,000–300,000 Huns at that battle (Roberts 1985: 8). That's a lot of lost warriors.

Alexander always made skillful use of his intelligence sources, and his enemy Darius failed to do so. Darius lost his first major battle at Issus to Alexander because he refused to listen to his spy, Amyntas (formerly one of Alexander's soldiers), who urged Darius to stay on favorable ground and wait for Alexander to come to him. Darius listened to his courtiers instead and was trapped in the narrows at Issus where he could not use his numerically superior force to full advantage. In contrast, Alexander waited for his intelligence sources to report on Darius' position. When he was sure that Darius was in the narrows, Alexander attacked. Result: Alexander wiped out Darius' army, losing only 450 men to Darius' 100,000 (see Arrian 1971: 121). Darius didn't learn from the debacle at Issus. He was later routed again (for the last time) by Alexander at Arbela—the "famous" battle.

Smart business people will emulate Alexander's use of intelligence. It is common for General Motors to collect and disassemble competitors' cars. They learn a lot this way. Some Japanese electronics companies have recently been accused and in some cases prosecuted for stealing trade secrets from American firms. A person who takes the marketing warfare stance must agree that the Japanese were doing what was necessary to ensure victory. Business is war, right? (My belief is that business is not war, and that a company will win bigger in the long run by doing what is best, that is, virtuous. More on that later.)

The fourth marketing war principle listed is *concentrating resources* at the decisive place and time. A classic example of failing to concentrate resources is when the Carthaginian generals Hannibal and Hasdrubal split their forces. The Roman general Nero feigned a pursuit of Hannibal but then turned, led a forced march against Hasdrubal, and attacked his left flank. Nero won.

The marketing application, according to Ries and Trout, is to concentrate resources on a narrow front, that is, a weakness in the market leader's strength. The example they use is Avis' narrow front attack on Hertz' service weakness. The idea was that Hertz was so big it just couldn't offer the service that Avis could. Customers had to wait in line to rent cars from Hertz. So Avis, capitalizing on Hertz's weakness in its strength, advertised "Rent from Avis. The line at our counter is shorter."

The idea of concentrating resources, a column attack, has been practiced by Alexander and other generals for thousands of years. It can work for big armies against other big armies that are arrayed in long rows. But for smaller armies or companies, an indirect attack (flanking, blitz) is usually better. This brings us to our fifth principle, *maneuver*.

Lawrence of Arabia, master of maneuver, not only attacked indirectly, but often split his Arab army to harass Turkish railroads, bridges, and telegraph lines. He would trick the enemy into concentrating its resources and entrenching, and would then fade away to fight another day. This is guerrilla warfare. Instead of fighting the great battle with great commanders to utterly destroy the enemy, as Clausewitz preferred, Lawrence preferred to engage the enemy indirectly or not at all, for a dead man cannot enjoy the freedom he has fought for. Lawrence believed it was unnecessary to destroy the enemy's army. All that was needed was for the invading army to leave. His job was to persuade the Turks to do just that. Undetected mobility was the key.

While planning his famous raid on Akaba, Lawrence (1926: 195) mused on the Turkish predicament in trying to invade Arabia:

> And how would the Turks defend all that? No doubt by a trench line across the bottom, if we came like an army with banners; but suppose we were (as we might be) an influence, an idea, a thing intangible, invulnerable, without front or back, drifting about like a gas? Armies were like plants, immobile, firm-rooted, nourished through long stems to the head. We might be a vapour, blowing where we listed. Our kingdoms lay in each man's mind; and as we wanted nothing material to live on, so we might offer nothing material to the killing. It seemed a regular soldier

might be helpless without a target, owning only what he sat on, and subjugating only what, by order, he could poke his rifle at.

His guerrilla strategy of attacking materiel (and sometimes troops) and then fading away into the desert like a mirage worked well. The Turks couldn't communicate or move supplies. Thus they were prevented from launching successful attacks and were kept in their garrisons where they could do no harm.

Lawrence's mobility and combat intelligence won many small victories which added up to winning the war in Arabia. His successful strategy was to disperse rather than concentrate resources. This is important for small companies competing against giants. It also shows that principles are not laws, but merely ideas to be considered when competing.

Clausewitz believed a flank or rear attack brought greatest success. Napoleon was a master at flanking, as was Alexander the Great. Alexander used flanking decisively in his victory over Darius at Arbela. He personally led the attack of his right wing on Darius' left. Darius tried (almost successfully) to flank Alexander's left by sending his chariots up the center, but Alexander's men let them pass through, then took command of the chariots, turned them around, and used them against Darius' forces. Meanwhile, Alexander headed straight for Darius. When Darius realized he was about to be captured or killed by Alexander, he fled (just as he had at Issus) with Alexander in hot pursuit. (Alexander was a master of pursuit).

And now, the rest of the story. Darius got away, but was eventually betrayed and murdered by his kinsman, Bessus. Bessus named himself the new king of Asia. So Alexander pursued Bessus, caught him, tortured him in public, then had him executed. Alexander now ruled the Persian Empire!

Here's another example of a successful flanking maneuver on a smaller scale, but closer to home. In the late 1800s, the U.S. cavalry pursued the Nez Percé Indians all over the Northwest because the Nez Percés balked at going to a reservation. The cavalry decided to raid the Nez Percé lodges in White Bird Canyon. Led by a Captain Perry, they were composed of 100 men; some were civilian volunteers. The Nez Percés had 70 men, led by Pile-of-Clouds or Looking Glass, but probably not Chief Joseph. The cavalry spotted the Indians in a narrow part of the canyon and rushed in to attack. Through a tactical error, they left their rear unprotected.

The cavalry didn't realize they were being lured into a trap. The Indians retreated, hiding behind boulders and taking potshots at the cavalry. Suddenly, 60 Nez Percé warriors popped up at the sides and rear of the cavalry and started shooting. The cavalry became confused, broke ranks, and hastily retreated. One squad was isolated and wiped out.

The remainder were pursued but eventually escaped. According to Howard (1941: 162–176), the cavalry lost 33 men; the Indians lost three. This was the second worst defeat (in casualties) to Indians that the U.S. cavalry suffered. (The worst was Little Big Horn.)

As effective as a flanking maneuver is, a rear attack is even more powerful. Lawrence of Arabia's rear attack on the Turks at Akaba was astounding. Lawrence mustered together several warring tribes of Arabs to cross the dreaded Nefudh Desert and attack Akaba, a Turkish stronghold with big guns pointed seaward. It seems the Turks believed that it was impossible to be attacked from behind. But then came Lawrence with his motly host of Bedu warriors on camels. Lawrence took Akaba without a shot, for the Turks were persuaded that they would be massacred by the restless Arabs, who were itching to fight.

Flanking maneuvers are good strategically and tactically for businesses who favor the indirect approach over frontal assault. Strategically, flanking involves taking possession of an uncontested market. Ries and Trout (p. 85) insist a company must be the first to occupy the market segment to achieve a true flanking move. They give several good examples of strategic flanking feats in business. Miller flanked the beer industry leader (Budweiser) with Lite. Volkswagen flanked General Motors' big car market with small cars. Close-Up flanked Crest in the toothpaste wars with its mouthwash and whitening ingredients.

Flanking can also be used in a geographic sense. Wal-Mart moves into rural areas to flank urban mass merchants. (Wal-Mart directly confronts small drug stores in rural areas, and since Wal-Mart is bigger, guess who wins.)

Michaelson provides other military/marketing maneuver examples. For blitzing, he naturally describes the German blitzkrieg of World War II—lightning-fast attack flowing around resistance to reach the objective. His marketing examples include a rapid movement of sales teams into a territory before competitors can react. Advertising blitzes to launch new products (such as Thomas' English muffins in San Francisco and Los Angeles) is another example provided by Michaelson.

For encirclement, Michaelson quotes Frederick the Great, who believed starvation was a good way to win a war. We can look at civil wars in North Africa today for starvation tactics. Custer's last stand serves as another example of how encirclement works. In marketing, Michaelson cites the DeBeers monopoly on the world diamond supply as an example of market encirclement. AT&T had the telephone communications market encircled, although they were forced by regulators to share it.

All marketing warfare authors discuss guerrilla maneuvering, which is appropriate, since most companies entering most markets today *are* guerrillas trying to carve a niche. They have to take what they can get. Their game, at least initially, is to survive. Later they may thrive, but that depends on many factors. One of these factors centers on the sixth principle, economy of force.

Economy of force refers to optimizing resources and delivering powerful attacks upon the enemy with the least amount of energy. Clausewitz (p. 221) wrote that inactive forces or armies doing an action for no purpose are badly managed. This applies readily to both military and business operations. Lawrence beat the Turks by keeping them idle while he was busy everywhere at once. Ben Franklin (1955: 201) railed at British General Loudoun for being less than economical during the French and Indian War:

> Loudoun, instead of defending the colonies with his great army, left them totally exposed while he paraded idly at Halifax, by which means Fort George was lost; besides, he deranged all our mercantile operations, and distressed our trade, by a long embargo on the exportation of provisions, on pretence of keeping supplies from being obtained by the enemy, but in reality for beating down their price in favor of the contractors, in whose profits, it was said, perhaps from suspicion only, he had a share.

It seems Loudoun not only wasted time and resources, but skimmed a profit when he shouldn't have. (This behavior is still practiced in American business.) The topper to this story is that Loudoun failed to pay Franklin money he rightfully owed him. However, winning the War of Independence more than made up for any losses Franklin and other colonists suffered due to British wastefulness and impropriety.

In business, we daily see companies fail because of inefficiency and inappropriate spending—sometimes on excessive advertising and sales promotions. Frugal Franklin wouldn't like it.

Economy of force is paramount in martial arts. To save energy, a martial artist would try to subdue an opponent with a decisive blow or move as soon as possible, using the line of least resistance on a vulnerable point. This is why promotional feats are important. Organizations can't just continually spend money on advertising (or any promotional tool) just because that is what has always been done. Doing nothing might be better. It is stupid for companies to continue investing time and money on ineffective promotions when a simple, well-timed, decisive promotion delivered to the appropriate target market would be so much more efficient—and effective. Later in this book I offer a variety of examples and show how to make promotional feats—efficiently.

Exploiting the initiative, or pursuit, is another important principle of war appropriate for marketers, especially flankers and guerrilla marketers who may fail to keep attacking once they have achieved a small

market niche and then suddenly find themselves ousted by new competitors scrambling to fill their place.

We can observe nature to witness the importance of pursuit for the
survival of predators. Wolves in the Canadian Arctic trail herds of migrating caribou. The wolves, usually in teams of two or three, look for
signs of weakness or injury in the caribou. If they see or smell no weakness, they create it by stampeding the herd, hoping that one caribou
will stumble and be slightly hobbled. When the wolves notice a wounded
caribou, they pursue it doggedly until a wolf is able to tear at its flanks,
hobbling the caribou further. Eventually, if all goes well for the wolves,
they kill their prey and feast. If wolves were lax on pursuit, they would
grow steadily weaker from hunger, and then they would be another
animal's prey, probably a guerrilla raven, who will eat anything it can
get and bug out at a moment's notice.

If armies are lax on pursuit, they free their enemies to regroup and
fight again another day. Alexander gave up the chase for fleet-footed
Darius after their encounter at Issus, and Darius was able to fight Alexander again at Arbela, costing Alexander the lives of 500 men and 1,000
horses. (Darius of course fared worse; estimates between 40,000 and
300,000 deaths were reported, with many more soldiers taken prisoner.)

Arrian's book on Alexander is full of pursuit. Here is a typical example
of Alexander's tenacity. After Arbela, Alexander was settling adminis-
trative affairs in Bactria when Oxyartes the Bactrian refused to be a vassal
and fortified himself and some of his people on top of the Rock of
Sogdiana, believing it unassailable. Alexander knew that if Oxyartes
could be subdued, then he would own the region. So off he went to get
a piece of the Rock.

When Alexander arrived at the Rock, he found it featured sheer cliffs
on all sides. To complicate matters, Oxyartes was well provisioned and
prepared for a long siege. Alexander asked Oxyartes to surrender, telling
him he would allow them safe passage. (Alexander usually kept his
word.) They laughed down at him and said only winged soldiers could
capture this fortress of stone.

It looked hopeless, but Alexander was determined. He offered huge
bonuses to any soldiers that scaled the Rock; 300 climbers took this
challenge. Thirty fell to their deaths but the rest made the top after
climbing all night. Alexander pointed to his "soldiers with wings" and
Oxyartes, awed and disheartened, surrendered. Alexander magnani-
mously married Oxyartes' beautiful daughter and gained an ally in Oxyartes. What a feat.

Pursuit is important in marketing. Miller put big money up when it
introduced Lite beer. Gillette spent over a $100 million dollars in early
1990 introducing its new Sensor razor. But some companies fail to exploit
the initiative, and then they vanish. Who offered the first personal com-

puter? Right—MITS. Altair was its name, but it received inadequate promotional support and faded away. Apple, Tandy, Compaq, Commodore, and Big Blue quickly filled the Altair void. MITS needed a promotional feat but became disheartened too soon.

Maintain the objective is the eighth principle. According to Michaelson (p. 51), this entails "choosing a strategic direction or a specific tactical goal and sticking with it." He reports that in Vietnam, instead of maintaining a single objective as the North Vietnamese did, the U.S. maintained twenty-two independent objectives. It's difficult to concentrate resources when objectives may be at cross purposes to each other.

Maintaining the objective is akin to a duck hunter keeping his aim on one duck and shooting it. If he points at one duck, then another, and then that big fat one, they all fly away and the hunter shoots at phantoms.

Alexander the Great had one objective: rule the world. You may scoff, but he almost made it. In 334 B.C., at the age of twenty, after receiving the throne from his slain father Philip under dubious circumstances, Alexander set off from Macedonia to Greece with 12,000 infantry and 1,500 cavalry. He subjugated Greece, Phyrigia, Syria, Libya, Armenia, Media, Bactria—in short, the Persian Empire. Every time he won, he convinced the opposing soldiers (and sometimes their leaders) to join him until he commanded the most powerful army on earth. When Darius was dying, he said he was glad that Alexander, rather than someone else, was succeeding him to the throne.

After the battle of Arbela, enemies fought Alexander with guerrilla tactics. He changed his tactics to defeat them, but he never changed his objective. He established seventy cities, constructed the world's greatest library (later destroyed), civilized nomads, and might have conquered the entire known world had he not taken ill and died at thirty-three. While dying, Alexander was asked who should be the one to continue pursuing the objective. He replied, "The best man." The best man wasn't good enough, and soon Alexander's empire crumbled.

Cortez, not mentioned by Clausewitz or any of the marketing warfare writers (perhaps he was too warlike for them), maintained one fanatical objective: conquer Mexico at any cost. On a personal crusade for gold and fame, he landed at Vera Cruz with four hundred Spanish warriors. Through amazing feats of courage and gall, and often deceit and treachery, he succeeded in converting 200,000 Indians to his cause against the Aztec emperor, Moctezuma.

Aztecs were highly civilized and centered their culture in the exquisitely beautiful city of Tenochtitlan, which Cortez razed through one of the greatest naval sieges of all time. He set up his capital there and called it Mexico City. He met his objective; Mexico was his.

Marketing strategists and managers must also fix their sights on one objective so it can be attained. Neutrogena positioned itself in consumers' minds as premium soap and related products and it has been very successful over the years.

Conglomerates, or any big company with several product lines, must set and meet many objectives. This means that each division or company within the conglomerate must have its team to set its own objective, one that is consistent with the parent objective.

A good example of this is the Grumman Corporation. They make high-quality canoes that are fun to zip around in. They also make another high-quality vehicle that's fun to zip around in—the F–14 Tomcat, the world's finest fighter/bomber. Both are successful products, and though very different, both feature the Grumman reliability of performance, an important quality in water and air.

Yet some big companies mix too many diverse objectives that do not blend well. Exxon's jump (and fall) into office products was an example of incongruent objectives. Ries and Trout (p. 197) humorously ask, "Did General Mills have a strategic plan before they lost their shirt on Izod?"

An army or business enterprise cannot maintain objectives without effective *leadership*, the ninth principle. All the military marketing authors agree on one thing—America's businesses need leaders, not more human resource managers who sneak their way to the top by never making a wrong decision (or a right one). Not that we don't have some good ones (e.g., Iacocca in Chapter 7). We just don't have enough.

What are the qualities of a good leader? Michaelson (p. 151) correctly states that every business and military commander "must be a manager, a theorist, and a leader of men." That is, a good leader must be able to administrate, understand and plan strategy and tactics, and motivate an army or an organization to perform at a consistent level of excellence.

Only this kind of woman or man can successfully lead a business enterprise (or a country) to greatness. That we produce so few people of this caliber is due in part to what I said in Chapter 1—we teach people to specialize rather than generalize, to conform rather than initiate, to follow tradition rather than seek new answers and new outlooks.

For the last few years, many corporate leaders have exhibited caution over courage. Some are cowards afraid to risk their capital and egos (remember, their lives are not on the line in the corporate jungle), but they arrange golden parachutes for themselves so they can bail out and tough beans for their employees and stockholders.

Here is a typical example. Through dirty deals (à la General Loudoun), Drexel executives made their company look good with other people's money. When the bottom fell out, Drexel declared bankruptcy and its 5,000 employees were suddenly out on the street (Eichenwald 1990: A1). A story in the *Los Angeles Times* pointed out that Drexel's creditors were upset with Drexel when they learned that it doled out up to $350 million worth of bonuses to its brokerage unit executives just before filing bank-ruptcy. Strangely, Drexel filed bankruptcy because they couldn't get bank loans of $300 million or more to help with their liquidity crisis.

Sadly, the Drexel example is one of many. We wouldn't have to search far to find impropriety and mismanagement in the savings and loan industry. Is this the image our corporate leaders wish to project to the world?

This must change. But how did we get this way? What would the founders of our nation say if they saw us now? The problem of weak leadership prevails not just in business, but in the military. Our generals don't lead soldiers into battle any more. (The last leaders on the battle-field were a few World War II generals such as Patton.) Now they strategize from a safe distance and let lieutenants in tactical situations provide leadership.

There is a saying in the navy: "In the old days, ships were made of wood and men were made of iron. Now, ships are made of iron and men are made of wood." If the men are made of wood, it's because their commanders are made of Styrofoam. They float to the top.

Here's another naval adage: "The captain goes down with the ship." That means the captain is totally responsible for his ship and crew—and all that happens. If the ship sinks, he makes sure everyone else gets off before he does, even if that means he goes down with the vessel. To the credit of the U.S. Navy, I believe most ship captains take on that immense responsibility. I only wish captains of industry would do the same.

If we check out the great leaders of the past, we will find that they inspired their men to achieve greatness by personally leading the charge. This includes Genghis Khan, Attila, Napoleon, and Alexander the Great. Alexander was a great warrior and received many wounds. In the battle against Darius at Arbela, Alexander made the first charge and hacked his way to his tactical objective—Darius himself. After witnessing Alex-ander's courage and ferocity, his men felt it their duty to emulate their godlike leader.

Cortez, the murderous conquistador, was similar to Alexander in that he inspired his men to give their all, then led the charge with berserk abandon. His most remarkable military feat occurred after he and his men slashed their way out of Tenochtitlan (itself a feat).

The Spaniards fled to Otumba, where they were surrounded by the largest assembly of Indian forces ever recorded in North America (Tomp-kins 1976: 11). Tompkins wrote that "tens of thousands of Indians . . . crowded into the valley . . . convinced they had come to witness the death of every Spaniard." The Spaniards (most were already wounded, including Cortez) numbered about 500, augmented with perhaps 1,000 Tlaxcalan Indian allies.

What did Cortez do? He charged right down the center with his cavalry and aimed for Indian war chiefs wearing bright feathered headdresses. One by one, the Indian war chiefs fell, the massive army became confused, and the Aztecs fled, with Cortez' mounted lancers in hot pursuit. This is an example of strong leadership making up for vast inferiority of numbers. (Cortez created unique visual displays to convince his 500 men to follow him on foot across Mexico to conquer 400,000 Indian warriors—like burning all of his ships so they would conquer or die!)

A good leader will use all the principles described thus far in concert to achieve military or marketing objectives. But there is one more principle that Clausewitz (p. 199) says "lies at the foundation of all undertakings without exception." That is our tenth principle—*surprise*.

There are three ways to achieve surprise in war: sneak attack, feinting (deception/strategem), and using new techniques and technology. Let's examine each of these.

Guerrillas like Lawrence of Arabia and the American Indians successfully used sneak attack. Franklin (pp. 174–177) describes a successful sneak attack during the French and Indian War in which British General Braddock was thrashed by a force less than half his. According to Franklin, General Braddock bragged to him that he would quickly take Fort Duquesne from the French, and then proceed to Niagara. Franklin pointed out to Braddock that his troops would march many miles on narrow roads and might be flanked by Indians. But Braddock, used to European-style fighting (superior forces lined up in rows and columns engaging in frontal assaults), would not listen to Franklin. The colonists gave Braddock Indian scouts to help him, but he slighted them and they left. (Recall that Darius also refused to heed competitive intelligence.)

The French and their Indian allies waited until Braddock was nine miles from Fort Duquesne before they attacked from behind trees while he was reassembling his forces to continue the march. Braddock directed his officers and men forward to where the attack was, then more French and Indians, still hidden by trees and bushes, flanked the British. Franklin (p. 175) relates what happened next:

> The officers, being on horseback, were more easily distinguished, picked out as marks, and fell very fast; and the soldiers were crowded together in a huddle, having or hearing no orders, and standing to be shot at till two-thirds of them were killed; and then being seized with a panic, the whole fled with precipitation.

The wagon drivers carrying supplies fled, leaving all provisions and artillery to the enemy. Four hundred French and Indians, suffering no losses, killed 800 of Braddock's 1,200 picked men, including three-fourths of his officers. This happened in 1755. The military historian and theorist Clausewitz (and the British) could have learned something important from it.

But that's not the end of our story. The sneak attack so terrified Braddock and his men that they ran (without pursuit) back to their reinforcements of 1,000 men under Colonel Dunbar, who abandoned all supplies and joined the flight, plundering and abusing the settlers they were supposed to protect, and finally ending up cowering in Philadelphia. General Braddock, mortally wounded in the skirmish, said on his deathbed, "Who would have thought it?"

The irony of this sad tale is that Franklin and the colonists had asked the British if they could form a militia and defend themselves, but the British, fearful that the colonists might become too "independent," denied their request. Franklin (p. 176) commented: "This whole transaction gave us Americans the first suspicion that our exalted ideas of the prowess of British regulars had not been well founded."

This story dramatically illustrates the power of the sneak attack. The American colonists used it often in their revolution. We all remember the story of Washington crossing the Delaware on Christmas night to catch the Hessians off guard and defeat them.

In marketing, the sneak attack is seen in a sudden flanking move into an unoccupied market segment, taking the competition by surprise. The beer market in general was surprised by Miller's sudden leap into a new market with Lite. Miller responded quickly to the latent need for light beer.

The feint is another form of surprise. Clausewitz used the term *strategem* to mean "concealed intention, deceit." He noted that *strategy*, and *strategem* are derived from the same root, yet he belittled strategem (pp. 206–207) as a dangerous trick that may be done in vain.

But Napoleon thought deceit was a good thing and used it regularly. Evidently, he had read Machiavelli's *The Prince*, for Napoleon was a master of deceit, both in diplomacy and on the battlefield. Austerlitz, his most successful battle, was won by deceit. According to Herold (1983: 145), Napoleon left the Heights of Pratzen to attack the Austro-Russian forces, and "stationed the larger part of his troops behind the heights and ostensibly made preparations for a rearguard action designed to protect his retreat."

He conned the enemy into making a flanking movement on his right by having his troops feign a cavalry advance and retreat, as if awed by the sight of the enemy. The next day he lured the Austro-Russian forces from the hilltop. As the enemy descended, Napoleon's troops suddenly attacked, split the enemy forces in two, and took the vacated heights. This confused the enemy and they were routed. The enemy lost 26,000 men; Napoleon lost 9,000. Napoleon gained not just a victory on the battlefield, but a psychological advantage over the Austrian and Russian emperors, which he later used to outwit and outflank them in treaty negotiations.

In business and marketing, deceit against competitors to gain advantage often ends in lawsuits. Deceit against consumers, once detected, is organizational suicide. Northrop (Weinstein 1990: A9) pleaded guilty to thirty-four criminal charges and paid the government $17 million, a hefty fine for defrauding the military by falsifying nuclear-armed cruise missile component tests. You can be sure their future bids for defense contracts will be carefully scrutinized.

Still, some companies try to deceive. Sometimes they get away with it and sometimes they don't. Shell got into trouble when they advertised that their gas was so great because it had platformate. It turned out that platformate is a standard ingredient in gas.

The STP ad, featuring Andy Granatelli dropping screwdrivers coated with STP, helped sell a lot of STP. STP earned a net profit of over $6 million in 1976. The problem was deceptive advertising. Did STP actually do what Andy (and later actor Robert Blake) claimed? Who knows? We do know that STP paid a $500,000 fine and spent $200,000 on corrective advertising. Caveat emptor.

Throughout history, strategic use of new technology in warfare has contributed significantly to battle outcomes—and in some cases, began and ended wars. When new weapons are combined with strategem and sneak attack, the results can be deadly for the enemy.

When the Iron Age succeeded the Bronze Age around 2,000 B.C., strong metal swords and other weapons brought a sharp edge to disputes in Asia. The Greek phalanx defeated the Persians at Marathon in 490 B.C. In 451 A.D., the Romans defeated Attila's Huns by using bronze armor and helmets against stone axes. The English longbow defeated the French in 1346 at Crecy.

The advent of gunpowder and TNT changed warfare forever. In the American Civil War, the new Gatling gun killed and maimed many on the battlefield. Over the years, true machine guns were developed, and the Germans introduced the heavy machine gun at the beginning of World War I. In its first day of use at the River Somme, 50,000 English and French troops were slaughtered.

As aerial warfare rapidly developed in World War I, machine guns were put on planes. Fighter planes emerged and the Red Knight of Germany ruled the skies. Bombers were developed in this war, as were the tank, submarine warfare, and the first use of carriers to support planes carrying torpedoes. All of these were "new and improved" by World War II.

The second World War introduced radar to track airplanes and sonar to track submarines. Since then, electronics and wireless communications, including satellites, have dramatically changed the face of warfare. In 1945, the Germans bombed England with V–2 rockets. They also developed a Messerschmidt jet airplane and stealth aircraft, but the war ended before these were operationalized.

On the "day that will live in infamy," the Japanese started their war with the U.S. with a surprise—the sneak attack aerial bombing of Pearl Harbor. The U.S. ended the war with a surprise—the atomic bomb.

Modern Military and Marketing Technology

Marketing warfare authors don't talk about surprises such as "the bomb" because it smashes their battlefield analogies to atoms. It makes war look like hell, which is no surprise. If Clausewitz could have foreseen what weapon innovation would produce, he would have changed his basic principle from superior forces to superior technology. Ask novelist Tom Clancy about the importance of modern military technology.

Marketing generals, along with everyone else, have difficulty fathoming modern superweapons such as thermonuclear bombs, neutron bombs, MIRVs, ICBMs, and cruise missiles. One nuclear bomb delivery system now in production is the B–2 Stealth bomber. Each bomber will cost only $270 million, once economy of scale has been achieved (Cole 1989: 62). The plane's selling points are its 6,000-mile unrefueled range, a 50,000-pound internal weapons load, and the radar profile of a crow. The bad news is that a peasant with a deer rifle might plug this unarmed, hardly nimble, low-flying, subsonic, ultrawide-winged crow from a mile away. Ask A–6 Intruder aviators how dangerous it was flying low-level bombing missions in Vietnam against peasants with rifles.

If the B–2 is a crow, the Trident submarine is an orca—the predator on top of the ocean food chain. It can hide under the polar ice cap for as long as it wants—years if desired. It can launch its full complement of nuclear missiles in a few minutes and you can bet that the planet would look different afterward. The Trident is a vital part of our strategic effort to keep the peace. In the twenty-first century, we'll likely see the advent of the Seawolf submarine (Alden 1987: 180). The only thing it won't be able to do is fly.

The Americans and Soviets are busy working on Star Wars projects that will make the *Starship Enterprise* phaser banks a reality, though we throw only "bright pebbles" today. And nations also research chemical and germ warfare, though the Geneva Conventions prohibit deploying such weapons.

Many people believe that innovations used for military purposes are bad. They worry that mankind may purposefully or accidentally destroy civilization. Some Americans don't like the fact that 25 percent of our federal budget goes to defense ($300 billion a year). Congress is responding to pressure from citizens and questioning possibly unneeded military expenditures (Broder 1990).

Marketers are not pressured to create and produce ever more powerful weapons that hopefully will never be used. Lucky for us, surprises we release on the market enrich consumers' lives. Some new products are capricious, even frivolous, but they usually cause no harm.

In the twentieth century, marketers have brought essential and enriching inventions and innovations to American consumers. Executives from the Soviet Union studying business at my campus, California State University at Hayward, were astounded by our supermarkets, which display a myriad of foods and beverages conveniently packaged and reasonably priced. No lines here! Meanwhile, in 1990, Soviets stand in line for six hours at McDonald's to enjoy an American hamburger!

Thanks to marketing efforts, Americans enjoy a wide selection of stylish and functional clothes, major appliances, and recreation opportunities. Marketers give us new and better automobiles that match our needs. Even past military research has paid dividends to consumers: jet planes (with radar) for fast transportation, microwave ovens, and satellite navigation.

Communication products are among the best gifts marketers have made available to consumers. Communication hardware products include telephones, radios, televisions, VCRs, satellite dishes, video cameras, fax and copy machines, computers, and stereos. I bet that everyone reading this book owns at least three of the products listed here. Every year more communication products and services become available, and communication software (music, films, and other entertainment) is available everywhere.

As communication access proliferates, marketers and consumers become more symbiotically linked. Both groups need and want to communicate with each other. Through communication channels, marketers have ever more ways of reaching target consumers. But we were not the first to create images and use media to disseminate these images. The great military masterminds used words, symbols, and deeds to communicate with the populace and the enemy.

IMAGE AND PROPAGANDA

Throughout history, emperors have used image and propaganda to control the hearts and minds of their people. The battlefield in war, as in marketing, is really the mind. Here are some outstanding examples of image manipulation and propaganda proliferation from military history.

In my opinion, Alexander the Great, in addition to being the greatest military leader and conqueror ever, was also the greatest military pro-

pagandist of all time. When I first researched him ten years ago, I was
so moved that I named my first son after him. There have been over
twenty books written on Alexander, including classics by Arrian, Cur-
tius, Diodorus, Plutarch, and Ptolemy. His own journal and letters have
been published and critiqued by numerous scholars. Over a hundred
journal articles have been written about him from differing fields—military, religion, art, administration.

Back in 330 B.C., media channels were considerably less available than
now. There were three ways to distribute information: word of mouth,
public event (oratory or ceremony), and writing. Alexander, educated
by Aristotle, the father of rhetoric, was a master of all three forms. He
employed an official propagandist named Callisthenes to ensure that
events were recorded to his liking.

Alexander believed he was the son of Zeus, and he made his soldiers
believe it also. They worshipped him as a god. When he spoke to his
men, he named several of them and detailed their deeds of conspicuous
heroism. As he briefed his troops before his battle with Darius at Issus
he said: "Remember, that danger has already threatened you and you
have looked it triumphantly in the face. . . . They, no match for us in
bodily strength or resolution, will find their superiority in numbers to
no avail. . . . And what, finally, of the two men in supreme command?
You have Alexander, they–Darius!" (Arrian 1971: 112).

Alexander's oratory motivated his men to fight—and convinced some
Greek states to follow him on his conquest of Asia. He had statues,
monuments, and entire cities erected in his honor as he travelled. Whenever a city or state voluntarily welcomed him, he presided over athletic
contests and festivities—and always paid tribute to the local deities, from
Artemis to Zeus. In Babylonia, he honored Marduk, their equivalent of
Zeus. In India, he conducted religious ceremonies to their local gods.

In Thebes, conspirators alleged that Alexander was dead and incited
the Thebans to revolt against his rule. To prove the conspirators wrong,
Alexander came and gave them ample opportunity to repent. They
wouldn't, Alexander attacked, and a battle ensued. The Thebans fled
into their fortified city in such a panic that they forgot to close the gates,
and a massacre resulted as the Macedonians rushed unopposed into the
city.

Later, the Greeks, probably trying to reconcile the horror of the Theban
slaughter, declared that the massacre was due to the wrath of the gods,
for Thebes had earlier betrayed Greece in the Persian War. To serve as
a warning to other Greek states, Alexander razed Thebes and sold its
remaining citizens into slavery. Later, as he hosted the Olympic games,
the word went around that the statue of Orpheus sweated when Alexander entered Thebes, a sign to the superstitious Greeks of Alexander's
godlike power.

One of Alexander's greatest publicity coups was his untying of the Gordian knot. Legend had it that whoever could untie the knot would rule Persia. The complex knot bundle showed no beginning or end, so how could he untie it? The most popular account of what occurred was that Alexander cut the knot in two with his sword and proclaimed, "I have undone it!"

The tales of Thebes and Gordius spread fast by word of mouth. A few days later, Alexander approached the Cilician Gates, which were heavily fortified. When the defenders saw him in the flesh, they fled. On many occasions after that, Alexander's enemies ran when they saw him or immediately surrendered. Those who didn't were awed by his daring in battle, and when defeated were often converted to his cause. Alexander used pomp and ceremony to advantage. He married his Macedonian soldiers to Persians to cement ties between the peoples, and he even adopted Persian dress.

Alexander was loved by most of his subjects and soldiers, which is more than can be said of Genghis Khan and Cortez. Machiavelli (1910: 66–67) wrote that Alexander came to an unhappy end (Machiavelli believed that Alexander was poisoned, though this has not been proved) because he would play lion but not fox, and Machiavelli claimed a leader must do other than good to maintain authority. Machiavelli's words have inspired slimy politicians throughout history to create false images to induce the populace to believe anything so the politicians can stay in power. We'll discuss a few of these tyrants presently.

Alexander wasn't the only lion to create and manipulate a true image to accomplish his goals. The sight of Attila the Hun caused his enemies to quake in their sandals. According to Roberts (1985: 50–51), Attila's beautiful horse and sword were legend. These trappings furthered his image of super-warrior and destined leader of Huns.

In the thirteenth century, Ghengis Khan led the Mongols in plundering Eurasia and established what would become the largest geographic empire of all time. (It lasted for only a century.) According to Rossabi (1988), Genghis would send an envoy to communicate to the Chinese, Koreans, Hungarians, Polish, Afghans or whomever was next that they should surrender. Genghis' image of power and ferocity were well known throughout Eurasia, and when his envoys spoke, people listened and surrendered. If they refused the envoy's offer, they were massacred.

Genghis' grandson, Khubilai, was set up to rule China, a sophisticated civilization compared to the Mongols. He did more than deliver edicts; he listened, mostly to leaders of Confucian, Buddhist, and Taoist sects. By securing their favor, he made peace with the Chinese to a degree where he trusted them to administer their own affairs (as long as they paid taxes). His delegation of authority to the Chinese freed him to pursue more important matters, like becoming Khan of Khans, which he did.

Then came Napoleon, Machiavelli's lion and fox. In his book *Napoleonic Propaganda* (1950), historian Robert Holtman devotes 130 pages to Napoleon's organized attempts to manipulate public opinion through various papers and books, military and political publications, public gatherings, education, religion, and the arts. Napoleon, truly expert at propaganda and image manipulation, said, "The truth is not half so important as what people think to be true."

Holtman (p. 201) concluded his study of Napoleon with: "Thus, Napoleon, in his use of propaganda devices, frequently relied on a slim, necessary base of truth. Consequently, it was the skill of his various distortions that gave the measure of his artistry and of his success."

Napoleon propagandized so well that he is still romanticized to this day. In movies, he is portrayed as a gallant hero and lover. *National Geographic* featured a 48-page lead article on Napoleon (Putnam 1982). Others also manipulated images, though they are remembered less fondly than Napoleon.

Cortez distorted truth to the Aztecs and his superiors back in Spain (although he was forthright and democratic with his men). He capitalized on a lucky situation. It seems the Aztecs, especially Moctezuma, believed Cortez to be Quetzalcoatl, the god of learning, who was supposed to return to Mexico and perform godlike activities. Though this seems more legend than truth, Cortez, by staging visual displays that the Aztecs recorded with picture-writing, conned Moctezuma into welcoming Cortez and his five hundred soldiers to Tenochtitlan. That was the beginning of the end for Moctezuma and the Aztec civilization.

During World War I, in the isolated deserts of Arabia, T. E. Lawrence performed his daring military feats—and all the world knew of it. Why? A photojournalist named Lowell Thomas paraded Lawrence's exploits in newspapers around the globe. Colonel Lawrence was one of the first media darlings. (Colonel North take note.) Since then, Lawrence has been immortalized through book and television biographies. The 1962 movie about his life (a very abbreviated version of his actual deeds) won Academy Awards for best director and best picture. The cinematic re-release in 1989 of a longer version of the film brought a new audience to appreciate the life of this soldier hero.

It wasn't until World War II that a military leader was able to deceive millions using all available media, including large-scale dissemination of propaganda films, the most notable made by Leni Reifenstahl. The dictator's name was Adolph Hitler, the man who said that if a lie were big enough, people would believe it.

If Alexander was the first propagandist, and Napoleon the first to systematically use propaganda, then Hitler was the first mere politician (and not fighting soldier) to systematically use propaganda to win the battle of the mind. We all know how successful he was in his efforts to manipulate opinion.

Americans also used propaganda quite effectively during WWII. Oscar-winning director Frank Capra made two hard-hitting documentaries about Germany and Japan called *Know Your Enemy*. These films were designed to rally Americans behind the war effort. They served their purpose; Americans were churned up and eager to contribute in any way they could (fighting, buying war bonds, or working in munitions factories). Uncle Sam wants you!

Meanwhile, Mao Zedong was quietly rising to power in China. Napoleon called China the sleeping giant. Mao made the giant stir, not with manipulation of media channels, but through word-of-mouth proselytizing. While Chiang Kai-shek was attempting to consolidate power in southern China, Mao indoctrinated subordinates who in turn indoctrinated millions of peasants in northern China to Mao's form of Communism. Mao's promise: Freedom and land for all.

Hundreds of millions of Chinese believed Mao and helped him defeat Chiang. However, more than forty years later the Chinese still wait for freedom and land for all.

Modern Image-Makers

Modern day marketers, military leaders, and politicians have gleaned much from the propaganda successes of past conquerors and dictators. From Alexander to Zedong, we have learned the importance of systematic use of all communication modes: oratory, print media, films, public displays and ceremonies, listening and delegating, and word-of-mouth indoctrination down the chain of command. Some leaders lied; others spoke truth. The common link among them was the innovative use of communication to influence people to relinquish their minds, property, and lives.

Ronald Reagan, dubbed "the Great Communicator," used his affable personality to get elected ("There you go again Jimmy, with the facts") and extricate himself from trouble ("I don't remember"). Only Teflon-coated Reagan could joke about pushing the button, call the Soviet Union "the evil empire," and still assist ace propagandist Gorbachev achieve glasnost.

It seems that esteemed members of Congress have also learned something from the classic rhetoricians—how to look good without actually doing anything. Barry Goldwater (1988: 4–5) laments that today's senators can't hold a candle to those of the past. "Appearances—media attention, staff-generated bills, and professional packaging like some mouthwash—often replace legislative tenacity." He believes many

Americans are "more concerned with money and appearances than genuine accomplishment." This is probably reflected on the Senate floor, "a babbling marketplace of pet projects and personal promotion instead of measured debate on major issues."

Even if Congress is showboating instead of dedicating itself to solving our nation's big problems, others in government use promotional activities to achieve good. Upon assuming office, President Bush envisioned "a kinder, gentler nation." I believe he will live up to this ambitious dream.

If we look around, we see there were many other individuals in history who changed the world without killing or subjugating anyone. To date, many have used persuasion and communication feats to help humanity, and some gave their lives in the process. Among the notables: Jesus, Sir Thomas More, Gandhi, and Martin Luther King, Jr.

Perhaps marketers, as we pursue our goals, should strive to emulate peacemakers rather than warmongers. I think we have the opportunity in this decade to use marketing communications to offer good alternatives to consumers rather than to trick them into buying junk they don't need.

BEYOND MARKETING WAR

The reason I devoted so much evidence to showing the horror along with the glory of battles and war toys is, as I mentioned at the start of this chapter, war *kills*—needlessly. Great conquerors such as Alexander are unquestionably brave and brilliant, but to what end? Alexander's superlative military feats won him land—later lost to mismanagement and new invaders.

Indeed, if we examine the history of part of Alexander's world, say Mesopotamia (the area around the Tigris and Euphrates rivers in what is now Iraq), here's what we would find. The Sumerians ruled in 2800 B.C. They were succeeded chronologically by the Akkadian Empire, the Empire of Ur, the Old Babylonian Empire, Babylonia, the Assyrian Empire, New Babylonian and Median empires, the Persian Empire, Alexander's empire, and the Seleucid Empire. This was all before the birth of Christ. After Christ, Mesopotamia was ruled by the Roman and Parthian empires, the Sassanid Empire, the Mayyad Empire, the Seljuk Turks, the Abbasid Califate, the Mongols, the Ottomon Empire, Persia (Iran), and Iraq. The Iraqis and Iranians warred over certain parts of the area through much of the 1980s. In 1990, the Iraqis annexed Kuwait and war tensions rose to their highest levels ever. Who knows what will happen next in Mesopotamia? It all seems kind of senseless.

Millions have suffered, and for what? To temporarily change borders, names of countries, and rulers? War pits the greedy against the needy.

If the greedy win, the needy have less. If the needy win, the greedy have less. The irony, according to Buckminster Fuller (naval historian and strategist, scientist, professor, futurist, inventor of the geodesic dome, and Nobel Peace Prize nominee), is that there is plenty for all. In the big picture, there is no scarcity of resources, hence, there is no need to fight as if there were. We just need to acknowledge this, use our intellect a bit, and act. Now.

We hope to learn from history. As Santayana said, "Those who cannot remember the past are condemned to repeat it." Marketers can benefit from military experience without repeating it. As Bismarck said, "Fools learn by experience. I prefer to learn by other people's experience."

If we go as far back in written history as possible to a foremost war strategist, we stop in 500 B.C. to heed the words of Sun Tzu: "To win 100 victories in 100 battles is not the acme of skill. To subdue the enemy without fighting is the acme of skill." (See Griffith 1963.) By analogy, we learn that we can compete in business without marketing warfare.

I believe that business, through a free market system, can lead the way to find and implement effective and peaceful solutions to many world problems. Thus, even though business is inherently competitive, we marketers should ease off the military marketing paradigm.

Rather than glorifying past military feats, which produce fruitless subjugation, we should applaud exploration, scientific invention, and virtuous deeds—and use our business acumen and marketing communication skills to improve the standard of living worldwide. That's not too much to ask, is it?

FAMOUS ADVENTURES

Before the 1400s, the known world for Europeans was Eurasia and North Africa. The Americas (named after Amerigo Vespucci) were considered legendary, like Atlantis. During the middle ages, extensive trade routes crisscrossed the Mediterranean Sea and linked Europe with spice-producing Asia. Commerce flourished. The great Italian explorer Marco Polo led several expeditions to Asia, met with Khubilai Khan, and opened new land and coastal routes for trade.

That was great for the Italians, but the Portuguese wanted to get in on the spice action. As in the best-selling science fiction novel *Dune*, whoever controlled spice trade controlled the world. Believing that the earth was round instead of flat, the Portuguese set out to discover a westerly route across open ocean to Asia. (For details on the Portuguese Age of Discovery, read Boxer 1969; Dos Passos 1969.) Let's examine how a desire for domination in commerce led to exploration of the Americas.

Great Sea Captains

Who discovered America? All schoolchildren answer: Christopher Columbus in 1492. What a promotional feat! How did Columbus get the credit for this important discovery? Simple. He convinced Ferdinand and Isabella of Spain to finance, document, and publicize his voyages, which they did, and that's why he is in *The Dictionary of Cultural Literacy* (Hirsch, Kett, and Trefil 1988) and João Vaz Corte-Real of Portugal (who discovered America in 1472) is not. The funny part is that in four voyages, not once did Columbus set foot on U.S. soil, yet I would bet that many Americans think he landed at Plymouth Rock or Daytona Beach or some other prominent place in America. That's the enduring power of publicity for you.

Marketing communications professionals can learn from Columbus on how to exploit an innovation, even if they're not first. But was even Corte-Real the first to discover America?

Carthaginian coins dated 400 B.C. have been found on the Azores. Did Carthaginians venture all the way to America? Maybe Phoenicians? Perhaps ancient Japanese explorers landed in Alaska or British Columbia centuries before Columbus. Evidence shows that Vikings landed in North America around 1000 A.D. Erik the Red and his sons (notably Leif) plied the southwestern waters off Greenland. It would have been no big deal to sail 300 miles or so to Canada while fishing.

At any rate, the argument is moot; Columbus gets the credit. It is worth noting, however, that Prince Henry the Navigator set up a pilot/navigation school in southern Portugal in the early 1400s that was attended by every European sea captain of note, including Columbus. When Henry died in 1460, the Portuguese ships sailed from Lisbon, but their destinations were kept secret—to this day. The penalty for disclosing a Portuguese shipping route was death. Loose lips let the word out that the Portuguese had discovered a gold-filled utopia across the Atlantic called Brazil. It was believed by some that the Portuguese sea captains secretly ruled the world south and west of Europe. But we may never know, because no genuine documents have been discovered to provide evidence for or against this claim.

According to Innes (1969), Columbus (a Genoese) married a Portuguese woman and then discovered papers and perhaps a log of a sea captain relative of hers. He made some bucks copying and selling the captain's maps, but he wanted to go to the new lands. He tried to convince King John of Portugal to support him, but John said Columbus brought him nothing new. So Columbus entreated with Isabella and Ferdinand, who wanted their share of the secret goodies, and the rest is history.

Here's the relevance of this long sea story. Because Columbus' voyages were documented and publicized, interest in the new world exploded. Soon, everyone wanted to check out America, including the British. The British were smart; they sent colonists to North America. After initial hardships, they flourished. A few (180) years later, the year is 1776 and the colonies adopt the *Declaration of Independence*. A competitive interest in commerce fueled new world exploration and led to our nation's birth.

After losing America, the poor British concentrated on tea trade with China. To increase their profits, the British coerced the Chinese into becoming opium addicts. The British stopped in India on the way to China and purchased opium, sold it to the unwilling Chinese, filled their holds with tea, and sailed home to merry England. The pesky Americans wanted tea (not opium), and designed the great clipper ships. These fast ships beat out the British clunkers on the high seas. Soon, the resourceful Americans led the tea trade. When gold was discovered in California, most 49ers traveled by clipper around South America to San Francisco—and then to fields of gold. The clipper ship era was a time of high adventure and marked America's emerging dominance in commerce.

Through continued land exploration in the 1800s, the rest of America was "discovered." Native Americans were killed or sent to reservations, French and Russians were bought off, and Mexicans were fought off. Through manifest destiny, we managed to expand to our current size of fifty states. At that time it was thought there was plenty of room and opportunity for all Americans, but we have become crowded, so what's next for modern adventurers to explore? The next frontiers—undersea and outer space.

Modern Adventurers

Humans have explored most of the ocean's surface, but not much of the bottom has been explored in detail. Scientists and environmentalists such as Jacques Cousteau have made concerted efforts to study the ocean's depths. Thanks to the ongoing promotional feats of Captain Cousteau, we are aware of how fragile the ocean ecosphere is. Though many people today are worried about the rain forests, few know that most of our oxygen comes from plankton in the ocean. Cousteau fears we are creating a worldwide toxic dump in the ocean, and if those little plants in the ocean die, we die. It's something to think about. If there are any marketing communications people out there looking for a good cause to promote, this is it: Save Our Seas—SOS!

Now it's a whole different ballgame in space for adventurers, businesses, and marketing communications professionals. Tom Wolfe's blockbuster *The Right Stuff* (1979), a book on test pilots and Mercury astronauts, immortalized today's adventurous explorer—the rocket jock.

Based on Wolfe's book, nobody can deny that these guys had the right stuff. These pilots performed some remarkable feats, some you know about, some you don't. Here's a sample quiz to test your space pilot knowledge.

Who was the first man to fly the X–1? Slick Goodlin, of course. Who broke the impenetrable-world-is-flat-can't-be-done-demons'll-get-you sound barrier, also in the X–1? Chuck (AC Delco) Yeager. Believe it or not the "Sound Barrier Broken" headline didn't appear for a long while after the event. Why look for trouble? Must keep these events secret— just as the Portuguese sea captains did.

Who was the first man in space? Yuri Gagarin. Dang. Who went up less than a month after Yuri? Alan Shepard.

Did Shepard walk on the moon? Yes, but what did Neil Armstrong say while he was on the moon? Hint: It wasn't 'Veni, vidi, vici."

Who made the first space walk? Aleksei Leonov. Valentina Tereshkova was the first what? Woman in space. How come the Russians beat us to the punch in so many categories? The Cold War became the Space Race. It's survival of the fittest out in the cold void of space.

What test pilot was passed over as a Mercury astronaut but later went into space four times? Pete Conrad. What test pilot stuff was going on behind the scenes when Mercury astronauts were making headlines, appearing in *Life*, and talking with JFK? The X-rocket speed and altitude tests. Let's talk about X-planes.

Who's the fastest pilot in the fastest plane at the fastest speed? Joe Walker, X–15, 4,105 mph (Mach 5.92). It ain't Mach 6, but close enough. Who flew highest in an X–15? Bob White, who flew nine miles into space (that's 59.6 miles above the earth). Too bad he didn't go 60 miles, for then they might have gotten more funds. No Buck Rogers, no bucks, no Buck Rogers—Catch–22.

What plane was jokingly called a "Dyna-Soar," but was made "to go into orbit with a pilot at the controls from beginning to end, a pilot who could land it anywhere he wanted, eliminating the tremendous expense and risk of Mercury ocean-rescue operations" (Wolfe, p. 349)? The X–20. The space shuttle didn't come around for nearly 20 years, and to think we had shuttles with us all along.

Since the *Challenger* accident, NASA has been plodding along, afraid to make any big moves in public. The shuttle *Atlantis* quietly placed another military satellite into space in March 1990.

Meanwhile, Japan put a moon probe into orbit and several aerospace companies are working together to make a space plane for commercial use. This is a good trend. Let's get some healthy competition in space exploration and research—for peaceful means. Let's get more navigation, communication, and weather satellites into space. Let's make commercial space stations and use them as platforms for joint ventures to

Mars and other celestial ports of call. These stations could serve as depots for moon tourists, microwave relays for solar and cosmic powered energy for earth, pollution-free mining and manufacturing factories, and platforms for scientific studies and galactic probes, such as the Hubble Space Telescope (Perlman 1990).

Because of thawing relations with the Soviets and subsequent reductions in arms and troops, America may soon enjoy a "peace dividend" due to military spending cuts (Kershner 1990: A1). Though I wouldn't count my "golden age" before it hatches, the peace dividend may signal an opportunity for big defense contractors such as Bell Boeing, Martin Marietta, Raytheon, Tenneco, and Textron to gear up for new adventures in space exploration and commerce.

These ideas may seem like something out of a Jules Verne novel, but we could have space planes and stations right now if we would have pursued the X–15 program more vigorously—and cooperated more with the Soviets, Japanese, and European Space Agency. We can still begin space commerce by 2001 if everyone works together and cooperates.

Imagine marketing moon rides. From here, it seems like a giant leap into Tomorrowland for mankind; but remember, 100 years ago the airplane had yet to be invented. Air transportation by jet is now commonplace and inexpensive. And they even serve meals!

As we look forward to more bold feats for the good of humanity in this decade, we marketers should heed the words of the late astronaut Gus Grissom, who's three-word speech to Convair workers (my grandfather among them) became their motto: "Do good work."

3

Media Events

"If there is no excitement ready-made, some must be manufactured."
—Silas Bent

MARKETING IS ENTERTAINMENT! There is one industry that America leads. That's *entertainment*. That's right folks, step this way. The line forms to the rear. Hurry, hurry. You ain't seen nothin' yet. The one, the only, really big show, the greatest show on earth. So let's get on with the show. And away we go-o-o-o.

In our first chapter we saw that all aspects of marketing are communication and marketers should coordinate all communication aspects of a product and create promotional feats to nourish healthy demand. In Chapter 2, you were entertained with military feats. I argued that marketing is competitive and certain military principles apply, but we can go beyond marketing war and create exciting feats that enrich rather than subjugate life.

In this chapter, I propose that good marketing communication increases demand (sells) by providing entertainment. A promotional feat is a feat only because it entertains. The entertainment aspect is causally instrumental in persuading a prospect to try or buy your product.

What does it mean to entertain? Webster's definition: "to engage the attention of, . . . to divert, to please, to amuse." Here is an axiom that explains it. "For customers to entertain a purchase, you must first entertain them." That's a fair deal.

Why is it that people love and seek entertainment? Admit it, as a child you craved entertainment. You read books (comic books at least), listened to the radio, watched TV, and listened to stories, preferably scary ones. If you weren't engaged in these things, you amused yourself in some way—going on an adventure in the neighbor's orchard or the mall, playing pretend (house or doctor or army), or inventing something devious.

When I was a kid, I liked to be entertained a lot. I read my first real book, *Treasure Island*, when I was ten and knew what I wanted to be when I grew up—a pirate. I watched Lloyd Bridges in *Sea Hunt* and longed to be a frogman—but I was a tad too young. After viewing *The Wizard of Oz* a mere eight times as a youngster I grasped the main theme: Tap your heels together three times and say, "If I only had a brain." Now that I'm grown up, I am a pirate, I enjoy exciting movies, and I still read comics. (See Chapter 8 to find out more).

As adults we still seek lots of entertainment. That's what advertisers bank on, that people will wade through the ad to get to the entertainment. I say the ad (maybe a better word is *appeal*) should entertain as much or more as the entertainment; otherwise why would anyone waste a moment of precious time responding? I agree with Ogilvy that an appeal should sell (create specific demand for a product), but it must first compel a consumer to pay attention, or else it will be ignored, zapped, or scorned.

Successful promoters tap into the human need for drama and deliver original, entertaining appeals. The appeal can be for a product or service such as a cologne or airline transportation, or an event, like a prizefight or a concert benefit. The trick is making the event so appealing that people go out of their way to watch.

In this chapter, we look at media events—stunts that made it on media. I'm not focussing specifically on stunts for traditional manufacturing and retail business (see chapters 4–8 for that), but on general stunts, for *fun*, *fame*, or *fortune*.

One element all these stunts share is excitement. Some are cheap (like a demonstration); others are expensive (movies). Some are simple, other complex. Some last a minute, while others are ongoing. All serve as illustrations, ideas, possibilities for marketers to learn from and use when appropriate. By experiencing these ideas that have worked in the past and present, you may be stimulated to create something entirely new for the future. Just don't bore us.

Here's the order of entertainment. We begin with adventure stunts and follow that with athletic feats. Then we marvel at circus, sideshow, and magic acts. We next explore the wonderful world of movies. Finally, we look at promotional feats from art and music.

Enough talk. It's showtime! Lights, camera, action!

ADVENTURE STUNTS

Military and sea exploration feats described in Chapter 2 comprise the bulk of adventures before the twentieth century. During the past century, adventures for "firsts" have flowered. Magellan's crew may have been the first to sail around the world in 1520, but nowadays circumnavigation by sea is no big deal. Now people sail around the world to see who's fastest. The Whitbred Yacht Race, a round-the-world yacht speed marathon held every four years for the past 16 years, is the quintessential example of a current sailing feat. Today, seaworthy examples of firsts exist in many categories: first to sail around the world in a small sailboat, alone, fastest, underwater, you name it. I wonder who will paddle first around the globe in a kayak (anyone but me).

Aviation Adventures

Air shows have been popular since WWI, when returning fighter pilots barnstormed the countryside. Modern military precision flying teams such as the Blue Angels and Thunderbirds continue to draw huge crowds. Tip: If you want to see military flyers do death-defying deeds daily, camp in the southern California high desert and bring your binoculars. Admission's free.

The venerated SR–71 Blackbird, the spy plane that made "peace through strategic reconnaissance" possible, retired from service in a blurring display of speed as one of the planes set an official record in March 1990 by crossing the U.S. in 68 minutes (a feat it performed regularly on active duty but never officially). The SR–71 landing at Dulles International Airport made front-page news across the nation.

Though military and NASA pilots have set many of the world's flight records, civilian pilots have garnered their share of firsts. Who holds the absolute record of speed around the world, nonstop, nonrefueled? No, not Chuck Yeager or an SR–71 pilot. The answer is Richard Rutan and Jeana Yeager. They flew around the world (25,012 miles) roundtrip from Edwards Air Force Base, in 9 days, 3 minutes, 44 seconds.

A picture of their aircraft, the stiff-paper-and-plastic Voyager, adorned the front page of the 1986 Christmas Eve editions of the *New York Times* and *Los Angeles Times*. After they landed, Rutan said "This was the last major event of atmospheric flight. That we did it as private citizens says a lot about freedom in America" (Blakeslee 1986: A1).

Rutan was not joking when he said "private citizens," for corporate sponsors spurned the effort, and Rutan and his brother Burt (the designer) built it with their own money, according to Jones (1986: A1). Heavily in debt, the Rutans pursued their dream despite the cost and cut safety corners when necessary to lower weight. "Obviously this flight was not insured," Rutan laughed (Browne 1990: A10).

Yeager (no relation to Chuck) and Rutan received a good deal of positive publicity from their feat. The *Los Angeles Times* devoted three front-page stories and four sidebars to the event. Former space shuttle test pilot Richard Truly said the flight was marvelous and compared it to Charles Lindbergh's solo transatlantic flight. President Reagan said Rutan and Yeager " . . . are a living example of American Pioneerism at its best." He later presented Yeager and the Rutans with the Presidential Citizens Medal.

The saga was covered by *Aviation Week and Space Technology* (Mordoff 1986), and *Newsweek* (Marbach and McAlevey 1986), among dozens of other publications, including *Reader's Digest, Wall Street Journal,* and *Sports Illustrated.* They appeared on television and finally cashed in with their book, *Voyager* (Yeager and Rutan 1987). Additionally, they received materials from King Radio and Scaled Composites (Stein 1986) and advertising sponsorship (during and after the flight) from Home Insurance and Shaklee.

Their determination, courage, and willingness to do it without a multimillion dollar budget is moving testimonial to the right stuff they abundantly possess. They eclipsed their biggest rival, Paul MacCready, inventor of the Gossamer Albatross, but have faded into obscurity over the past four years. Their stunt remains in the record books, but it and they have not made the news since 1987. The lesson: One great stunt will put you in the record books but it won't sell planes.

Mountain Man Messner

Human flies, without ropes or other equipment, scale Half Dome in Yosemite in hours instead of days. The trend in rock climbing is toward doing more with less. Ironically, the move toward simplicity flies in the face of old-style mountaineering, which urged use of more and more equipment: ropes, pitons, jumars, chocks, oxygen. Young men and women climb acrobatically these days. Soon, they'll leap from hold to hold. Spider Man lives. You can see him making the news by climbing city buildings and then getting arrested.

The sport of mountaineering (expedition climbing in a variety of alpine conditions) is also undergoing change. Since Edmund Hillary and Tensing Norgay first climbed Everest (also called Qomolangma—"goddess mother of the world") many have clambored atop it, setting sundry climbing records. One man achieved notoriety by skiing (or rather tumbling) down a face of Everest. It's all on a film entitled *The Man Who Skied Down Everest*—one hour of ennui, one minute of excitement.

In the past three decades, the person who has made the most firsts in alpine climbing is the great Italian superman, Reinhold Messner. After zooming up most major peaks in Europe, and telling everyone about it, he went after the fourteen really big peaks (over 8,000 meters) in Nepal and Tibet. His first Himalayan climb was Nanga Parbat in 1970. He climbed more peaks in the Himalayas, gathering industrial sponsors along the way, and writing articles and books (twenty-four books in all).

In 1978, Messner (1979) and Peter Habeler (1979) scaled Everest together without oxygen, "and the mountaineering world gasped" (Murphy 1986: 106). Actually, he climbed all fourteen of the major peaks without oxygen, an amazing feat.

In 1979, Messner conquered K2 (Messner and Gogna 1981). Then, in 1980, he went after Qomolangma again. But this time, things were different. "This time there were no porters. No fellow climbers. No bottled oxygen. No radio. I was attempting the greatest challenge, to me, in mountaineering—to climb the highest mountain on earth completely on my own" (Messner 1981: 556).

Did he make it? Naturally. But that's not all. He went on to climb the remaining 8,000-meter peaks, without oxygen of course. By 1986, Messner accomplished what no one had ever thought possible: he climbed the fourteen highest peaks in the world.

The difference between Messner and the Voyager pilots is that Messner made a name for himself early in his career and then banked on it. He lives in a castle and is recognized all over Europe as a super hero. Messner knew that one feat was not enough to stay in the limelight, and hence the big bucks. So he daringly accomplished feat after feat, capturing the adulation of the world. In 1986, he told the media that he was out to document the abominable snowman, the legendary yeti. Did he discover it? We have yeti to find out.

Pole Vaulting

Polar exploration is as exciting, dangerous, and competitive as mountaineering. In 1909, Robert E. Peary arrived at the North Pole by dogsled, but his feat was contested by a rival explorer, Frederick Cook. *National Geographic*, using scientific tests, finally verified Peary's claim 90 years later (Davies 1990) to end that debate.

The Arctic region has other firsts worthy of mention. Naomi Uemura of Japan reached the North Pole by dogsled in 1978. He accomplished the deed alone, accompanied only by a polar bear that tried to eat him.

In 1982, British explorers Ranulph Fiennes and Charles Burton circled the earth from pole to pole, at a cost of $18 million. An explorer, as of this writing, is attempting to repeat the deed, alone, with no sponsors. Go for it; get Goliath!

Nowadays, people race in dogsleds 1,158 miles from Anchorage to

Nome. The Iditarod Sled Dog Race attracts women as well as men. In fact, women have won the last five of six races. Susan Butchart has won four of these races.

Exploration and adventure in the Antarctic is just as exciting and competitive as way up north. A dogsled race to the South Pole found Norwegian Roald Amundsen the winner in 1911. A month later, his opponent, Captain Robert F. Scott, arrived. Not only did Scott lose the race, but he and everyone in his party perished in the cold.

Admiral Richard E. Byrd established Little America, a scientific colony, in Antarctica in 1929. By 1940, Byrd had charted most of the Antarctic coast. In 1989, two American women, Victoria Murden and Shirley Metz, skied to the South Pole with nine men. They were the first women to ski to the South Pole. These are impressive accomplishments. But there are more firsts in Antarctica.

In 1989, Will Steger led a dogsled trek (with lots of media support) on a 3,800-mile excursion north to south in Antarctica. Their purpose was to bring international attention to the environment. The team was composed of six men from France, the Soviet Union, China, and Japan. They completed their trip with lots of hoopla on March 3, 1990, according to Crary (1990: A4).

This trip, though arduous and expensive, was upstaged by guess who? Reinhold Messner. Messner and Arved Fuchs, who crossed Antarctica in 91 days, finished their 1,550-mile trip on February 12, 1990. The feat was another first for Messner—it was completed on foot! No dogs. The men used sails to pull their sleds and were able to cover over 50 miles a day. The German magazine *Der Spiegel* bought exclusive rights to the story and Messner scored yeti again.

What we learn from these exploration adventures is that only the first or fastest are remembered. Also-rans don't rate. And being first doesn't guarantee longevity in peoples' minds, even if you receive lots of publicity. Being first in a major category is more memorable than being first in a subcategory. For example, we all remember Hillary's climb of Everest, because he and Norgay were the first to climb the highest mountain in the world. Rolex watches still use this feat in their print ads (apparently Hillary wore one on the expedition). But we don't hear about or remember who was second on Everest, or the first Japanese climber, or even the first woman. However, people who are into climbing probably know the answers to some of these questions. So a feat, even in a specific category, can be remembered by a relevant market segment.

Another point worth considering is being the "greatest" in the adventure. People remember Messner because he made himself the greatest by publicizing his outrageous feats. People remember Peary, but not Cook. People remember the Wright brothers and Charles Lindbergh because their feats were great and not obscured by other events. I bet a nickel you don't remember Ms. R. M. Sharpe's 1950 record for speed over 100 kilometers in a light airplane (322.78 mph in a Supermarine Spitfire 5–B).

Promoters should note that first, fastest, greatest, and most are things to strive for when creating and executing promotional feats. "Me too" and "We tried" count for nothing. Let's check out the world of sports and athletics for more memorable feats.

ATHLETIC FEATS

Who's the greatest athlete there ever was? We agree there are many contenders, both amateur and professional. Let's see, how about Jim Thorpe? Bruce Jenner? Jesse Owens? Florence Griffith Joyner? Jean-Claude Killy? Martina Navratilova? Mikhail Baryshnikov? Magic Johnson? Babe Ruth? Jim Brown?

If you said Bo Jackson, you don't know diddley. On January 29, 1990 (which just happened to be one day after the Super Bowl), I asked 290 college students at campuses in the San Francisco Bay area: "Who's the greatest athlete there ever was?" Although all the names I presented above were mentioned at least once, the overall winner on that day was . . . Joe Montana!

Commentator John Madden said what we all were thinking during the game. "I think Joe's the best quarterback ever." After the game, the best selling t-shirt in the Bay area was inscribed with these memorable words: Joe Knows Super Bowls!

If you were to ask Joe Montana if he's the greatest athlete there ever was, he'd say no. He'd say he's only good because of his teammates. Why, did you see Ronnie Lott? Hey, how about those receivers and running backs? I've got the best line in football. My guys really protect me. . . .

This greatest athlete thing is important because although Joe may not be the best ever, he was chosen because he was in the media limelight when it mattered. The "greatest" athlete ever could be Hercules, Reinhold Messner, one of the people I discuss in this chapter, or someone no one has ever heard of. The trick to being great is getting others to notice—through a promotional feat like kicking Denver's butt in the Super Bowl.

I Won the Olympics

I bet you didn't know that at age 15 I broke all Olympic swimming records set by Duke Kahanamoku (the father of surfing) and Johnny Weissmuller (Tarzan). My high school swimming coach, Barbara Fish, told me so. I checked it out and she was right. I went around bragging to everyone, "Hey, I can beat Tarzan!"

Well it turns out that every decent swimmer in 1968 had beaten Tarzan. People improve in swimming so fast that in the 1988 Olympics a new Olympic and/or world record was set in twenty-six of thirty-one events. And two new swimming stars emerged for the United States, Matt Biondi and Janet Evans. Of course, we mustn't forget diver Greg Louganis, who smashed his face on the diving board and still took two gold medals to put on the mantel next to his two 1984 Olympic golds.

This swimming discussion is leading up to something. Yes, the greatest amateur athlete ever is a swimmer. He didn't win any individual events in 1968 and everyone was disappointed—he had a bad day— okay a bad week. But in 1972 he was the greatest amateur athlete ever. He won *seven* Olympic gold medals (four individual events, three relays). In every event he won he established a new Olympic record. No one before or since has won seven Olympic gold medals in any sport in one year. The poster of him in his American flag swimming suit adorned with the heavy medals broke all sales records. He was the idol of every red, white, and blue-blooded boy and girl in America. His name is Mark Spitz.

After his swimming career, he entered the exciting profession of dentistry and later became a TV commentator for yacht races. While he was sailing in the doldrums, every record he ever set was broken, over and over again. Mark was down, but not washed out. In fact, he's in the swim of things. The word in the water is that Spitz is making a flip turn and coming back. He plans to compete in the next Olympics. I can't wait to see what happens in Barcelona in 1992. Can you?

Other Outstanding Olympians

Jim Thorpe and Bruce Jenner, both American decathletes, won Olympic gold in the most demanding series of events in the games. Bruce Jenner made some money from ad sponsorship (he even had a shirt named after him) and then later became a sports commentator. Thorpe didn't fare so well. He was stripped of his medals because he had played baseball for money. Seventy years later, Thorpe's medals were restored posthumously. A movie biography of his life, with Burt Lancaster portraying Thorpe, keeps him alive in our memory.

In track, Carl Lewis was bested by Canada's Ben Johnson in a thrilling 100-meter run in the 1988 Olympics. But in this era of accountability, Johnson ran but couldn't hide from his steroid use. Johnson's gold medal and world record were taken from him and he was savaged by the media.

There were winners and lugers who made headlines in the Winter Olympics. In 1968, Jean-Claude Killy, like Anton Sailer before him, won all three men's alpine skiing events. But Killy was handsome and charming and thus became a media sensation, while Sailer, a regular guy, was left floating in the breeze.

Peggy Fleming and Dorothy Hamill, Americans who won gold medals in women's singles figure skating, both went on to professional skating careers and have served as commentators. Scott Hamilton, the men's 1984 singles figure skating winner, made big headlines in his hometown of Bowling Green, Ohio, where he was a local hero. He also used his Olympic achievement to help him in a professional skating career. Now that the Berlin Wall is down, the ice princess herself, Katarina Witt, will grace American ice rinks. The public eagerly awaits her next provocative move.

It's too bad there's no professional market for speed skaters. Eric Heiden, "Spitz on ice," won all five men's speed skating events in the 1980 Winter Olympics held at Lake Placid. There was nothing placid in his performance, yet it went unrewarded, at least commercially. How many people remember Heiden's great feat?

For that matter, who can name the greatest Olympic men's gymnastic team in history? It has to be the 1988 Soviet team that won seven of eight events, including best all-around and team. If the Soviets had been into capitalism in 1988, the names Artemov, Kharikov, and Bilozerchev would have adorned their nation's cereal boxes. Maybe in 1992 the Soviets will capitalize on outstanding athletic feats.

Which Olympic athlete has the most heart? Al Oerter, who won the discus throw in four consecutive Olympics, was still trying out for the team in the 1988 Olympics at age 51! What's more remarkable is his sense of sportsmanship. To Oerter, winning is less important than striving for excellence. In an interview (Widner 1988), Oerter said he disliked seeing Olympic contenders psyching each other out before competition. He noted that "the athletes who played the mental games did poorly" (p. 6).

To win in 1964 and 1968, Oerter had to overcome injury and pain. But the medals were less important to him than the journey to the Olympics. Oerter thinks the Olympics are about "stretching the limits together, seeing what we could collectively achieve in a celebration of capability (p. 7).

I admire Oerter and respect his views on competition. He believes the best should win—fairly. I agree. Applied to business and promotions, it is best in the long run if a product or promotion succeeds on its own merit, rather than on the disparaging of another brand. To become a promotional feat, a promotion must be entertaining—and excellent.

Famous Fighters

As we can see from the above examples, many Olympic athletes— even gold-medal winners—never get to cash in on their physical prowess. But some do. Teofilo Stevenson, the Cuban super-heavyweight Olympic boxing champion and arguably the best boxer ever, never took commercial advantage of his Olympic gold medals (three of them). But other Olympic boxing champions (e.g., Floyd Patterson, Sugar Ray Leonard, the Spinks brothers, Joe Frazier, George Foreman, and the stinging bee Muhammad Ali) made good money by capitalizing on their Olympic fame.

At one time, Muhammad Ali was the most famous man in the world. When he fought Joe Frazier in the "Thrilla in Manila," the event was televised by satellite so all could watch. From then on, gladiators were people that everyone wanted to see. Now, on any given day, we can flip on the telly and choose between boxing, American Gladiators, and the very entertaining "sport" of professional wrestling, led by the incomparable Hulk Hogan.

But what about Olympic wrestlers? Do they ever make TV? No. Neither do Olympic judokas or tae kwan do competitors. But one man made martial arts big business. There is a 99 percent probability you know of him. His name is Bruce Lee.

Dubbed "the little dragon," Bruce Lee did more for martial arts than anyone in history. He gave Chuck Norris his first fighting role in a blockbuster martial arts movie (*Fists of Fury*). His last film, *Game of Death*, was also a big hit. By far his greatest success came from his first major film, *Enter the Dragon*, which catapulted him to international stardom. This film made kung fu popular. A few years later a TV show sporting the name *Kung Fu* was well received. This was due to Lee's groundwork in making martial arts so appealing. Today, *Teenage Mutant Ninja Turtles* reigns as a favorite kid show. It started as a comic, and made it big as a motion picture. Of course, Ninja Turtle merchandise is available everywhere.

Ironically, Bruce Lee never reaped the rewards of stardom. He died in 1973 at the age of thirty two. But thanks to his pioneering in quality kung fu films, here is what has happened in the martial arts market. Lee wrote six kung fu instructional books (four with M. Uyehara); five were bestsellers. There have been at least seven biographies of Lee; one was written by Robert Clouse (1989), the director of *Enter the Dragon*. Universal Studios is working on a movie of Lee's life. There have been at least six books written by Lee's proteges in his eclectic martial arts non-style called jeet kune do. Several of Lee's best students and their students (e.g., Dan Inosanto, Paul Vunak, Tim Tackett, Chris Kent, and Larry Hartsell) are popular instructors and seminar leaders around the world. Dan Inosanto has five instructional videos on the market; Paul Vunak has seven. The magazine *Inside Kung-Fu* has a monthly column devoted to Bruce Lee's jeet kune do. Almost every issue of every martial arts magazine (there are at least seven) has some word on or about Bruce Lee and his philosophy.

Chuck Norris has probably reaped the most money from the martial arts. He has several feature films to his credit and endorses Century martial arts equipment. He recently received a star on the Hollywood Walk of Fame.

A few years ago, the ninja craze swept the country and several hit films were released. In all, there have been nearly a hundred martial arts entertainment films made since Lee's death. And that's not counting top grossing war movies and shoot-em-ups like *Rambo, Lethal Weapon,* and *Batman,* which feature many martial arts scenes.

To date, there are hundreds of martial arts how-to videos and books available by a wide range of Asian and American stylists and competitors such as Bill Wallace, George Dillman, Tadashi Yamashita, and Benny Urquidez. There are dozens of martial arts equipment manufacturing and distribution companies in the United States. There are hundreds, perhaps thousands, of martial arts studios across the nation. Fred Villari's kempo karate schools have over two hundred locations worldwide. There are over a hundred martial arts studios located in the San Francisco Bay area alone. Almost every college and university offers some kind of martial arts classes and intermural competition (usually wrestling, boxing, fencing, judo, karate, or tae kwan do).

Though most studios and retail outlets are small businesses, as you can imagine, collectively the martial arts market may approach a billion dollars a year. Although judo and karate were popular before Bruce Lee, the explosion of interest in the martial arts since 1973 has been phenomenal. Most martial arts professionals would agree that Bruce Lee's popularity was the cause. He performed a tremendous promotional feat when he starred in *Enter the Dragon*. The rest is history.

The First Bodybuilder

Martial arts are part of the many sports and activities which comprise the booming recreation market. People participate in competitive sports, swimming and running, aerobic conditioning, ballroom dancing, weightlifting, and a host of outdoor leisure activities such as kayaking, sailing, skiing, climbing, and just walking. I'll discuss marketing communication and sporting events a bit more in chapters 6 and 8.

For now, we need to determine who founded the vitalic fitness movement. It could be the originators of the ancient Greek Olympic festivals which started in 776 B.C., 440 years before Alexander's time. Or maybe it's Baron Pierre de Coubertin, credited with starting the modern Olympic Games in 1896. (I wonder how festive the 100-year anniversary Olympics will be?)

Physical fitness interest may have been fanned by creators of the Boy Scouts or YMCA. Every activity boasts a few pioneers and trendsetters. For example, Joe Weider contributes to the weight training industry, especially with commercial products that sell well. But all things considered, I believe the granddaddy of the health craze is still going strong at age seventy-five.

Dee Dunheim's (1990) headline gives it away: "Jack LaLanne: Leader of the Revolution That Shaped Americans." Dunheim (p. 6) claims that "Iron pumping television exercise evangelist Jack LaLanne was the super man responsible for shaping American physiques and the entire physical fitness movement." I must agree.

LaLanne was one of the first people to design and make muscle development equipment back in the 1930s. Many innovators and inventors never obtain the success they dream of when they create new products and ways of living. But LaLanne succeeded. LaLanne learned as a teen that sugar was bad. So he ate right and kept fit.

He started the first modern health club in 1936. His clubs often feature a stunning statue in the foyer of Atlas holding up the world. His television fitness show for women first aired in 1951 and was broadcast for 25 years. It still plays in syndication. He claims to have been the first person to encourage exercise with free weights. Amazingly, many years ago, doctors and health experts berated LaLanne for his fitness advice. But they came around and now totally support his philosophies.

His company, BeFit Enterprises, produces health products and services. You can eat the Jack LaLanne Fruit and Nutrition Bars, or read one of Jack's or his wife Elaine's fitness books. You could purchase a few of their exercise videos or catch them in person at one of their public lectures.

Yes LaLanne is still going strong. But how did he thrive in the fitness industry when others withered? Simple. He was a master at promotional feats; in his case, physical feats of strength and endurance. He received tremendous amounts of print space and broadcast time by performing a physical stunt every year to celebrate his birthday. The result? LaLanne's been a household name across the nation for 40 years. Let's review a few of his incredible feats.

At age forty-two he wowed television viewers on the show "You Asked For It" by doing 1,033 pushups in 23 minutes. Three years later he did it again on TV; this time he performed 1,000 pushups and 1,000 chinups in 1 hour and 20 minutes. Wow.

When LaLanne was forty he swam from one end of the Golden Gate Bridge to the other—underwater, with 140 pounds of gear. The next year he swam handcuffed from Alcatraz to San Francisco.

Jack loves the water around Alcatraz. When he turned sixty LaLanne repeated the Alcatraz to Fisherman's Wharf stunt—only this time he shackled his wrists *and* ankles—and towed a thousand-pound boat. (I once swam from Angel Island to Alcatraz towing a kayak full of water during a 50-knot gale with eight-foot waves breaking all around me, but I didn't do it on purpose, and I wasn't shackled.)

LaLanne's love affair with water and boats produced ever more outlandish feats. He swam a mile across a lake in Japan towing 65 boats full of 6,500 pounds of Louisiana Pacific pulp—at age 65. At seventy Jack swam a mile across Long Beach harbor towing 70 boats with 70 people aboard. He wanted to swim from Catalina Island to Los Angeles towing who knows what, but his wife talked him into swimming the bathtub towing her. My company, Tsunami Products, would like to convince Jack to paddle one of our kayaks from Catalina to LA, towing the *USS Enterprise*. We think he could do it.

LaLanne has made the fitness field profitable for himself and many others. Look at health and racquet clubs, health food products and stores, and home gym and training equipment manufacturers. They all gained from his pioneering efforts. Companies such as Nike, Diversified Products, Nautilus, Soloflex, Patagonia, AMF Voit, and even Hobie Cat owe something to LaLanne, for his products and his herculean deeds have intrigued Americans for years. Not only do health, fitness, and recreation industries benefit from the health trend, but consumers do as well. We get to be healthier and live longer.

Everyone loves heroes' tales, but how about clowns'? Let's find out.

CIRCUS STARS

Since court jesters entertained kings, everyone has loved clowns. Some clowns are brightly colored harlequins. Others are sad hobos. Modern slapstick clowns such as Gallagher are marquee features in Las Vegas, the desert entertainment mecca. The Smothers Brothers, Jay Leno, and Johnny Carson are popular political satirists on television. And some jokers like Dan Aykroyd, Bill Murray, Eddie Murphy, and Robin Williams have starred on stage, on TV, and in films.

Sophisticated clowns such as Bob Hope and the late Jack Benny make people laugh at life with just a quip. Gentle, honest cowboy humorists like the great Will Rogers live on, thanks to one-man shows by actors such as Burgess Meredith.

But the activity most people associate with clowns is the circus. From the 1800s to the present, American parents have taken their kids to see clowns in the traveling circus. But there are more than just clowns at the circus. You can also marvel at tight-rope artists, acrobats, lion tamers, human cannonball acts, magicians, maybe a few elephants stomping around, and sideshow freaks. The circus puts a world of wonder right there before your eyes. It fulfills a need in humans to experience activities that are beyond what seem possible.

Barnum's Ballyhoo

Though the street circus and carnival have been around for centuries, Phineas T. Barnum is credited with organizing the "greatest show on earth" back in the 1870s. Though many small circuses thrived at the time, Barnum and Bailey's big traveling circus left them in the dust. Now, Barnum and Bailey have teamed with the Ringling Brothers to offer the world a truly colossal circus.

As interesting as Barnum's circus was the way he first promoted it. According to Fuhrman (1989), in her book *Publicity Stunts*, Barnum was a master of ballyhoo. *Ballyhoo* is defined in Webster's as "loud, exaggerated, or sensational advertising or propaganda." Barnum began his career by staging sideshows featuring George Washington's nurse, Tom Thumb's midget family, and the bearded lady. Barnum made these shows sell out by ballyhooing. Whenever attendance slipped, he wrote angry letters under assumed names to local editors in which he attacked or defended his show.

He created bogus backgrounds and stage names for his characters. The practice of changing stars' names continues to this day. (John Denver is really Henry John Deutschendorf Jr., Doris Day is Doris von Kappelhoff, Alan Alda is Alphonso D'Abruzzo, Lee Majors is Harvey Yeary, Englebert Humperdinck is Arnold Dorsey—or is it the other way around?) But false biographies remain a thing of the past. After all, this is the era of accountability.

Barnum (who made it into the *Cultural Literacy* book), was sometimes called the "Shakespeare of advertising." He was certainly a master promoter. His circus traveled by train, and he dedicated a railroad car to the publicity and advertising team. Fuhrman (pp. 20–21) describes how the publicity/ad system worked. His ad team swooped down in three waves. The first wave consisted of posters slapped up everywhere in town. The second wave featured stories planted in local newspapers (and more posters). The final wave occurred just before the circus came into town. The team made sure all was ready for the circus and the big parade that preceded it, so everyone could gawk and get fired up about the upcoming entertainment. The circus was always a big hit.

In Barnum's heydey, he was criticized for misusing the media and staging hoaxes, but everyone came to the circus. He believed people needed illusion and liked his shams. He was the crown prince of humbug.

To this day, the name P. T. Barnum stands for sly showmanship.

MTV revealed a hoax perpetrated on its viewers concerning a pirate signal invading MTV's programming. The feat was meant to interest viewers in MTV's new show, "Pirate TV." And it worked, for the show tripled Friday night ratings for MTV and made national news. In *Newsweek*, writer Harry Waters (1990: 55) commented, "Turns out it was just a promotional stunt, but one even Barnum would salute."

The Modern Circus

Barnum's circus remains popular in 1990. Only now it can be seen on TV along with other modern "circuses" such as the IceCapades. But even the old European street circus is regaining popularity. The grandest "street circus" (no animal acts) might be the Cirque du Soleil from Quebec, Canada. Formed by a group of street performers in 1984, this travelling circus led by Guy Laliberte, with help from the government of Quebec, began touring the world. They carry their big top (which seats 1,750) with them, along with their portable ticket booths and auxiliary equipment.

Benny Le Grand, their clown, plays practical jokes on the audience and the ringmaster. This guy is anything but sad. In addition to acrobats, jugglers, and balancing acts, this circus features the most amazing physical feat I have ever witnessed: a hand balancing act. You'll have to see it to believe it.

In 1984, the troupe performed 50 times before 30,000 spectators. By 1988, they made 312 performances for 502,000 people. They advertise nominally, yet every show sells out. There are two reasons for their phenomenal success. First, they seek out publicity (they've appeared twice on Johnny Carson's "Tonight Show" and have been reviewed favorably by all major American newspapers and newsmagazines). Second, they rely on word-of-mouth advertising, still the best way to get a promotional message across. In short, Cirque du Soleil succeeds because their product is great and everyone wants to talk about it, including me.

Buffalo Bill's Wild West

I would be remiss if I failed to discuss the greatest show of the American frontier, Buffalo Bill's Wild West. (Yes Virginia, Buffalo Bill and Annie Oakley were real people.) William F. Cody really was a colonel and Indian scout. And he did avenge Custer. And Sitting Bull "buried the hatchet," became his friend, and joined his show.

I visited the Buffalo Bill Historical Center in Cody, Wyoming and was enthralled with the memorabilia from his illustrious life. He was a scout, sharpshooter (it is claimed that he shot 69 buffalo [for food] in 8 hours, and 4,280 in 17 months), author, actor, and creator and promoter of his show. He was also one of the first famous men to support women's suffrage.

Near the end of his scouting career, Cody met Ned Buntline, an extremely popular dime novelist, who wrote about Cody. Buntline's novel became so popular in the East that a play was written about Cody. A publicist invited Cody to attend, and the audience cheered when he was introduced. Later that year (1872), he played himself in Buntline's play, *Scouts of the Plains*. He ad-libbed a lot, which critics abhorred and audiences loved.

By 1876, he tired of theater, so when he heard about Sitting Bull's uprising, according to Arpad and Lincoln (1971: 6), "he rushed onto the stage shouting to the audience that he was through acting Indian warfare—that he was returning to the frontier to fight in a real Indian war." He polished his image of frontier hero with that remark. So off he went to Little Bighorn, two weeks after the massacre.

Cody avenged Custer by killing and scalping a Cheyenne warrior named Yellow Hand. Cody promoted himself as part of the Custer story and came to be known by Plains Indians as "the other Pahuska" (long hair).

Cody returned to the stage to play himself. By 1877, it was time for Cody to publicize the first of many farewell tours, a trick used today by performers. Bill sort of retired from the East and took his Buffalo Bill Combination show to San Francisco, where the westerners ate up his fictitious portrayal of western life. In 1878, he worked on his ranch in Nebraska and got to know some "cowboys" who were organizing a "round-up." Cody later popularized both terms in his show.

In 1879, Prentiss Ingraham wrote a play for Cody called *The Knight of the Plains*. It was popular, though critics, as they do today, lambasted it. In all fairness, the play was probably nothing to write home about, but it established a relationship between Cody and Ingraham which made Buffalo Bill famous the world over. According to historian Don Russell (1960: 263), Ingraham wrote "one thousand adventure yarns," of which two hundred were about Buffalo Bill.

Russell (pp. 265–266) claims that Buffalo Bill actually wrote several dime novels bearing his name as author, although it is popularly believed that the novels were all ghost-written by Buntline or Ingraham. In all, twenty-four dime novels were penned by Buffalo Bill himself. Being the publicity hound that he was, he wanted to get his name spread everywhere. It worked.

By 1882, Cody was semiretired back at his Nebraska ranch. He was asked to officiate at a rodeo, a "round-up" where steer roping, bronc busting, and sharpshooting were featured. Cody spiced up the event by adding horse races, a buffalo drive, and a simulated Indian attack on the real Deadwood stage. The event was so successful that Cody and actor Nate Salsbury beefed up the show and took it back East where it was a tremendous smash.

In a few seasons they grossed over a million dollars a year. The "Wild West" ran from 1883 until 1913, with Buffalo Bill at the helm all the way. Although Cody ran a loose outfit, his publicity people managed to gather sellout crowds by staying just a few days ahead of the show. Learning from Barnum's success, they plastered posters everywhere. During the show, agents distributed handbills with key performers' biographies. This souvenir maintained spectators' interest in Buffalo Bill long after the exhibition.

The "Wild West" was never a show to Cody; he was recreating the West. Cody changed "Wild West" often to keep it interesting, but always retained skill exhibitions (lassoing, shooting, racing, riding) and theatrical vignettes of western life (Indian ceremonies, Custer's Last Stand).

After four years, Arpad and Lincoln (p. 9) report that his show was so popular that "Cody owned his own train of white railroad cars with his name emblazoned in gold letters on the sides. As his publicity agent boasted, Cody 'out-Barnumed Barnum.' "

When that train chugged into town, everybody came out to watch. And when his ship pulled into London and Paris, the royalty showed up. Cody had his advance men secure endorsements from military officers to make him credible to the British. It worked; they loved him. In 1887, Queen Victoria, who had not attended a public event in 25 years, came to London to see "Wild West." Cody rode up on horseback, followed by his band of fierce-looking Indians, and doffed his hat to the lady. She, in turn, bowed to the American flag—the first Brit to honor Old Glory.

On that day, he put four European kings in the Deadwood stage, and as the Prince of Wales rode shotgun, Cody tore around the stadium as wild Indians attacked it on horseback. He repeated this stunt with the Shah of Persia and Queen Isabella of Spain in Paris. Can you imagine such a spectacle today?

By 1890, Cody had made cowboys and Indians look like respectable heroes instead of renegades. After all, Europe's aristocracy was duly impressed. He retook America by storm.

In 1893, President Cleveland introduced "Wild West's" Buffalo Bill and "The Congress of Rough Riders of the World," composed of top equestrians from Mexico and Europe who competed with each other to see who could best American cowboys. Teddy Roosevelt was so impressed with Cody that he later called his own cavalry Rough Riders. Posters compared Cody with Napoleon, the other man on a horse.

Arpad and Lincoln (p. 9) write that Cody's show "was not quite a circus, and it was more than a rodeo." After the show began to lose its popularity, Cody joined up with James A. Bailey (of Barnum and Bailey) in 1898 and added sideshows which included jugglers, a snake charmer, and a sword swallower. Pawnee Bill later joined Cody. By 1913 the show was over—but it had lasted 30 years!

When "Wild West" was rising to its zenith in 1883, it was something to behold. An announcer would tell the audience to hush and witness entertainment that was not acting but "an exhibition of skill." Then a parade of cowboys, Mexican vaqueros, and several Indian bands with their chiefs would ride by. Then, in the script written by Cody and Salsbury, the announcer said:

> I next have the honor of introducing to your attention a man whose record as servant of the government, whose skill and daring as a frontiersman, whose place in history as the chief of scouts of the United States Army under such generals as Sherman, Sheridan, Hancock, Terry, Miles, Hazen, Royal, Merritt, Crook, Carr and others, and whose name as one of the avengers of the lamented Custer, and whose adherence throughout an eventful life to his chosen principle of "true to friend and foe," have made him well and popularly known throughout the world. You all know to whom I allude—the Honorable William F. Cody, "Buffalo Bill."

What a buildup! Buffalo Bill would ride up as a bugle called. He would then announce the remaining events: a horse race between a cowboy, a Mexican, and an Indian; a Pony Express demonstration; a race between an Indian and a pony; a recreation of Buffalo Bill's fight with Yellow Hand; various shooting exhibitions, including acts by the Cowboy Kid, Annie Oakley, and Cody; the Deadwood stage attack; more horse races and riding stunts; Pawnee and Wichita war dances and ceremonies; an African riding a wild elk; and an attack upon a settler's cabin by marauding Indians who are repulsed by scouts and cowboys.

What a show! Buffalo Bill was responsible for romanticizing the western way of life. Every western movie ever made owes its market to Cody. John Wayne, Gary Cooper, Clint Eastwood, "Shane" and the "Lone Ranger" owe him. Western writers such as Zane Grey and Louis L'Amour are indebted to him. Television shows such as *Gunsmoke*, *Bonanza*, *The Big Valley*, and my favorite, *Rawhide*, were popular in their day thanks to Cody.

Although rodeos live on, "Wild West" is just a memory and the grand spectacle is gone. When Bill died, it's rumored he said, "Let my show go on." His friends tried, but failed. They sold it to Ringling Brothers in 1929, but it faded away. Yet Buffalo Bill has remained in our memories.

No American has received so much written publicity. Several plays, hundreds of novels, hundreds more short stories, innumerable newspaper articles, and dozens of biographies were written about Buffalo Bill. Poster and handbill reprints of his shows are still available. Russell wrote (p. 407) that Buffalo Bill stories appeared in 1,700 weekly publications.

Sell and Weybright (1979) tell of Cody's promotion adventures in addition to his plays and shows. He started the Irma Hotel in Cody, Wyoming (imagine a town named after you), which was successful in its day (with Cody occasionally playing bartender), and is still operating. Cody always wore Stetson hats, and naturally endorsed their hats and appeared in their ads in the early 1900s. Sir Robert Baden Powell, founder of the Boy Scouts, admired Cody as a scout. By providing publicity, Cody helped Powell and Dan Beard organize the Boy Scouts of America, who adopted his kerchief around the neck and made him a patron saint with Teddy Roosevelt.

His fellow stars loved him. Annie Oakley, who toured with the show for 17 years said, "His word was better than most contracts. Personally I never had a contract after the show started. It would have been superfluous" (Sell and Weybright, p. 240).

Artist Frederic Remington sketched Cody and "Wild West." E. E. Cummings and Carl Sandburg wrote poems about him. He's mentioned twice in *Cultural Literacy*. When he died nearly broke in 1917, 25,000 attended his funeral. The *Denver Post* said, "It was the most impressive, the most notable funeral ever witnessed in America."

When we think of cowboy heroes, names like Wyatt Earp, Bat Masterson, Kit Carson, Geronimo, Wild Bill Hickok, and Jesse James come to mind (thanks mostly to movies). But Russell (p. 476) says these people contributed but one event to the great rodeo. "The man of many lives and legends, the all-around champion in popular opinion—publicity opinion, if you will—was Buffalo Bill. You need name no other."

Daredevils

Some performers don't quite fit into the circus mold, so they opt to go out on their own and perform death-defying feats for pay. The Wallenda family, a team of high-wire acrobats, performed complex acts, often without a net. The public paid to see if they could perform their act without falling. Sometimes they did fall, once with tragic results.

Earlier in this chapter I mentioned human flies—people who climb walls for fun and fame. Sometimes these daring climbers fall and die. In 1990, a father-son team climbed a building in Los Angeles. The father fell to his death and the son was arrested on site for illegally climbing buildings. He received no sympathy from LA's finest.

According to Fuhrman (p. 156), the president of Abercrombie and

Fitch once rappelled up his building to "publicize the company's excellent outdoor department." He didn't fall, and neither did Abercrombie and Fitch's prices—or sales.

Some people leap instead of climb. We all have heard tragic tales of suicide-bent people who jump to their deaths from buildings and off bridges. But some do it just for the publicity. My company, Tsunami Products, prepared to throw one of our kayaks (the toughest in the world) off the Golden Gate Bridge with a dummy strapped in just to show how tough our bulletproof, Kevlar-constructed Tsunami X–1 Rocket Boat really was. We chickened out on the bridge when we considered the negative publicity of arrest and a whopping fine, plus we secretly worried the boat would shatter into a million pieces, and that wouldn't help our sales any. So we threw it off a hundred-foot cliff instead.

Other companies have leapt into the spotlight with good results. The president of Original New York Seltzer beverage company plunged ten stories off a building into an air bag with the company brand name written on it. He lived and his company thrived on the publicity.

Two years later, in 1984, a stuntman was paid $1 million to leap off the top of the Vegas World Hotel into an air bag. The stuntman made the world record plunge (326 feet), walked over to the hotel owner and collected his million bucks. Not bad pay for a few seconds' work.

The Evel One

Evel Knievel is one of the greatest daredevils of all time. It's hard to believe that a man who once sold life insurance would later jump cars for a living. But that's just what he did. After cheating at cards and thieving for a living until he was twenty-five, Evel settled down into the car-and-fountain jumping business. To say he is an enigma is an understatement. He was described by Biebuyck (1971: 22) in the *New Yorker* as having "the wary eyes of a cardsharp, a thief's nerve, the combativeness of a brawler, the aplomb of a professional athlete, the flamboyant instincts of a promoter, and the glibness of a con man."

During the height of his car-jumping days, he drove into town in a large bus pulling a matching trailer. He sported a red, white, and blue jumpsuit. He liked to brag about making a big jump on his motorcycle over nineteen cars. He made hundreds of successful jumps.

By 1971, he had already made nine major crashes. In 1967 he didn't quite clear the fountain at Caesar's Palace and "broke his back that afternoon, and his pelvis—and his head and his shoulder bone and his motorcycle, and drove his legs up into his hips so hard that one of them fused there and never came loose" (Dexter 1985: 45).

Undaunted, he came back and jumped more cars, again and again.

A movie bearing his name was made starring George Hamilton as Evel. That was before Knievel did his really big jumps. He planned to jump the Grand Canyon but officials wouldn't let him do it. He could've sneaked in and done it, but that would not draw publicity, a crowd, and lots of money (he doesn't do this for free). So he decided to jump the Snake River Canyon in Idaho instead. He promised to climb on his rocket-powered Harley and jump the Snake on Labor Day in 1972. But sensible folks didn't want to cooperate in his suicide attempt.

Finally, after two more years of negotiation, he got permission. In the final months before the jump, Knievel was merchandised like crazy. Helbros sold Evel watches, Addar made the hobby kits, Krypton offered Knievel radios, Mego made bicycle accessories, and Ideal hawked Evel clothes for boys. Ideal also sold $6 million worth of a 12-inch "sky cycle" toy that looked like Evel's—before he made the jump attempt over the canyon.

One of Knievel's merchandising executives claimed that the products would bring in $200 million in gross revenues, with at least $5 million of that going to Evel. Top Rank Productions planned on making up to $20 million on the canyon jump from broadcast royalties.

You can see that Knievel's planned stunt jump over the canyon brought in a lot of revenue. A few weeks before the jump, Pete Axthelm interviewed Evel while Evel zoomed around Montana in a Ferrari signing autographs for patrolmen who stopped him for speeding. Axthelm (1974: 78) reported, "Evel had happily signed autographs for the officers and counted them among the millions who will make that leap the most lucrative and widely watched daredevil feat in history."

Here's what happened at the event. Two weeks before his mile jump across the Snake River Canyon, Knievel warmed up by clearing 13 Mack trucks in Toronto. Meanwhile, bikers and other curious people started filtering toward the canyon to begin the "blue-collar Woodstock." *Time* correspondent Leo Janos (1974: 64) wrote, "Fans from every state in the union formed a camper city that was soon awash in beer, dope, cocaine and false rumors of savage beatings and rapes."

About 16,000 people surged forward to the edge of the 600-foot cliff on the day of the event. Some fans were rooting for Evel, others, including many media personnel (who were physically abused by Knievel and the crowd), were favoring the canyon. So, on September 8, 1974, Evel Knievel fired up the rocket and shot out into space. To make a short story brief, he nowhere near made it to the other side, but did manage to bail out and live.

He almost bit the big one in London in 1975 when he failed to clear thirteen buses. After that, he decided he didn't want to jump anymore. However, he still made the news. A man named Sheldon Saltman wrote a book about Knievel's fizzled jump. Knievel beat him up and went to jail. Then his son Robbie started jumping over cars and pickup trucks—with no hands (Lidz 1986). Now Knievel senior makes money as an artist and claims that people like his paintings better than Picasso's or Van Gogh's.

Knievel was still in the news in 1987. A *Wall Street Journal* article (Guiles 1987) related how "Muhammad Ali floated like a butterfly into Kmart Corp.'s annual meeting yesterday, but he let Evel Knievel do the stinging for him." Knievel, a partner in Ali's shoe polish company, read a statement to Kmart brass which said they wanted the big retailer to sell Ali's products in all stores. The Kmart chairman said they would consider it.

Evel Knievel, the "last gladiator," lives on. What he will do next is anybody's guess. As of 1990, he is serving as a pitchman for Clarion Inns. Knievel epitomizes the one-trick circus and his publicity antics have ensured he will be remembered as an American folk hero. It's amazing what some people will do for fame and fortune. His big mouth and audacity made him rich. Knievel says he earned $50 million in his 16-year career. How many executives can make that claim? What can we as marketers learn from Evel Knievel's success?

The Most Magnificent Magician and Marketer

There is one man who Knievel may have taken publicity and daring lessons from. This man is in the *Cultural Literacy* dictionary, which means he is someone that every culturally literate American is supposed to know. The man was ace magician, king of escape artists, and grand self-promoter. His spectacular publicity stunts made him one of the most famous people ever to emigrate to America. Indeed, during his time, he was the most publicized one-man act around. He was far better than his competitors, and he practiced what he preached. He made "the impossible possible." His name was Harry Houdini.

Houdini practiced his magic at the same time as Barnum and Buffalo Bill, only Houdini was a one-man act, not a major circus. After initial hardship, he became the most famous single act in the world. To this day, no one has come close to repeating his escape feats. And his accompanying publicity stunts were almost as remarkable. Let's look at his magic—on stage and in the press.

We've all seen magicians conjure up doves. Houdini made a live eagle appear. Many magicians can make things suddenly vanish. According to Christopher (1969: 7), "Houdini fired a pistol and a 10,000-pound elephant disappeared!" Now that's magic.

Houdini claimed he originated the "challenge" handcuff act. He would publicly challenge anyone in the audience to produce manacles and shackle him. He would then escape. He played in San Francisco for a week in 1899. The *Examiner* printed a story saying that Houdini's escapes were no big deal. He "challenged" the police department in San Francisco to handcuff him with the best they had. He was stripped naked, shackled every which way, straitjacketed—and he escaped. The *Examiner* then wrote another story, retracting their previous statements and boasting about his talents. Harry then bought advertising in newspapers and billboards which said: "Who created the biggest Sensation in California since the Discovery of Gold in 1849? WHY! HARRY HOUDINI! The ONLY recognized and Undisputed King of Handcuffs and Monarch of Leg Shackles."

His "Naked Test" was such a big hit in San Francisco that he became a headliner in vaudeville back East. Every time he would play in a new city, he would challenge the police to shackle him. He escaped every time, newspapers touted his success, and theaters were always packed.

When he played in Kansas City, he did a new publicity stunt. He challenged prison officials to lock him in jail while he was manacled. They did, he escaped, and added "Champion Jail Breaker" to his title. He made the papers nationwide.

Houdini then sailed to London without a booking. No one would sign him on, so he arranged to have Scotland Yard manacle him. They locked him up with everything they had, and laughingly said they would return and free him in a few hours. Before they had shut the door behind them, Houdini was free. Houdini was destined to be a big hit in England.

During his act, Cirnoc, a rival who claimed to be the "Original King of Handcuffs" ran on stage and called Houdini a fraud. Houdini let Cirnoc chain him, and then Houdini immediately escaped. He then fastened the cuffs on Cirnoc and handed him the key. Cirnoc could not escape and admitted defeat. The crowd cheered Houdini and Cirnoc reluctantly shook Houdini's hand. The British press lauded Houdini's talents and he was soon in demand everywhere.

Imitators and detractors tried to upstage him in Germany, but Houdini bet them money that he could escape from anything they came up with but that they could not free themselves from his shackles. Time and again Houdini proved victorious. Houdini became so popular in Germany that one night the audience, which packed the aisles, shouted down all other entertainers and demanded that only Houdini perform. He obliged, took over the show, and did whatever he wanted. He was truly king on the continent.

When he played in Paris no one answered his challenges to produce handcuffs for him to escape from, so he also performed regular magic tricks. To beef up attendance, Houdini hired seven bald men to sit at a busy Paris cafe and periodically remove their hats, exposing the word H-O-U-D-I-N-I for all to see.

Later, a German policeman wrote an article calling Houdini a fraud. Houdini sued him for libel and had to appear in court to prove he could remove any cuffs. Houdini performed a remarkable escape in front of the judge and jury, won the case, and enhanced his reputation even more.

Not long after, Houdini went to Holland and shackled himself to a windmill blade as it was turning. The blade broke and Houdini fell but was only slightly injured. He received great publicity from that accidental stunt.

Houdini heard that another escape artist named Kleppini claimed he had bested Harry. Houdini blew up. He dressed as an old man and challenged the man as Kleppini was doing his act. Houdini jumped on stage, removed his disguise, pulled out 5,000 marks, and wagered he could escape from Kleppini's cuffs but Kleppini could not escape from his. A few days later, they had their showdown. Houdini let Kleppini see that his combination lock handcuffs could be opened by spelling the French word *clefs* (keys). Kleppini grabbed the cuffs and hid backstage to test and make sure they opened to *clefs*. They did. He came back on stage and said he was ready. Houdini scuffled with him a moment, then suddenly shackled Kleppini with the cuffs. Kleppini said he would open them and then let his wife do it to show just how easy it was. Houdini replied, "Ladies and gentleman, you can all go home. I do not lock a cuff on a man merely to let him escape. If he tries this cuff until doomsday, he cannot open it."

Kleppini tried for hours but could not open it. Finally, Houdini removed the shackles by spelling out the word *fraud* on the lock. Houdini had changed the combination during their little skirmish on stage. Once again, Houdini had proved the master in public. His fame grew.

He played in England again two years later and was an extremely big draw. When theater managers complained about his requested salary, he agreed to take a percentage of ticket sales in lieu of salary. He ended up being paid double what he would have received in salary. Spectators were turned away in droves. He had to play extra matinees in the biggest theaters they could find.

Houdini the showman was still not satisfied with his fame, so he concocted false stories for the press. He offered to sell his escape secrets for $50,000 (a lot of money in 1900). He advertised a challenge for all would-be escape artists: Houdini would pay $2,500 to anyone who could duplicate his escapes. There were no challengers.

Houdini invited manufacturers of boxes, coffins, and manacles to devise contraptions he could escape from. One contractor wrote Houdini a letter asking if he could make a box that would be nailed shut by the contractor. Houdini, publicity expert, made thousands of handbills which reproduced the letter and Houdini's acceptance, along with Harry's promise to pay $200 to a hospital if he failed (which he didn't). As always, the house was packed.

A rival escape artist named Cunning claimed he could escape from any handcuffs. Houdini had his brothers appear wherever Cunning was playing and expose the man by challenging him with handcuffs he couldn't free himself from. Harry had all rivals challenged and debunked. He didn't want any competition. Talk about marketing warfare!

He challenged his protege, Jacques Boudini, to an underwater escape contest. They were thrown overboard in the Atlantic, each shackled and tied. After a minute, Houdini came to the surface and said, "Is Boudini up yet?" Harry showed his hands were free. Two minutes later he showed his legs were free and clambered aboard. Boudini was dragged up and had to be given artificial respiration. He said he had swallowed some water. Whether they were in cahoots is anybody's guess, but they both received a lot of press.

One of Houdini's most successful stunts was performed at the federal jail in Washington, D.C. He was stripped naked and placed in the cell which had once housed President Harding's assassin. In a few minutes Harry was free. He walked around Murderer's Row nude and put all the prisoners in different cells. When the stories hit the papers, Houdini's Washington engagement was sold out.

Houdini performed other daring jail escapes. He also would allow himself to be tied and manacled inside an iron-bound hamper which was strapped and locked shut. Somehow, Harry escaped with no evidence of the strappings being touched.

But that was nothing. When attendance started to fade in 1908, Houdini created a dazzling new feat. He had himself put inside a large milk urn filled with water. He invited the audience to hold their breath along with him as he was handcuffed and stuffed into the urn. Then six padlocks were placed on the urn. After a minute or so, everyone in the audience had already run out of air. Franz Kukol, Houdini's assistant, walked up to the cabinet which hid Houdini. Kukol held a fire ax in his hand. After three minutes, Kukol raised the ax to break through the cabinet and locks on the urn. Just then a smiling Houdini walked out to roaring applause.

He later performed the water-can trick at Harvard University. He wore "Yale blue" swim trunks. The all-male audience wanted him to wear Harvard crimson. Houdini didn't have red trunks so he did the trick naked. He received a lot of publicity for this spontaneous act.

He jumped off several bridges and boats while handcuffed or manacled and freed himself underwater. The public loved these daring physical stunts. He always stayed underwater long enough so that observers feared he was drowned; then he would surface, displaying the opened manacles.

In late 1908, Houdini stopped accepting handcuff challenges. There were just too many imitators around taking away his publicity. So he instead escaped from straitjackets and other torturous devices in full view of the audience, rather than from behind a cabinet or curtain.

Houdini was also an aviator. In 1910, between magic acts, he became the first person to fly a plane in Australia. He later became friends with the Wright brothers, who thought Houdini was only a pilot. When a stunt pilot died during an air show, Houdini raised money for the widow by leaping out of a plane with hands and feet manacled. He fell 50 feet into Lake Michigan and freed himself. The Wright brothers were impressed.

Harry then escaped from a sea monster (really!), a locked diving suit, a box banded with steel and thrown overboard, and the "Chinese Water Torture Cell," in which he was shackled upside down in a locked metal cage suspended underwater. He freed himself from straitjackets while suspended upside down 100 feet above city streets as tens of thousands watched for free. Needless to say, people lined up for blocks to see the rest of the show.

He was one of the first to use red hot radio to promote his magic shows. He also wrote columns in local newspapers while appearing at city theaters. He edited three publications on magic; wrote hundreds of magazine articles, souvenir booklets, monographs for back-of-room sales, and 17 books (some were about magic or fraudulent spirit mediums, others were fiction). He also made a few movies (more on these later). All his writings and other creative works complemented his magic and escape shows, helped pack houses, and made him a household word to this day.

According to Gresham (1959: 215), one of his publicity agents actually managed to get the 1920 Funk & Wagnalls dictionary to include the word *houdinize*, which he coined. *Houdinize* means "to release or extricate oneself by wriggling out." Houdini was so good at publicity events that he often spoke to the Advertising Club and other business associations about his publicity methods. At one of these meetings he said, "I get more advertising space without paying for it than anyone in the country."

MOVIE MANIA

Advances in filmmaking and now videography make these media very attractive to marketers to complement existing marketing communications efforts. Both Buffalo Bill and Houdini dabbled in filmmaking, although neither made any money directly from movies. However, they both successfully used movies as ancillary vehicles to draw attention to their money-making product—their shows. Houdini showed clippings from his movies during his shows in the 1920s and so became one of the first to feature multimedia presentations.

The advantage of film and video is that special effects can replace or augment physical stunts and other dangerous or impossible screen acts. Thus, the magician's illusions become commonplace in movies. Now, animation and special optical effects (some created by computer) can be used in lieu of expensive and dangerous activities. Douglas Trumbull, Industrial Light and Magic, Disney, and other companies manufacture special effects. That's why science fiction movies seem so realistic today, and good technical effects are commonplace. Many of these optical effects and new, sophisticated editing equipment (especially in video) make film and video production affordable for marketers. Buffalo Bill and Houdini could make money if they used video today.

But with movies, the medium *is* the message—or the product. And movies are one of America's biggest and most successful industries. What's remarkable is that movies are an intangible product, providing nothing but amusement. Like athletes, adventurers, and circus performers, movies that make big money have to be excellent to cut through the clutter of competition. Technical and artistic excellence are needed to compete.

Stunt Artists

We know that movies feature stars who act. It's obvious that actors are needed. But in many films, athletic and adventurous circus-like performers called stunt artists perform standard superhuman feats such as fights, falls, acrobatics, car chases and crashes, and specialty stunts such as catching fire, acrobatic parachuting, and swimming with sharks or in river rapids. These stunts inject physical drama into movies and are often the parts most remembered by audiences. Do you recall when Butch Cassidy and the Sundance Kid jumped off the cliff into the river? Very exciting, right? Remember any other scene from the movie? Not likely. That's the power of a good stunt.

Every Western, war flick, and thriller depends on stunt artists. I think *Indiana Jones and the Temple of Doom* featured more stunts than any other movie in history. The January 1989 issue of *Variety* rated this movie eighth in all time rental sales (behind *Raiders of the Lost Ark*, which was number seven—and chock full of stunts). The last film of the trilogy, *Indiana Jones and the Last Crusade*, released in 1989, grossed $165 million in its first eight weeks of theatrical release. It featured thirty feigned deaths and a multitude of fantastic stunts coordinated by master stunt-man Vic Armstrong (who doubles for Harrison Ford). The Indiana Jones trilogy earned $609 million at the box office, which shows that people love to watch dangerous stunts.

The *James Bond* series of spy/adventure films have featured some of the most interesting movie stunts as Bond grapples with goons underwater or in outer space using futuristic gadgets that get him in and out of trouble. Naturally, he always escapes by skiing down a mountain on a cello box or off a cliff with a British flag parachute. Or he may drive the latest car or airplane (or carplane) to nab the bad guys. In *Licence to Kill*, the most exciting stunt of 1989 may have occurred when a truck zoomed off a cliff as an airplane flew underneath it.

We at Tsunami Products hope that someday Bond will begin one of his movies by donning our body armor, climbing onto one of our X–1 kayaks, and getting shot out of a submarine's torpedo tube at dawn. He surfaces in a storm on the ocean near an enemy beach. He surfs our boat through rocks to shore, does a daring deed onshore, and escapes in a hail of bullets back through the raging surf where he is picked up by Navy frogmen in a high-speed hydrofoil. The question is, who would perform this stunt? I would. Can you think of a better way to promote an adventure product than to get paid for featuring it at the beginning of a Bond movie—with the company president as the stuntman?

According to John Hagner (1989), president and founder of the Hollywood Stuntmen's Hall of Fame located in scenic Moab, Utah, the trick to stunts is to make them look dangerous and exciting while minimizing the risk to the performer. His stuntmen's museum showcases devices used to protect stunt performers. For example, in cowboy stunts, windows that people fall through are made of resin or sugar candy, chairs that smash over heads are made of balsa, horses and riders fall into pits filled with soft compost and cork, rocks used in explosions are made of foam. Hagner says that stunts are well-planned and executed—and thus are fairly safe.

Generally, star actors do not perform their own stunts. However, there are exceptions. Burt Lancaster did the fantastic acrobatic stunts in the spoof *The Crimson Pirate*. In one scene, Burt swung off the ship's mast, flipped through the air, bounced off a sail, landed on the deck, and engaged in a cutlass duel. Burt Reynolds performed many of his own stunts. In *Deliverance*, Burt executed the canoe capsizing stunt where he rolls and tumbles down a steep river chute and lands in a pool below the rapid. By the way, this movie started the river running craze, which is still gaining in popularity and has become a major recreation industry.

So who's the greatest stuntman of all time? Believe it or not, it's possible that Harry Houdini was the greatest movie stuntman ever. Why? Because he performed stunts that no one else since has been able to duplicate. Here are some examples. In one scene, while hanging by his thumbs from the ceiling of a locked room, he scissored his legs around the bad guy's neck and choked him. Houdini kicked off one of his shoes, rifled through the man's pockets with his toes, retrieved the key to the door, swung to the door and unlocked it with the key between his toes, opened the door with his feet on the knob, walked up the door with his feet, climbed atop the door, then freed his thumbs.

In another movie made in 1919, the bad guys put Houdini in a strait-jacket and hung him upside down over the side of a roof. He extricated himself from the real straitjacket (no phonies here), dropped down onto an awning and then to the street where he rolled under the wheels of a moving truck and held on to the chassis as the truck sped away. Modern stunt makers could spice up today's films by "houdinizing" out of impossible situations with magical contortions.

Buster Keaton, the silent film comedian, performed some of the first and best film stunts. In one movie, Keaton walks through an open door as a 2,000-pound wall (no balsa) falls around him. In the old movie days, stunt making had not yet become a scientific art.

Yakima Canutt, who died in 1986 at the age of ninety after a 65-year career, "is credited with changing stunting from a rag tag occupation to a respectable part of the film industry" (Edwards 1986: 4).

Hagner dubbed Canutt the "incomparable stuntman." He was famous for horse stunts. In a John Wayne movie, Canutt stayed with a team of horses connected to a wagon as he led them over a cliff at full running speed and into the Missouri River. No one was hurt, including the horses. The stunt was the hit of the movie.

Canutt also staged the chariot race in *Ben Hur*. One of his most famous stunts occurred in *Stagecoach*. Playing an Indian, he brought his horse to a gallop and jumped off, grabbing the reins of the horses pulling a wagon going at full speed. He then fell between the horses and lay motionless as the horses and coach dragged him along and left him in the dust. What a stunt.

Dar Robinson, whose specialty was leaping off extremely high towers, ended his meteoric career when he died in a motorcycle accident during a movie chase scene in 1986. By age thirty-nine Robinson already held twenty-one world stunt records and was considered by many to be the best in the business.

Another person vying for best stuntman is Dave Sharpe. Or maybe it's Jock Mahoney. Some believe it may be the King of Stuntmen, Loren Janes, who has wrestled 27-foot anacondas and performed stunts in hundreds of movies and television shows.

There's no use in arguing who's best at stunts. All men and women who perform stunts are the best in their demanding profession—and they are the people who create the exciting action which makes movies worth watching. In effect, they are the heart of the movie; the actor is only the face.

Metamovie

For a movie to hit the big time, everything has to congeal and cook properly, just like the ingredients in a lemon meringue pie. The whole, the gestalt, must be greater than its parts. Acting, make-up, stunts,

special effects, cinematography, editing—every subteam must work together in harmony to make a product that will appeal to the ever-changing tastes of the American public.

The summer of 1989 is one period in which several movies managed
to get the gestalt of their product right—and consumers responded by
flocking to theaters for a record-breaking summer of good movies enjoyed by all. Movies released in the summer of 1989 grossed over $2
billion before it was all over. This is a big industry!

David Ansen (1989: 60), a movie critic for *Newsweek*, concluded: "Even
Hollywood is slightly stunned by its own success. The conventional
industry wisdom that there is a finite amount of money to be made in
the movie marketplace has been challenged this year."

This comment shows that there is room for every "excellent" product
in the market (at least in the entertainment market). But marketing
communications play a major role in a film's commercial success.

Let's take the case of the *Star Trek* movie series (five as of this writing).
The first four movies made good money: they were top–10 moneymakers
when released in theaters (a total of $300 million), and two made the
Variety 1989 all-time top–50 bestselling videos list. The last film, directed
by William Shatner, didn't fare as well—he's better at commanding
starships. Still, dedicated Trekkies pay good money over and over again
to see their heroes. The question is, how did *Star Trek* become so popular?

There's no simple answer, but it seems that in the 1960s, when the
three-year television series aired for the first time, people were ready
for a glimpse into a future where humanity continued to push the envelope of space, the final frontier. After the television series was axed,
it immediately went into syndication and has been shown on network
and cable TV ever since. Fans organized and held Star Trek conventions
around the U.S. where they could share Trek scuttlebutt, meet Kirk or
Spock in person, watch bloopers, and buy memorabilia (pins, decals,
posters, models, t-shirts). These conventions kept Star Trek foremost in
the minds of fans.

When VCRs became commonplace, Paramount released videos of the
movies and TV shows. Paramount, through its publishing company
Simon & Schuster, produced Star Trek novels. As of 1991, there are over
fifty such titles released through Pocket Books. DC Comics (a Warner
subsidiary) now produces a successful *Star Trek* comic book. So a Trekkie
can read a book and a comic every month, see a new movie every two
years or so, watch the reruns on TV just about every night (or plunk
one in the VCR), and attend a couple of conventions per year. In 1991,
Star Trek will celebrate its twenty-fifth anniversary. You can be sure
some big media happening will occur to make more money for the
intrepid space travelers.

However, people age: Kirk and Spock aren't getting any younger. So

Paramount created *Star Trek: The Next Generation*, set 70 years farther in the future (that's 370 years from now). The new show's special effects are as good as the Trek movies, and the characters and plots are great. The show's a big hit. It began in 1987 and was an instant and steady moneymaker. It is shown on cable channels and was ranked fifth in syndicated TV programs according to a 1989 Nielsen Cassandra Report. *The Next Generation* is finally receiving the admiration of Trekkies and now sports its own DC comic and Pocket Book novels (at least fifteen as of this writing).

The Star Trek phenomenon continues to keep Paramount in the black. Amazingly, Paramount gets all this exposure and doesn't advertise much (they are not one of the one hundred leading advertisers—Philip Morris spends over ten times as much as Paramount on advertising). *Star Trek* remains continually in demand, thanks to a good product and the fact that Paramount controls several media. Other industries can learn from Paramount's promotional feat. People want to be entertained. General Foods, Post, Ralston, and Kellogg know this. Just look at cereal boxes.

Movie Publicity

According to Fuhrman (1989: 8), "It seems that the Golden Age of Hollywood, roughly thirty years from the early 1920s to the late 1940s, was also the golden age of publicity stunts." Today, most films are publicized through newspaper ads and billboards, and trailers shown on TV and during movie previews at theaters. *The Hunt for Red October* combined yesterday's publicity stunt with today's advertising trend. The film's advertising began with billboards announcing, "The hunt is on." A few TV spots reminded us that the hunt was still on a week before the premiere. Then the Soviets announced that the "Red October" event really happened (sort of) and so author Tom Clancy appeared on radio and in papers discussing the movie and the actual incident. This pre-publicity helped. If I didn't know better, I would bet that Paramount made an arrangement with the Soviets to break the news just a few days before the opening. Movie critics liked it well enough. (Siskel and Ebert gave it "two thumbs up.") When the film finally debuted in March 1990, Paramount ran newspaper ads featuring Sean Connery's face with the submarine conning tower below. It sold well. Overall, the movie promotion was a feat.

There were some good publicity stunts done for movies during those golden years of Hollywood to boost attendance at film openings. A publicity man named Harry Reichenbach created a few good ones. One of his better stunts was for *The Return of Tarzan*. A few days before the film opened in New York, Reichenbach checked into a prominent hotel under the name Thomas R. Zann. He had a huge crate carried to his room. It turns out that the crate contained a lion. The lion's appearance made headlines. Mr. T. R. Zann said the lion was appearing at the opening of the Tarzan film. This gag helped promote the movie.

Reichenbach and other publicists were in big demand from movie studios in the 1920s. MGM, Paramount, Warner—all the big movie studios hired "exploitation departments" whose job was to publicize movies. They held Charlie Chaplin and Jackie Coogan lookalike contests. Then there were Elvis lookalikes. Douglas Fairbanks and Mary Pickford put their footprints in the cement outside Grauman's Chinese Theatre when it opened. It was a publicity stunt then; it's commonplace now. Exploitation teams staged Marilyn Monroe's walk over the grate blowing air under her dress. When MGM began its nationwide search for an actress to play Scarlett in *Gone With the Wind*, the film started receiving headline attention which continued until its premiere at the Loew's Grand Theater, where Gable gave a few words to the thousands lined up outside. Alfred Hitchcock used lots of publicity stunts for his movies. For *Frenzy*, Hitchcock arranged for a dummy of himself to float down the Thames River. When *Lassiter* opened on Valentine's Day, a publicist named Marty Weiser pasted up a 14-foot picture of Tom Selleck that women could kiss to see who had the most kissable lips. Hundreds of women kissed the poster, including seven women reporters from TV stations.

There are many more good examples of movie publicity from the past. These days, it seems many marketing types are afraid to take as many risks as exploiters used to. Still, today's marketers manage to create novel ways to market movies that draw the public's attention. We'll look at some of these in subsequent chapters. Stay tuned.

PROMOTION FOR THE ARTS

The movie stunts just depicted were planned. Sometimes a promotional event opportunity comes accidentally and can be exploited by an alert marketer. *The Last Temptation of Christ* was released early to take advantage of all the publicity it received when fundamentalists raised a ruckus and picketed theaters. Salman Rushdie's book *Satanic Verses* sold many more copies than it merited after Ayatollah Khomeini issued a $5 million reward for Rushdie's death because he felt the book was blasphemous. However, this was one instance when publicity got out of hand. Rushdie went into hiding (and is still in hiding as of this writing), book burnings and firebombings ensued, and six people were killed in riots. This example shows how the power of mere fiction can move people to censorship and violence.

Fortunately, most fiction does not produce death threats against authors, but censorship in many forms still plagues creators of fiction, art, movies, promotion campaigns, and other legitimate business products. We'll discuss censorship, lobbying, and promotional campaigns against business products in the next chapter. For now, let's turn to promotional feats used by painters.

Dalihoo

Although art (paintings, sculpture) is one product that sells on looks alone, it still needs promotion so people know it exists. Art galleries showcase works by contemporary artists, but this is not the only way to get good (and bad) art publicized. Painters now have lithographs made of their successful paintings. They often print these in limited editions and sometimes the artist autographs the print. This way artists earn more money than they would by selling originals alone. But some artists do wacky stunts to promote their work.

Surrealist painter Salvador Dali performed publicity stunts to get his art in the news. One time Dali was commissioned by Bonwit Teller department store in New York to design surreal window displays, which he did. Passers-by complained to the management. Officials tried to conceal the displays, but Dali got mad and pushed one of his exhibits (a bathtub with a mannequin floating in it) through the window. He made headlines and incited thousands to visit the gallery where his paintings were exhibited. Fuhrman (1989: 144) reported, "Overnight, Dali became one of the richest artists in the world."

A print entitled "September Morn" was used by ace publicity man Harry Reichenbach to publicize an art gallery that sold prints. "September Morn" shows a naked girl standing in a pool. Reichenbach placed the print in a window and called the local Anti-Vice Society to inform them of the shameless work of art at this gallery. He kept pestering them until they took notice. The subsequent publicity from court action helped sell $7 million worth of the mundane print. In 1913, that was a lot of money for one print.

Marketing Warhol

While he lived, Andy Warhol was the most-publicized pop artist of the second half of this century. Somehow, he managed to make paintings of Campbell's soup cans salable. His friendships with rich and famous people in New York helped get his art and name in the news. He was shot by one of his acquaintances in 1968 and almost died. *Time* and *Newsweek* ran stories on the shooting.

Warhol was also a filmmaker, originator of the "marathon motionless movie." He made exceedingly long and boring films of people doing everyday activities like smoking a cigar. As the American public yawned, critics applauded. David Bourdon (1971: 48) wrote: "Currently, there is a fairly broad consensus that he is among the most important, provocative and influential filmmakers of the sixties."

There are probably thousands of artists with styles similar to Warhol's that never made it. But Andy knew how to get and stay in the limelight. To this day, everyone knows Andy Warhol. By the time he died of a heart attack in 1987, he had managed to capture the imaginations, if not the hearts, of Americans. *Rolling Stone* (Loder 1987: 36) listed his accomplishments. He helped start a magazine called *Interview*, painted portraits of rich and famous folk, mentored blossoming new pop artists, and *didn't* create paintings of Brillo pads and Burpee flowers (although everyone thought he did). He starred in two cable TV shows. "He appeared in commercials, in rock videos, on *The Love Boat*. He left behind an estate of at least $10 million. Warhol was a promotional success." The *Newsweek* headline (Kroll 1987: 64) about his life and death best describes Warhol: "The Most Famous Artist."

The lesson of Andy Warhol is that art is truly in the eye of the beholder. He managed to make everyone behold his work. Apparently enough people liked it to make him a millionaire. And now that he's dead, Hollywood's going to make a movie about him (Johnson 1990).

Promotion managers and marketers should note that any product needs lots of public exposure to thrive. Managing to stay in the public eye was Warhol's promotional feat.

MUSIC IN THE MEDIA

Frank Sinatra lives! He's sung with big bands, his daughter, Sammy Davis, Jr., and Shirley MacLaine, among others. He won Grammy awards in 1966 for best record and best album. His name is prominently displayed on casino marquees in Las Vegas, Tahoe, Reno, and Atlantic City. He's starred in a slew of movies. Oldies radio stations feature "Sinatra Days" where they play his tunes for hours. "Old Blue Eyes" continues to dazzle the world with song—but he ain't no opera singer. How do singers with less-than-spectacular voices (e.g., Willie Nelson, Bob Dylan, Johnny Cash, any heavy metal band) make it big? They do it with promotional feats, for music is in the ear of the listener.

Beatlemania

Like Elvis (whom some people think is still alive), the Beatles were well promoted. In their heyday, they eclipsed all other pop music singers and bands. They produced hit song after hit song, gold album after gold album. They stayed in the vanguard of rock music, always a step ahead of their competitors. Their managers and agents got rid of much of the competition from England. The Zombies, Dave Clark Five, and many other British bands quickly faded after the Beatles reached the top of the pop pyramid. The Beatles' songs were good on several levels—they were danceable, had meaningful lyrics, and had good technical quality. And they were promoted like crazy. The Beatles appeared on the Ed Sullivan Show, produced four hit movies, won a Grammy, licensed their songs to other artists, toured the world, and had thousands of articles written about them. They were the most famous rock band in the world. John Lennon said "We're more popular than Jesus Christ now"—and then they were on the hot seat and in the papers.

Since the group broke up in 1970, victims of "creeping maturity" (Goldman 1970: 38), much has happened to them all. Ringo made movies and records and recently starred in an Oldsmobile television commercial. George followed a similar path (with no commercials). Paul recorded a series of albums and made a few tours. He received a lifetime achievement Grammy award in 1990, which coincided with his U.S. tour (sold out everywhere).

John Lennon made a few albums which sounded more like therapy songs but were nevertheless enthusiastically received by his fans. Lennon and the Plastic Ono Band performed numerous peace concerts which drew publicity. John and Yoko even held a "bed-in" during their honeymoon in 1969 ostensibly to promote peace—although they received most of the publicity.

Then came Lennon's *Double Fantasy* album and his murder. The album made number one and received a Grammy for best album in 1981. Lennon's flame is out but his fame lingers.

After the Beatles split, they stayed in the media, making money. Cartoon shows appeared on TV along with docudramas and biographies. Compact discs of past albums and new anthologies were released in the 1980s and were accepted by consumers. Ressner (1988) reported that Michael Jackson bought copyrights to 250 Beatles songs and collects royalties from artists, filmmakers, and TV and record producers who use the tunes. Jackson also sells some Beatles songs to businesses for tasteful TV commercials. In short, the Beatles, even after their demise, managed to stay in the limelight by continuing to make products (songs) that entertained people.

The Beatles are the only rock 'n' roll group to be included in Hirsch, et al.'s *Dictionary of Cultural Literacy* (1988: 159), which includes everything a culturally literate American should know. They describe the Beatles phenomenon: "The intense devotion of the group's fans, especially the hysterical screaming that the Beatles provoked in large crowds of teen-agers, was called Beatlemania."

A Rolling Stone Gathers Media

The Who and the Rolling Stones, both contemporaries of the Beatles, were still touring as of 1989, when both groups swept across the U.S. in sellout shows. *U.S.A. Today* reported "First day ticket sales for the Rolling Stones' Steel Wheels tour broke records in four cities Saturday, fueling predictions that the band will eclipse the Who as 1989's top draw" (Gundersen 1989: D1).

Pete Townsend may have written "Hope I die before I get old!" in the Who's top-selling song "My Generation," but he was obviously just joking, for the Who are still a "smash" band. And the Rolling Stones are still the bad boys of rock. Both groups have worked hard to maintain their respective images in the minds of America's rock consumers, and have succeeded. Their longevity in a shooting star industry is a promotional feat.

Keep on Truckin'

No American rock group from the 1960s can boast of the following that the Grateful Dead enjoy. Their product is excellent, consistent, and appears often. They advertise minimally; in fact, for some concerts, fans must call a hotline to find out when and where the Dead are playing and then follow a precise mailing procedure to get in the lottery to get tickets. Now that is "deadication." Where many businesses offer an 800 number to draw customers, Grateful Dead fans have to pay the toll—and do it willingly. Deadheads (very deadicated fans), pursue the Golden Road across the U.S. to follow their heroes every touring season. Local Deadheads in the San Francisco area get to attend Dead concerts at least fifteen times a year. Their concerts inevitably sell out and kids who want tickets stand outside the stadium and say, "I need a miracle."

Every Grateful Dead concert is a renaissance happening. My wife took me and her parents to a concert at the Shoreline Amphitheater, a reclaimed landfill. Right after we parked our car, someone walked by hawking "Dead at the Dump" bumper stickers. My wife warned us that "This is not a Perry Como concert." Just outside the arena, vendors sold beads, t-shirts, posters, and all sorts of Grateful Dead memorabilia. The people attending the concert were mostly young, but older folks mingled in here and there. Tie-dyed t-shirts and baggie hippie pants made everyone look like gypsies. Once inside the amphitheater, the atmosphere transformed into a gypsy festival when the music began. The Dead looked as if they were jamming in their living room rather than playing live before thousands of people. They didn't wiggle around—but the fans did. In fact, just about everyone danced. Some people never sat down once the concert started. We all had a good time. Even Perry Como would have had fun.

You may wonder how a '60s rock band could remain so popular after all these years. The answer is simple—the Grateful Dead make their fans feel special—they exemplify the Customer is King philosophy.

Let me elaborate. They allow vendors to sell Dead merchandise for free—they don't extract a licensing fee. They share the wealth with loyal roadies. They let small-time entrepreneurs flourish at their expense. Bill Candelario, the band's merchandising manager in 1987, said in an article in *Forbes*, "On a good day, we're losing $200,000 in sales out there" (Frank and Cone 1987: 43).

What the Dead get in exchange is fanatical loyalty, almost fealty, from vendors and fans. They allow fans to record concerts for private use. Naturally, some fans make bootleg tapes which are traded, not sold, through fan-generated newsletters like the *Golden Road*. The Dead turn a benign eye on this activity which would infuriate most pop singers and their record companies.

The Grateful Dead sell nostalgia. They haven't changed their style or philosophy since the '60s. They are simple, spiritual, natural, and genuine. Fans sense the congruence between the Dead and their product—music. To advertise, they rely on the greatest advertising medium of all—word-of-mouth.

In 1990, the Grateful Dead celebrated entertaining people for twenty-five years. That's not as long as Sinatra, but we are talking ethereal rock 'n' roll. Here are a few figures that show how successful this rock group is. The band grosses at least $10 million a year from concerts alone. In 1973, they played to 600,000 people in Watkins Glen, New York. Fans promoted the official Deadhead book written by Paul Grushkin (1983).

Since their inception, they have produced five gold records. In 1987, Arista Records released "In the Dark," which went platinum and generated substantial airplay on traditional rock radio stations and made a lot of money for the Grateful Dead. They have had videos appear on MTV and receive ink from *USA Today*, the *New York Times*, the *Los Angeles Times*, *Time*, and a host of leisure sections of newspapers across the nation.

In effect, the Dead have been mainstreamed, and still they perform over seventy concerts a year. At this rate, they will have performed 2,000 concerts by 1993. Naturally, members of the band appear solo a few times a year. These guys are workaholics, and their fans love them for it. The Grateful Dead's promotional feat is longevity due to good product plus repeat purchases multiplied by word-of-mouth advertising, or rather, preaching.

Modern Music and the Media

How do pop groups clip through all the clatter on the airwaves to make themselves heard and purchased? One way is to create a new dance and a song or two to go with it, demonstrate it on American Bandstand or Soul Train, and the cash waltzes in like Fred Astaire. Here's a smattering of fad dances; some survive today as "ballroom" dances and others are just gone. Let's see how many you remember: Charleston, foxtrot, mashed potatoes, bossa nova, monster mash, twist, boogaloo, shingaling, samba, Watusi, locomotion, cha cha, filly, swim, tango, jerk, skate, crocodile rock, break, bump, slam, and da butt.

In 1990, a new dance craze almost swept the country. It was the Brazilian sensual bump-and-grind called "lambada." The dance was featured on TV (*Arsenio Hall* and *Hard Copy*) and written up in *Newsweek*, *USA Today*, *The Wall Street Journal*, and *New York Times*. Music videos were aired on MTV and music shows. So far, so good. Two lambada movies were released in 1990, but neither made it big and critics panned them both. Mick LaSalle of the *San Francisco Chronicle* (1990: F1) wrote, "I saw the two 'lambada' movies that opened this weekend over the course of a single afternoon, which was pretty rough going and something that no one but an experienced professional should even attempt."

The people pushing lambada should be congratulated for promoting the dance more than any other dance has ever been promoted, but it just didn't quite catch on like it should have. Perhaps the fact that no single lambada song rocketed to number one predicated an early death for the dance. But it may yet capture the hearts and feet of America.

Another way to make it big in music is to define a particular genre. Since rock 'n' roll rose in the '50s, many other types of related pop music have flourished: rhythm and blues, soul, acid rock, bubblegum, heavy metal, rockabilly, salsa, new wave, reggae, and now rap music. Rap is such a rage that in 1990 *Newsweek* devoted a cover and ten pages to it. With all this publicity, some rap group will make it into the mainstream.

ENTERTAINING MARKETING

I hope it is evident from the preceding examples that all forms of entertainment, from adventuring to athletics to magic shows, movies, and music, involve marketing, perhaps more marketing communication efforts than any other product or service. We have seen how most successful entertainers have combined an excellent product with varied promotional schemes to make America the entertainment capital of the world.

We see that the entertainment industry is very dependent on and very good at manipulating the media. Oftentimes the entertainment company owns media. Marketers in other industries need to learn how to establish good relations with the media in order to elicit more, especially positive, response from these communication channels.

It is up to us marketers to fit entertainment promoters' strategies and tactics to our products and services. This shouldn't prove too difficult. After all, business products and services offer consumers tangible benefits, whereas entertainment offers only amusement, correct?

4

Product Features

"The package is the most important component of the product as a communication device."

—T. A. Shimp

MARKETING IS PACKAGING! That's right, if you make a unique product that consumers need and package it correctly, it's half sold. This holds especially true in retail, where numerous brands compete in the battlefield of the mind as shoppers wander the aisles and scan shelves looking for that benefit, image, or value communicated by each product's design, packaging, price, and placement. As the consumer makes that big decision as to which brand to buy, all the advertising and sales promotions that money can buy go out the window if your product is not on the shelves, or is shelved inadequately, or is priced too high or low, or is unattractively or unclearly packaged or labeled. Think about that.

What do Joe Montana, Reinhold Messner, Buffalo Bill, and Harry Houdini have in common? They exemplify excellent "products" that were well packaged, priced, placed, and promoted. In this chapter, we leave "person marketing" and examine consumer products and their implicit promotion. "Implicit promotion" refers to what Dommermuth (1989: 3) calls "persuasive communication inherent in the product, its places of sale, or its price."

This chapter highlights implicit promotional feats—that is, marketing communication of marketing mix variables. We discuss and provide outstanding examples (and a few failures) of implicit promotion of the product itself (creation, function, design, packaging, and branding), product price, and placing the product. In each area, cost-effective tips are provided to help marketers maximize the impact of these neglected promotional tools and make them work together to reap profits and satisfy consumers. Let's begin by looking at communication elements of the product itself.

INVENTING PRODUCTS

Necessity may be the mother of Invention, but Profit is the father. Invention is ignored by uncle Finance, observed by aunt Research, altered by its stepsisters Caprice and Status, and finally bragged about and sold by big brother Marketing. Over the centuries, many useful discoveries and inventions have never made it to market, or if they did, became obsolete and/or were changed, dropped, or superseded by new, improved products.

The basic human need for clothing, shelter, transportation, food, and water has resulted in discoveries and inventions that were sometimes marketed to best address these basic concerns. But often enough, what seems to be a solution to a basic need actually causes a bigger problem. Companies that satisfy basic human needs must look at the utility of their basic product and ask the question, "Is it still needed, and if yes, are we meeting that need in the best way?" If the product is not satisfying a need in the best way, then perhaps the product should be dropped, changed, or remarketed.

Let's look at discoveries and inventions that relate to basic needs and see what their status is today. Let's begin with the fur industry, which addresses the "clothing" need.

Fur Better or Worse

One of the first discoveries humans ever made had to be that animal skins keep a body warm—and they look good. Fur trade comprised a major part of commerce from prehistory to the present.

Fur trapping contributed to the discovery and development of the American West. Trappers ventured ever westward in search of beaver, mink, fox, and otter furs. Russian fur traders hired Aleuts and other native Americans to hunt down sea otters along the coast from Alaska through California. Sea otters had particularly desirable pelts, and in a few years, they were almost extinct. Today, a few survive around Monterey, California, and are protected by law.

After fur-bearing animals became scarce, entrepreneurs set up ranches to breed and raise mink and fox for furriers. Business quietly boomed for decades until the 1980s, when animal rights groups labeled fox and mink ranching as cruel since the animals are raised just to be killed and scalped. Evidently, it takes quite a few minks to make one mink coat. The animal rights advocates argue that it is not a "necessity" to kill animals for clothing, since cotton, wool, silk, and synthetic fabrics are readily available. In other words, mink stoles are capricious items. Also, animal activists note that the meat is not eaten and is thus wasted.

By 1989, the animal rights people had mobilized and struck. Billboards were their weapons, fur wearers their targets. Their object was to shame people into not wearing or buying fur products. Billboards featured beautiful women hiding their faces behind their furs. The billboard headline usually said something like, "You Should Be Ashamed."

The anti-fur campaign worked. People wearing furs were ridiculed in public. A *National Enquirer* headline read: "Charles Gets Di to Burn Fur Coats Worth 120G." Duffy (1990: 16) also reported that Prince Charles " . . . threw a mink stink and got posh Harrods department store in London to close their fur shop."

By mid–1990, furriers were clearing their warehouses at drastically reduced prices. At this rate, by the year 2000, furs will be a rarity, perhaps a novelty.

The reason I brought this story up is that the fur industry may serve as a bellwether for similar industries. Furriers have done everything right in making and marketing their product, but increasingly, the public doesn't want it anymore. Perhaps the leather industry should take note—they may be next. And who knows, animal rights activists may learn that silkworms are also animals, even though they don't have big eyes. Perhaps sheep-shearing will be called cruel. And I hear that cotton plants don't like to be picked at either. That leaves synthetics (usually oil-based). Save the naugahydes and baby neoprenes! I wonder, do we really want our oil reserves to be used for clothing? What will the emperor wear next?

Undoubtedly, the emperor will wear waterproof, breathable clothing made of Gore-Tex. The fabric industry used to be generic, but now, like everyone else, it's brand-conscious. W. L. Gore & Associates were the firstest with the mostest in breathable, waterproof fabrics. Rich consumers pay triple to wear waterproof (would you believe water-resistant?) Gore-Tex instead of a fabric as common as coated nylon. The phenomenal success of Gore-Tex shows that good design is an implicit promotional feat.

But in these copycat, too-many-choices times, Ellen Reagan (1990) reports that several water-resistant brands now compete to be sewn into sportswear. Examples include H2Off, Gymstar-Plus, Microfine, Microft, Tactel Micro, Trevira Finesse, Tuflex, Versatech, Exeltech, Klimate, Neozoic, Thintech, Bion II, Sympatex, Celtech, Dermoflex, Helly-Tech, Permia, Ultrex, Aqua-Guard, Pandaflex, and Vent-X.

The big guns in the fabrics industry have joined in the fray. Du Pont, Burlington Industries, and 3M will undoubtedly shake out the weaker contenders. Meanwhile, poor shoppers will continue to buy waterproof plastic raingear from Kmart for unbelievably low prices.

Lumbering Along

Here's another example. Since the beginning of history, humans have chopped down trees to clear the way for civilization, make homes, and secure firewood. The ancient Sumerians cut down the forests in Lebanon 5,000 years ago to sustain their civilization. Since then, timber harvesting has never stopped. But now, things are different. People are worried about global warming, extinction of rare animals and plants that may have medicinal properties, and the needless destruction of old and beautiful trees (such as redwoods in California and alerce cedars in Chile).

In the 1990s, lumber products companies may face a bleak future for two reasons: environmentalism and new discoveries. Pelline (1990: C1) reported that Louisiana-Pacific laid off 195 timber workers in California because environmentalists limited the company's access to national forest timber—to save the habitat of the spotted owl. Other timber companies and pulp processors have also suffered.

Environmentalists have been pulling off promotional feats left and right. The entire twentieth anniversary issue of *Smithsonian* (April 1990) magazine was devoted to the environment.

Loggers are under attack from "ecoterrorists" who commit "ecotage." Jennifer Foote (1990: 24) calls radical environmentalists "eco-guerrillas" who are trying to save the planet by warring with what Earth First! members call "greedheads" and "eco-thugs." Groups such as Earth First! attempt to "rewild" America by sabotaging logging operations in various ways. Their antics sometimes get them arrested, but always make the news.

Michael Parfit (1990) details Earth First!'s publicity stunts. Usually, Earth First! finds a prominent place to display a banner, like in the middle of a tree, across a road, or on top of a crane. The banners say things like, "From heritage to sawdust: Earth First!," "No compromise in defense of Mother Earth," "Pacific Lumber, stop the plunder," and "Save our saplings." They painted a crack in the dam at Hetch Hetchy Reservoir and wrote "Free the rivers—J. Muir" next to it. They painted the word *Extinct* over statues of grizzly bears on the Klamath River bridge in California. They spike trees and pour sawdust in logging truck gas tanks.

They spread their gospel during large public gatherings in the wilderness and publish newsletters, a journal, and books. One of the founders of Earth First!, Dave Foreman, addresses large groups at colleges. In short, these guys are getting their word out not just to loggers and miners but to everyone, including the more conservative conservation groups like the Sierra Club and to business leaders.

Many logging companies are taking legal action against the eco-guerrillas; others whine. Some clean up their act and then advertise their corporate responsibility to help Earth First!ers and the rest of society see their efforts. The American Forest Council put out a print ad in 1990 which read, "For us, every day is Earth Day." Some logging companies are socially responsible. They own their own tree farms, cut scientifically, replant thousands of trees daily, process lumber in an environmentally conscious manner, and support conservation of our resources.

Much of the timber logged today is used to make pulp for paper products such as this book, boxes, tissue, and packaging. Scientists are working on a new paper product that can be grown, harvested, and renewed yearly, which would save a lot of timber. The product is called papyrus—the stuff used by ancient Egyptians, Greeks, and Romans. Actually, the product is some fancy genetic papyrus-like hybrid. But an ancient invention is being reinvented—because of necessity.

Applying high-tech communication inventions such as electronic word processing, electronic mail, facsimile machines, and the reliable old telephone saves timber. Recycling paper also saves trees. Conservatree Paper Company received an Earth Day environmental achievement award (Russell 1990: C1) for "almost singlehandedly" creating the recycled paper market. Business is booming in all these timber spin-off industries. Thus, in the next few years, timber cutting will be cut back.

Tobacco Woes

Furriers may go out of business, loggers may have to toe the line, but no industry has been besieged in the last few years like the tobacco industry. It seems like everyone is against them: the American Medical Association and all other health organizations, the Surgeon General, airlines, restaurants, senators, and President Bush's Secretary of Health and Human Services. Even some smokers are against tobacco products. Due to the efforts of consumer action groups, tobacco companies must negotiate a maze of obstacles just to market their products.

Here are a few tobacco industry problems. Tobacco companies are prohibited from broadcast advertising. California passed a bill that increased the tax on all tobacco products, and many smokers voted for it. The Surgeon General requires health warnings on all tobacco ads and products. Smoking is banned on interstate flights. Many cities and states enforce ordinances requiring no-smoking sections in restaurants. Many businesses and government offices post no-smoking signs. Smoking is prohibited in movie theaters (except lobbies). The American Lung Association and American Heart Association advertise against smoking.

Celebrities like Larry Hagman and the ex-"Marlboro man" act as spokespersons for anti-smoking campaigns. Billboards and print ads which say "Kick some butts" capture the attention of nicotine addicts. The AMA jumped on R. J. Reynolds' "smokeless" cigarette Premier because nicotine cannot be sold without a prescription (unless it's in tobacco). Reynolds lost $100 million on Premier. But there's more bad news for RJR and Philip Morris.

Morganthau (1990: 19) reported that Louis W. Sullivan, Secretary of Health and Human Services, "publicly denounced R. J. Reynolds . . . for test-marketing a new cigarette aimed specifically at African-Americans." The cigarette, called Uptown, was being test-marketed to see if blacks would switch to it from other brands. But after community protests and Sullivan's thumbs down, Reynolds decided to shelve Uptown.

Sullivan didn't stop with Uptown. He went after the Virginia Slims tennis tournament by urging athletes to refuse tobacco "blood money" for endorsements. Pictures of Sullivan holding an "Emphysema Slims" shirt were published in newspapers and magazines. He criticized tobacco companies for marketing to blacks, women, and young people. Reynolds was planning a new brand, Dakota, to compete against Marlboro and targeted especially to young, white, "virile females." But who knows what will happen with that new product.

According to Mabry, et al. (1990: 46) a man named Mandrake paints over billboards that advertise smoking or drinking to blacks in Chicago. Mandrake has become a sort of Robin Hood hero.

Marketing News (Barlas 1990: 1) described anti-tobacco bills being bandied about in Congress. A bill by Senator Kennedy would establish a watchdog organization to monitor and regulate tobacco companies and promote anti-smoking ad campaigns. Kennedy's proposal is tame. Two other bills "ban point-of-purchase ads and cigarette company sponsorship of sporting events, and restrict the kinds of graphics that can be used in cigarette ads on billboards and in magazines and newspapers."

What have tobacco companies done about all the bad press? Not much. Company spokespeople have calmly tried to explain that market segmentation by brand differentiation is just good marketing. People don't buy it.

Philip Morris has aired television ads which remind people about America's Bill of Rights. If you call their toll-free number, they'll send you a beautiful copy of the Bill of Rights, suitable for framing. Tobacco industry critics say that Philip Morris broadcasts the ads about individual freedom for their own purposes. (That's obvious.) Still, the TV and print ads, along with their Bill of Rights mail campaign, is a good promotional effort to point out to Americans that their basic freedoms are eroding. Unfortunately for Philip Morris and the tobacco industry, it's too little, too late.

The ACLU has defended the tobacco industry's right to free speech—that helps a bit, at least with congressmen. But tobacco companies need to take the threat to their livelihoods very seriously and do something decisive, now. The Marlboro man (speaking of promotional feats) needs to rescue the tobacco image.

The good news is that the marketing profession is taking notice. A front-page article in *Marketing News* (Schlossberg 1990a) warns marketers who segment to learn from cigarette companies' woes in trying to segment their markets. The Association of National Advertisers is joining the fight to protect First Amendment rights of businesses such as Philip Morris and RJR. Maybe the Marlboro man will join the Dakota woman to promote freedom of choice in America. Let's hope so. It would be ironic if free enterprise in America were curtailed just as the Soviet Union is embracing capitalism.

The tobacco industry should join forces with other legal vice industries (alcohol, coffee, cola) and promote everything pro-choice and anti-prohibition. Otherwise, like dominoes, companies in these industries (which advertise heavily) could fall, one by one.

If adversaries can make promotional coups against products such as furs, lumber, and tobacco, imagine what they can do in other industries. The good news is that invention got companies in trouble, and market-driven and marketing-directed invention can get companies out of trouble and back in the black. The key to success in invention is to think about the market and how a product must be designed, packaged, labeled, and branded to make the appropriate implicit communication to consumers, watchdog agencies, and consumer advocate groups. That way, you can spend your explicit promotion dollars to promote, not defend.

Some Inventions Still Fly High

Leonardo da Vinci dreamed of flying in 1496. Four hundred years later, Langley made an experimental airplane that worked. The Wright brothers put an engine in a plane in 1903. The first passenger flight occurred in 1923, from New York City to Atlantic City. When the DC–3 was rolled out in 1935, the airline business was established. You could fly from New York to California in less than 15 hours. Now you can fly from New York to Paris on a Concorde SST in less than four hours.

By 1996, the aviation centennial, commercial space planes may be offering international space travel. As it is, airlines sometimes compete to fly you from New York to California for $99. Even though customers often complain about delays, service, or prices, commercial air travel worldwide is available, efficient, affordable, fast, and much safer than car travel. From 1979 to 1988, there were an average of 5.5 million departures yearly, with an average of three fatal accidents a year (including sabotage). Not a bad invention, that airplane.

By 2006, we may commute to work in a vertical takeoff-and-landing, saucer-shaped aircraft that is computer-controlled and hovers 40 feet above the ground. Paul Moller, a former aerodynamics professor, invented the M200X plane and demonstrated it publicly on May 10, 1989 (M. Miller 1989). The plane is propelled by eight 120-horsepower rotary engines. Moller plans to have a four-seater version available by the end of the decade that will cost the same as a passenger car. If Moller develops, designs, packages, and promotes his invention correctly, he could end up a very rich man—and the world would be better for his invention.

I could go on describing inventions and discoveries that have made life so much better, but it's time to move on. The evolution of the airplane has long fascinated me. Evidently, the people at TWA, American, United, and all the other airline companies are pleased with the invention. Delta spent $108 million in advertising alone in 1987. USAir Group enjoyed 1987 gross revenues of $5.7 billion. The airline service industry has thrived, thanks to a feat of invention—and smart entrepreneurs turning it into a marketable service.

Food for Thought

Moller's plane may address the transportation crunch facing most major cities, but many other problems call for inventions and discoveries that can be marketed to help satisfy basic human needs. One basic need that has been addressed during the past decade is the need for nutritious food.

America's farmers have succeeded in providing good food. Recent advances in agriculture show that farmers are working more with nature now than they have in the recent past. Small farmers and sometimes even big corporate farmers grow produce and raise livestock more organically, using fewer pesticides, fertilizers, and growth enhancers. Marketers are capitalizing on recent advances in nutrition research to bolster their products so they provide more nutrients and fewer harmful additives. And marketers are quick to communicate good health to consumers.

After studies showed that oat bran reduced cholesterol, cereal-makers bragged about their cereals' oat bran content. According to A. Miller, et al. (1990c), oat bran is featured not just in oatmeal, but in Anderson pretzels, Van's Belgian waffles, Health Valley's pilaf, Frookie cookies, and of course Cheerios. Farmers, nutritionists, and food processors are working together to make America a healthier place. Now, all we need do is get our food surplus to starving people in other countries. Like Quaker Oats ads say, it's the right thing to do.

Water Needed Everywhere

In Chapter 1 I mentioned a few business scenarios that are likely to occur in the future. But there is one basic human need that should be addressed by marketers very soon. That basic need is water—cool, clear water.

The world, especially big cities, needs more potable water. Let's take Los Angeles. California has faced drought off and on for the past ten years. Rationing is normal for San Francisco, but Los Angeles has been using everyone else's water. Now, finally, they must also think about filling swimming pools only half way. Seriously, drinking water is a problem now and it may worsen. It's ironic that California would suffer water shortages with all that ocean out there.

I have often wondered why we can't desalinate ocean water and drink it. My engineer friends tell me that it takes too much energy to pump seawater through desalination facilities; thus it costs too much. Apparently, Los Angeles and the state don't want to assume that responsibility. Fair enough. Private enterprise developed the airplane, and it can develop profitable desalination facilities.

It seems that if a joint venture were undertaken by Coca-Cola or the entire beverage industry and an aerospace firm or industry and maybe a big construction company such as Bechtel, that ways could be found to efficiently convert the sun's energy into abundant electricity that could fuel a huge desalination plant that would manufacture and market pure water for the millions of people in California. This is an example of a modern necessity which calls for a modern invention, assisted and promoted by modern marketing.

FEATS IN PRODUCT DESIGN

How a product is designed is as important as its basic function. Tobacco companies offered low-tar cigarettes in response to consumer demand. Automobile companies such as Chrysler are beginning to offer air bags to increase occupant safety during an accident. Volvo has always designed their cars with safety foremost. Ford has opted for the aerodynamic look coupled with "Quality Is Job 1."

StarKist announced in 1990 that it will only can tuna caught without harming dolphins. Their labels tout this fact. StarKist's marketing research showed that environmentally conscious consumers are willing to pay a few cents extra to buy "untainted" StarKist tuna. StarKist received a flood of television coverage following their announcement. According to Parrish and Kraul (1990) StarKist's publicity stunt was immediately followed by similar proclamations from America's other big tuna brands, Chicken of the Sea and Bumble Bee. The three labels represent 75 percent of the U.S. tuna market and half the world market. By accepting only "dolphin harmless" tuna, they have redesigned their product's image. Everyone wins except traditional tuna fishermen. They will have to change their fishing methods or go out of business.

On Earth Day 1990, Arco released a four-page color magazine ad featuring a scented tree with tips on reducing air pollution. In the ad, they alert consumers that they developed the first "emission control" gasoline. Arco reformulated their gasoline to reduce pollution and they are letting everyone know about it. Front-page headlines announced that Shell (along with Conoco, Marathon, Sun, and Diamond Shamrock) has joined Arco in introducing gasoline that helps reduce harmful emissions in smoggy cities.

Conoco made the front page in a promotional feat by announcing it is ordering new double-hulled oil tankers to reduce spillage. Shell and other oil companies are setting up their own oil spill clean-up fund. These proactive efforts by oil companies will gain favor with an increasingly environmentally aware public.

These examples of basic needs product redesign and accompanying explicit promotion serve as benchmarks for manufacturers and service providers in industries that appeal to higher-order needs (such as self-esteem, social acceptance, achievement, personal fulfillment). According to Nussbaum (1988), design blends form, function, quality, style, art, and engineering. Let's look at designs of products which exhibit implicit promotional feats.

Aqua-Fresh, The Complete Toothpaste

We all know that baking soda is the perfect powder to use when brushing our teeth, but it doesn't taste good. Not very many consumers use baking soda for this purpose. Tooth powder became available in the U.S. in 1899 (Quelch 1989: 90), but it had to be mixed with water before it could be used. Smart marketers introduced Pepsodent, Colgate, Ipana, Dr. Lyons, and Squibb in 1936; these were our first toothpaste brands. They took off, with Ipana in front by a nose.

Colgate shared the lead with Ipana and Pepsodent for a few years, then surged ahead. Pepsodent continued to crawl, but the other brands couldn't compete and were dropped by the time Gleem and Crest entered the scene in the early '50s.

Procter & Gamble (Crest) were smart. They differentiated Crest from other brands by including fluoride in their formula. The perceived health value of fluoride earned Crest the first seal of approval from the American Dental Association (ADA) in 1960. That year, Crest became (and has remained) the market leader. Families stayed brand loyal to Crest (and to Colgate, which put fluoride in its toothpaste also).

Colgate introduced Ultra-Brite in 1967 to capture teenagers' need for white teeth and fresh breath. Meanwhile, also-rans such as Macleans, Pearl Drops, and Peak came and departed. Lever Brothers introduced Close-Up to compete with Ultra-Brite. It featured silica, which could be used in a gel formula. It communicated "freshness," and its Lavoris-like red gel helped it beat out Ultra-Brite.

Lever Brothers then introduced Aim, Close-Up's fraternal twin with fluoride, to capture market away from Colgate and Crest. Aim enjoyed moderate market success at the expense of its competitors.

Then came Beecham. Its market research showed that many families bought a therapeutic toothpaste such as Crest and a cosmetic brand such as Close-Up. They decided to formulate a toothpaste which featured therapeutic and cosmetic benefits. So Aqua-fresh was introduced through extensive sampling in 1979 and was an immediate success. After a few minor reformulations, the Aqua-fresh we know today appeared. The tube features a clear top with red, white, and aqua stripes showing through. The tube says "tartar control" in big red letters and claims that it "fights cavities, help remove plaque, and reduces tartar build-up," in addition to freshening breath.

The Aqua-fresh product and package were an innovative response to consumer needs. The product communicates that it offers everything a user could possibly want in a dentifrice. Couple the intrinsic promotion inherent in the product and package with the extensive advertising and sales promotion accompanying the product ($43 million in 1980), and Beecham had themselves a promotional feat. Triple Protection Aqua-fresh overcame Aim and slid into the third place slot behind Crest and Colgate. The marketing war in dentifrices continues to this day and Aqua-fresh is a steady competitor, averaging a little over 11 percent market share. (See Quelch 1989: 92.)

From Coffee Crystals to Whole Beans

In the old days, we had to roast, grind, and filter our own coffee. Then coffee companies roasted and ground it for us. That was convenient, but we still had to filter the stuff. Then instant coffee was formulated, and coffee brewing became as simple as scooping a teaspoon-full into your cup and pouring in hot water. Voila!

Instant coffee is a product design phenomenon. The problem lies in differentiating one instant coffee from another. Maxim instant coffee is chunky. Folger's coffee crystals are unique. Yuban instant coffee comes in an extra rich formula called Marabor Bold. Sanka instant is decaffeinated. Once Sanka brand became successful, imitators entered the arena. General Foods' International Coffees were a big hit; now Hills Brothers are right on their tail—only they use convenient plastic packages instead of nice cans. Both containers are reusable (more on this later). Very clever. But that's not the end of the story.

Many consumers like filtered coffee better than instant, but complain that filtering is too difficult and time consuming. Maxwell House, a Philip Morris brand, came up with pre-measured Filter Packs that fit standard automatic drip coffeemakers. All you have to do is drop one in, pour water into the machine, turn it on, and presto!

Over the past few years, consumers have expressed a preference for, you guessed it, fresh roasted, unground coffee beans from around the world. Small companies are filtering away big companies' profits by offering coffee drinkers what they want, even if the beans cost much more.

Yuban decided to fight back with its own unground coffee beans. When a consumer buys a competitor's coffee beans, she receives a cents-off cashier's checkout coupon from Yuban, good for the next purchase. That's a promotional feat. Yuban realized that a significant portion of the public wanted whole beans—and they responded. The checkout coupon, which is offered only if the customer buys a competing brand, is the topper to this feat. Other coffee brands will likely follow Yuban's lead.

A Cola's a Cola

It's hard to believe that Americans (and the rest of the world) have been buying colas for over a hundred years. It's just brown-colored sugar water. When Coca-Cola was introduced as a snake oil medicine, it contained cocaine from coca leaves and caffeine from cola nuts. It was originally advertised as an "invigorating beverage" and "a cure for all nervous afflictions." No doubt.

If you ordered "original Coke" today you might get arrested. We all know there's no cocaine in today's Coke, but America's most popular product around the world has undergone numerous formula changes over the years and no one complained. Then, in response to taste tests which showed that Americans preferred the sweeter taste of Pepsi-Cola, Coke made their formula sweeter and Coke loyalists revolted.

The irony is that a significant portion of Classic Coke fans cannot tell which cola is which. I replicated Coca-Cola's taste test experiment and found that only 15 percent of cola drinkers who reported they were loyal to Pepsi or Coke could discern their brand from a panel of brands. Most thought that the brand they liked the best was their regular brand.

The Coca-Cola debacle received nationwide media attention for weeks.

The new Coke and Classic Coke were shown on TV day after day. Pepsi and Coke presidents were on news shows with big smiles on their faces. The entire soft drink industry benefited from the millions of dollars of free exposure. The incident, though accidental, was certainly a promotional feat for Coke.

In response to perceived consumer demand and competition, Coca-Cola developed all kinds of strange beverages: Tab and Diet Coke, Cherry Coke, and decaffeinated versions of the above. The market share of New Coke dropped from 15 percent in 1985 to 2 percent in 1989. Miller and Smith (1990: 38) reported that Coca-Cola plans to give new Coke a new name—Coke II—with "real cola taste" and the syrupy taste of Pepsi. Good luck.

Here's a question. How could educated consumers spend 50 cents to a dollar for Caffeine-Free Diet Coke? The stuff has absolutely nothing in it, except brown fizzy water with aspartame added. Many Americans spend money on products with no nutritive value while millions of people in the world beg for food. The gods must be crazy!

From out of the brown came a company that recognized that some Americans eschewed no-nothing cola. Jolt Cola, a guerrilla product with a small market share but enough loyal buyers to earn a profit, brags that it has twice the caffeine and all the sugar of other colas. In other words, some smart consumers will get a bigger buzz for their buck. Jolt Cola's formula is a promotional feat in the product design category.

The Future of HDTV

Home electronics have come a long way. AM radio was king for decades, despite the fact that static-free FM was invented in 1933 by Edwin Armstrong. RCA kept Armstrong's invention under wraps because they didn't want to change their broadcasting equipment to handle FM, so the public had to wait until the early 1950s to enjoy FM. Most radio stations didn't broadcast in FM until companies designed and produced radios that could receive FM signals, so consumers had to wait for the 1960s before FM caught on big. Now, many radio networks offer the same signals on both FM and AM bands.

In the early 1960s, people bought tinny Japanese "transistor" radios at low prices. Now, we can buy a hi-fi Sony Walkman or a host of copycats at reasonable prices. The harvest of innovatively designed radio and other sound equipment (such as CDs) has greatly enhanced our listening pleasure. Many people have chucked their record collections and bought CDs of their favorite music to play on new CD players with small speakers that deliver big sound.

But if advances in audio technology seem remarkable, they pale beside advances in video technology. In the past, consumers shot home movies using 8-mm cameras. Now, high quality video cameras loaded with options are available for under $1,000. VCRs used to be so expensive only television stations could afford them. Now, VCR technology is so advanced and manufacturing so efficient that we can buy a good one for under $300.

So everyone's making home videos. One of the most popular television shows in 1990 was "America's Funniest Home Videos," which featured hilarious bloopers recorded by amateurs with camcorders. The show is flooded with thousands of videos weekly. We are witnessing a trend. Local television stations purchase home videos of accidents, crimes, and other newsworthy items, and even solicit them on the air. Freelance news videography may become a profession.

Television has advanced also. In the 1950s, you could watch TV in any color as long as it was black-and-white. In the early 1960s, when RCA came out with their color TV, their ads featured a happy consumer singing a jingle about the joys of color: "Wow, I got color TV—natural, wonderful, color TV! RCA Victor color TV! Wow, I got color TV!"

Soon, everyone made color TV. Sony's Trinitron had the quintessential sharp color picture. By the 1990s, all TVs except microportables offered high-quality color. Color picture quality has steadily improved. Now the television industry (broadcast stations and television manufacturers) face a dilemma. Do they switch to high-definition television (HDTV) and make expensive changes, or do they resist, as RCA did with FM?

HDTV, invented in 1988, will produce color pictures equal to film quality. In this early stage of development, it's expensive. (A few Japanese received HDTV broadcasts in 1989, but receivers cost them $60,000 each.) The U.S. Defense Department wants HDTV developed for their own uses, so they've offered over $30 million in research grants to aid electronics companies in producing HDTV. But they want more money, over $1 billion more, and they probably won't be given the handouts they seek. In 1990, there were only five groups left in the U.S. competing for the HDTV standard (the one that everyone would use). Zenith and AT&T allied to form one group, a Japanese public broadcasting service group (NHK) formed another.

The only cost-effective way that these companies are going to develop HDTV that Americans will buy is to pool their resources, as Zenith and AT&T have done. The problem, according to McMahon (1990), is that the picture is not that much clearer than what we have now. HDTV broadcasts will have to work on existing TVs to make it initially. By 1994, manufacturers hope to develop a 27-inch HDTV available for less than $2000. The world waits, but not with bated breath.

While HDTV research continues unabated, some TV manufacturers are giving consumers what they want now. People like *big* pictures. The trend of the '90s is home theater. According to Blumenthal (1990), a company called Stewart Filmscreen offers a 100-inch screen ($600) with high-quality graphics, a great projector (the Barcodata 1001—$23,000), and a surround-sound audio system from Fosgate-Audionics for $8,500. Total cost: $32,000. Still a bit high-priced.

Then, along comes big Wilt Chamberlain hawking the Sharpvision 100" on TV. I called the 1–800-BE-SHARP number and received a brochure along with a list of Sharp home theater dealers in my area. One of the dealers, Performance Audio, sent me a handwritten card inviting me to try out Sharpvision at their store. Now that's targeting customers. That's a promotional feat. I called the store and found that the portable Sharpvision video projector costs only $5,000 and operates with standard audio and video equipment (such as VCRs and conventional stereo systems). Sharp's minds have designed a Sharp product, one that will beat everyone else to the punch if they exploit their initiative.

Designing a Design

Business executives are conservative by nature. They don't change quickly. Often, incremental change saves money; sometimes it costs money. To compete, companies must take a hard look at their fundamental products and services and design them with people's true needs in mind. Well-designed products, such as StarKist dolphin-free tuna, Arco's lower-pollution gasoline, Sharpvision home theater, or Black & Decker's portable power tools and under-shelf home appliances will sell themselves. They will become implicit promotional feats. But to succeed, people from different departments of a company (R & D, production and operations, and marketing) must work together. In some cases, companies must ally with competitors to fully exploit an idea or invention whose time has come.

PACKAGING

A package not only contains and protects the product, it does much more. With the exception of the product itself, nothing communicates more than the package and its constituent elements: material, shape, size, colors, and labeling. For a package to attain implicit promotional feat status, it must be functional and inexpensive, convey the intended message to consumers, and be recognizable and desirable to buyers. In short, the ideal package must stand out among competing brands and almost compel the shopper to grab it.

Since the Smith Brothers began distinctive packaging of their cough lozenges to prevent merchants from selling inferior cough drops as a Smith product, smart marketers have designed packages to differentiate their products from all others. Consumers are so package-, label-, and brand-conscious that they often eschew a generically labeled, plain-packaged, less-expensive good for their preferred brand even when the two products are identical.

Obviously, distinctive packaging cues buyers in significant ways. They have the opportunity to see a package every time they shop. After a purchase, they may look at the package numerous times when using it (as in the case of shampoo or toothpaste). Oftentimes, the package is the medium as well as the message.

Astoundingly, many modern marketers don't realize the promotional power of packaging. Nickels (1984: 120) remarks, "Considering the promotional impact of packaging, it is a wonder that it has received so little attention among marketers relative to other promotional elements."

Food Packaging Feats

The beverage industries realize the promotion potential of packaging. I bet $50 that 90 percent of Americans would recognize a Coke bottle when they see it. They should, since the distinctive bottle has been around since 1915.

V–8 juice is now available in easy-opening cans, aseptic containers, and wide-lipped jars—but the label remains true to the original. V–8 still gets plenty of shelf space, in spite of the multitude of juice brands flooding the market.

While we are discussing juices, juice-flavored waters now compete with sodas for shelf space. Shoppers can choose from a variety of brands, each supporting a unique bottle. I bet most upscale water drinkers can distinguish a Perrier bottle from a Clearly Canadian bottle without seeing the labels.

GatorAde, the flavored beverage for athletes, still holds the greatest market share in its category (96 percent, with annual sales of $600 million), but is being challenged by a newcomer called Power Burst. In addition to resembling GatorAde in ingredients, taste, and price, the 64-ounce size of Power Burst comes in a wide-mouthed, reusable plastic bottle. Forget about recycling; the Power Burst bottle is used by recreationists as a canteen. Imagine a canteen that is cheaper and better than those sold in sporting goods stores, yet comes filled with an "advanced performance beverage." That's a feat.

A beer drinker can buy Bud in cans, seven-ounce bottles, or longneck bottles. I conducted a survey and found that nine out of ten college beer drinkers prefer longnecks. Although longnecks are difficult to shelve, retailers clamor for more and claim they cannot get enough longnecks of any brand. Beer drinkers will gravitate toward any longneck over their regular brand, that's how popular this package is. If I were Bud,

Coors, or Miller, I'd scramble to give the people what they want. And remember, bottles are re-usable.

Speaking of reuse and recycling, McDonald's Corp., long accused of overusing foam containers that are not biodegradable, now has recycling logos on its Happy Meal boxes. Kids may not care, but environmentally conscious parents do.

Food Packaging Failures

Whereas many companies take advantage of developments in packaging, a significant number of food providers do not. Most pancake mixes, flour, and other traditional foods still come in bulky boxes and bags that are difficult to open and nearly impossible to reseal. Someday, someone will come along and offer consumers an attractive, easy-to-use, inexpensive package that communicates "buy me." And if future pancake mix boxes are so constructed to ease the work of distributors and grocers, then they will be even more successful.

With the exception of Pepperidge Farm cookies (which usually get more shelf space because they are so popular among consumers), most cookies are still contained in cheap plastic packages that once opened are impossible to reseal. Consumers don't like this. They believe that cookies sold in awkward containers are somehow inferior to the unique, high-quality packages used by Pepperidge Farm.

Many Americans like to eat salsa. La Victoria makes several salsas for every taste. Unfortunately, their glass jars break and the mouths are too narrow to dip a corn chip into. Thus, a person must put La Victoria's (and other brands') salsa in a separate container to serve it. A reusable, wide-mouthed, plastic jar would work better and encourage more sales.

Why do cheap wines feature easily removable and replaceable plastic corks (or equally convenient metal screw-on lids) and expensive wines sport awkward, crumbly, permeable wood corks? Supposedly, consumers think that real corks bespeak quality, tradition, and romance. I bet many wine drinkers would welcome plastic corks on bottles of premium wines. Hopefully, some premium wine makers will soon brag about their convenient, reusable, wine-protecting plastic corks.

Some wines come conveniently packaged in Mylar bags. Why not permanently stamp the company logo directly on the Mylar, so when consumers reuse the Mylar bags, they will be reminded who provided the handy containers?

I could list more food packaging feats and failures, but suffice it to say that aware marketers should ensure that their products are packaged to communicate these benefits to consumers (and retailers): ease of use, ease of storage, and future reuse of the package. The environmental

consciousness trend is here to stay. Smart marketers will serve the buying community by stressing the benefits of reusable, recyclable packages.

To remind consumers who provided the package they are reusing
(e.g., a Power Burst bottle), be sure to emboss the package with your
logo, since labels don't last long. Of course, if you own a package of
proprietary design (such as a Coke bottle), embossing reinforces the
recognizable shape. Let's leave food packaging and look at packages for
other products that have earned implicit promotional feat status.

A L'egg up on the Competition

Hanes textile corporation pulled the biggest coup yet in promotion
through packaging and other implicitly promoted products (more on
that later). After the miniskirt craze faded in the late 1960s, the future
of pantyhose was uncertain. Hanes spent $400,000 researching the mar-
ket. They found that young women wanted non-sag pantyhose at reasonable prices. Hanes developed a pantyhose that contoured to most
legs and resisted running. To give it a unique appearance, Hanes put
the pantyhose in a plastic egg and called it L'eggs. The rest is hosetory!

Packaged for Your Convenience

L'eggs hosiery is put in a distinctive and convenient package. Other
companies have followed suit. Remember way back when motor oil was
packaged in cans that required a leaky spout to use? In the 1980s some
oil companies finally started caring about us poor consumers and placed
motor oil in easy-pour plastic bottles. The containers were an instant hit
and soon all oil was packaged in resealable containers. Two leading
brands, Pennzoil and Quaker State, exemplify the smart packaging
trend. Both packages feature embossed brand names and company
colors. The oil container example dramatically demonstrates the communication power of good packaging. Here's a question: would you buy
your brand of motor oil in the old cans if each can was only a quarter
cheaper than the new containers? Neither would I.

Here is another innovative packaging example. Liquid Tide, conveniently packaged in an easy-pour plastic bottle, revolutionized the laundry
detergent market. Suddenly, there was an alternative to conventional
powdered detergents. Consumers liked the liquid detergent and the
bottles, and Liquid Tide dominated that new market with an implicit
promotional feat. Naturally, competing companies immediately began
formulating their own liquid laundry detergent and unique, convenient
plastic bottles.

These examples show the promotional power of packaging. Promotions professor Terence Shimp (1990: 59) underscores the promotional

value of good packaging: "Clearly, the package is a vital element in the marketing communications mix."

So, when designing or redesigning packaging, carefully consider the cost and reusability/recyclability of the physical materials used in the package. In a way that is congruent with your company's mission and promotional strategy, your product's intended use, and consumers' needs and desires, design your package to achieve maximum sales impact. Pay attention to color, size, shape, and other important design features. Make your package cut through clutter and sell your product. Your package should be so compelling that it can sell your product without the help of explicit promotional activities such as advertising and sales promotions.

BRANDING

To help the package design promote, carefully note every word and symbol on the package. Check out brand names and marks, product information, warnings, and guarantees, for each of these factors must combine with the package, the product itself, and explicit promotion activities to create a gestalt that affects consumers in a powerful, consistent manner. Let's look at words and symbols that have achieved promotional feat status.

A Brand by Any Other Name

For years, western ranchers branded cattle to discourage rustlers from stealing stock. But ranch brands also serve to differentiate herd quality at auction. Over time, buyers learn that Bar-X steers are fatter than Bar-Y steers. Hence, buyers seek out Bar-X cattle and pay a premium for the high grade beef.

Distributors, retailers, and consumers emulate cattle buyers; that is, they are brand sensitized over time and actively seek out preferred brands. We all know elderly car drivers who have always bought Fords or Chevys and will continue to do so until they die. They ignore good foreign brands such as Volvo or Toyota in favor of the car makes they have purchased since 1946. In Chapter 3, we noted similar behavior among music concertgoers. Some rock music fans will ignore all other performers yet attend every Grateful Dead concert in the country. In short, these young consumers are brand loyal (though they might not admit it).

A revered brand will sell itself year after year once it has been firmly ensconced in consumers' minds. Often, only a bit of reminder advertising or an occasional sales promotion is needed to revitalize consumption of a famous, long-lived brand. Products such as Kellogg's corn

flakes, Bayer aspirin, Arm & Hammer baking soda, and Windex window
cleaner typify established brand names. Competing companies are
forced to promote aggressively to gain on these brands.

What are the most recognized brand names in America today? According to Lowry (1988: 31), the most popular brands are Coca-Cola,
McDonald's, American Express, Kellogg, IBM, Levi's, and Sears.

Sometimes consumers become so familiar with a brand that they un-
consciously attribute generic status to the brand name. Here are some
famous examples. After several lawsuits, most soda jerks today make
customers clarify when they order a "coke" and the fountain serves only
a competing cola. When a department store sells Wrangler jeans and
the customer asks for Levi's, the sales clerk delineates the difference
between "jeans" and "Levi's."

These are easy examples. But do you know the generic name of Styrofoam? Polystyrene foam is the product name. The moral of the story is
that it's good to be recognized the world over, but not when your brand
name becomes genericized.

So, create memorable brand names and marks, display them on packages and the product itself, and reinforce brand uniqueness through
advertising and other promotional efforts. Be vigilant in ensuring brand
value and differentiation from generic products. While you're at it, zeal-
ously protect your brand names and trademarks from competitors. And
remember, every time a consumer looks at a package with your brand
name or logo on it, the quality of your product is reinforced.

One more time again, how important is brand name? Zaltman and
Wallendorf (1979: 3) report that up to 40 percent of new product success
(or failure) can be attributed to brand name. Make your brand name a
promotional feat.

Labeling

Just as important as brand identifiers is information printed on the
package: package contents, quantity, price, warnings, use instructions,
guarantees. Intermediaries also need information on how to handle the
product. Obviously, written information should be clear, factual, and
complete. It must also comply with current regulations regarding the
product.

Photographs and illustrations should portray a realistic view of the
product; otherwise, consumers will be disillusioned with your brand.
We have all seen the plump, juicy cherry pie in the picture, only to be
disappointed by the actual product full of glaze and an occasional cherry.

Most of us would agree that mandatory information such as how to
use the product and warning labels can hardly be considered a pro-

motional feat. Yet, there is lots of room on a package for other label information that can promote the product. Here are a few examples.

The environmental trend is not a fad, as claimed by some marketing experts such as Hunter Hastings (1990: 4). Smart companies will figure out the best way to capitalize on environmental issues. Some companies, such as Chevron and AT&T, support environmental causes. Others tout the recyclability of their packages. Procter & Gamble's detergents (Tide, Cheer, Dash, Dreft, Bold, and Oxydol) now display the recycling mark of arrows spinning clockwise in a circle.

Other pro-environment seals now found on certain packages include the "Green Cross" for content composed of at least 25 percent recycled material, the "Ozone Friendly/No CFC's" for spray products, the "Nutri Clean" for vegetables and fruits that contain no pesticides, and the "Green Seal" checkmark for products that have some environmental benefit. According to Beckett (1990a: C1), consumers may get confused trying to figure out what all these seals mean. Environmental groups fear that companies may use the seals to sell products that have negligible positive effect on the environment.

Still, the seal system has been used with success in the past. We're all familiar with products that feature the Underwriters Laboratories and Good Housekeeping seals of product performance. There is no reason that environmentally beneficial products should not tout their benefits to consumers.

A pro-environment message is just one example of what can be done with labels to attract consumers. In addition to seals of approval, many labels contain interesting information: nutrition highlights (such as "Vitafort," "low cholesterol," "light"), games and contests, historical and scientific facts, and merchandise offers. Celestial Seasonings' popular herbal teas feature quaint, traditional, four-color illustrations and words of wisdom that many people like to read.

The best implicit promotional feats for labels can be found on the 140 brands of cold cereal that shoppers must choose from. Although cereals are almost all the same, they lure buyers with packages in bright colors and labels replete with celebrity endorsements, cartoon characters, nutrition claims, coupons, guarantees, slogans, promotions, and just about anything else imaginable that might persuade someone to reach out and grab that box.

All manufacturers can learn from cereal boxes. Gimmicks used by Kellogg and General Mills to sell cereal work. And don't forget to label your packages with old standards such as "new" and "improved."

We see that promotion managers must make full use of the product, package, brand identifiers, and labeling to create and maintain a consistent standard of value in consumers' minds. Advertising, sales promotions, and other forms of explicit marketing communications are not enough. Implicit promotional cues contribute significantly to sales.

THE PRICE IS RIGHT

Pricing is another underused implicit promotional tool that complements explicit promotional efforts. Marketers use a number of strategies to price goods and services. In a book dedicated to pricing strategies, editor Daniel Seymour (1989) presents a number of issues that marketers must grapple with when setting prices: direct and indirect costs of production and operations, competitors' pricing activities, marketing objectives, and consumer demand and perceptions. Let's examine these pricing strategies and see how they can become part of an implicit promotional feat package.

Cost-Plus Pricing Is a Minus

Many companies base price on break-even analysis of fixed and variable costs over time. Break-even analysis is necessary but insufficient as a price-setting practice. Good companies keep costs down by insisting on quality from purchasing to production to promotion.

By following quality control guru Ed Deming's advice of establishing a quality-oriented relationship with suppliers and carrying that over into promotion (so money is not lost by rejecting faulty items caught by inspectors or consumers), a firm can gradually acquire a reputation for quality. (See Mann 1989 and Dobyns 1990.)

Thus, economy of scale, increased sales at higher margin, and overall higher return on investment are achieved by quality consciousness at all levels. High-quality product combined with appropriate packaging, branding, labeling, and price signals consumers that their expectations will be met by purchasing said product. So, cost-plus pricing must be augmented by other factors when constructing price.

Ignore Competitors' Prices

Some "me-too" companies decide their prices based on what their competitors charge. If the competitor lowers its prices, me-too companies achieve parity by lowering theirs accordingly, and a price war ensues. Consumers go on a price-feeding frenzy, and perceived product value is replaced with pork belly commodity thinking. The me-too company loses profits in the short and long term. All market share gains are temporary; they evaporate with the next price reduction or discount salvo in the price wars. The reactive me-too company is sunk.

Even big companies lose in price wars, since the perceived quality of

their products or services is devalued permanently in the minds of consumers. Naturally, a successful company always knows what its competitors are doing in price and price-based promotions, but it does not
blindly copy competitors. In business, as in judo, you cannot win by
merely imitating your opponent's moves.

Deciding to base your price higher or lower than your competitor is
necessary to consider, but insufficient ground on which to finally determine your pricing policy. My advice is to study your competitors'
pricing strategy and tactics and then ignore it. Focus instead on your
own marketing objectives, natural and created demand, and the most
important component of pricing—consumer perceptions of value.

Set Realistic Marketing Objectives

If you perceive your product as low value in a high competition market
(such as raw lumber or steel), you have few pricing alternatives. All you
can do is discount for high-volume purchases and hope you can find a
cheap source of the commodity. (This is how rain forests get stripped.)

A better solution is to raise your product above commodity status by
creating product differentiation and increasing price to signal new value.
Putting platformate or some other additive in gasoline helps move consumers away from seeking the lowest-priced gasoline. Gas additives
coupled with price increases create brand identification with commodity
products. Consumers do not buy oil companies' rationale for higher
prices (i.e., the cost of crude increases a few cents per barrel, so gas
increases 25 cents at the pump). Consumers will pay more for what they
perceive as increased value.

For markets that have competition but in which product and service
value varies, price can and should signal quality. All providers of goods
and services should strive to make their products high, but not necessarily premium, quality. The important thing that a marketer needs to
remember when setting prices is that the price must communicate the
company's perceived value of the product to the consumer. As a marketer, you must ensure that the product matches the value that your
price communicates. It's as simple as that. Marketing research into consumer perceptions will quickly tell you if your perceived value is the
same as the consumers'.

Marketing strategy that deals with a product's price should center on
profit through volume, margin, or both. High-quality products can earn
profit through margin alone even if few units are sold, as long as enough
consumers pay high enough prices for the company to realize ROI. Sub-
Zero sells custom refrigerators at over $3,000 each and earns a tidy profit.
Sub-Zero knows their products are worth the price, and evidently their
customers agree.

The ideal situation occurs when a high margin product or service achieves high demand so the company can produce enough volume to achieve economy of scale. When this happens, as in the case of Hewlett-Packard (who achieved market penetration of calculators at skimming prices, at least for awhile), an implicit promotional feat occurs based partly on price.

Break Elastic Prices

Economic pricing models center on price elasticity based on demand and rational cognitive activity of consumers. The classic economic model states that under normal (perfect) conditions, price and demand are inversely related. As price increases, demand decreases. It must be noted that external factors affect this relationship. If consumers obtain more disposable income or the value of the dollar increases or a company dramatically increases promotional activities such as advertising, demand may shift upward without a price decrease.

The economic model shows that under given conditions, prices are said to be elastic (demand changes with price) or inelastic (demand does not change noticeably with price). When price is elastic, the classic response is to lower price to keep obtaining revenue.

Consumers are less price sensitive when the price for a product or service is low compared to their disposable income. Also, prices are more inelastic when there are no competing brands available (for example, when consumers live in a remote area and have access to only one brand). For marketers, the most important reason that price may be inelastic is due to consumers' perceptions of quality or uniqueness. Sony continues to sell electronic goods at higher prices than competitors because they are perceived as higher quality and innovative.

The economic model is useful but doesn't account for subtle promotional efforts to create brand uniqueness and quality in the minds of consumers. Another tenet of the economic model is that consumers think rationally when making purchases—at least for major purchases such as automobiles. Professional buyers may think rationally, but average consumers are often swayed by perceived value, unique "necessities," lack of confidence in their own judgment, brand-name-stimulated response patterns (buying brand names no matter what), and snob appeal of certain products. In 1990, teenagers were mugged for their snobby Nike athletic shoes. Apparently, in some circles, high class apparel is worth killing for.

In many buying situations, consumers use what Nickels (1984: 127) calls the doubt strategy. "When in doubt, consumers often buy either the cheapest or the most expensive brands. In other words, branding and pricing become surrogate indications of quality and value." In short, much buying behavior is not very rational; it is more black or white, cheap or expensive.

Price Is Perceived Value

Although the aforementioned factors contribute to a company's pricing strategy, a promotion-centered marketing executive should concentrate on establishing a perceived value of a product in target consumers' minds. Explicit and implicit promotion activities should work together to create a high perceived value of the product. A price set significantly and consistently higher than competing products helps convey this value.

Of course, for this to work, your products must be significantly better than the competition on key attributes. To find out if this is so, conduct research with target consumers and see how they compare your brand against competing brands and an "ideal" product. As best you can within your capabilities, give customers what they want.

The key to creating a promotional feat out of price is to remember to successfully differentiate your brand from others by showing its benefits, or its unique value to customers. For years, Curtis Mathes televisions were higher priced because they were presented and perceived as better and higher status due to fine craftsmanship. In recent years, Curtis Mathes sets were not rated significantly higher in performance and reliability than competing sets, and then other brands (e.g., Sony) began to make their marks as top-of-the-line brands.

Certain markets are just ripe for brand differentiation through price. Examples include liquor, fashion, cosmetics, and luxury items such as fancy, high-status automobiles. Capricious products and services always provide ample opportunity for implicit promotional feats such as sustained demand for high-priced products. Let's examine some price-related feats.

Toni at Twice the Price

The Toni story best illustrates the "perceived value" of a capricious product. According to Conover (1989: 103):

> when Toni home permanents were first introduced at a price around a dollar, sales were disappointingly low. An astute marketing manager decided to more than double the price, to a level closer to that of beauty-shop perms, and sales took off. Apparently, women who were interested in the product doubted its quality at such a low price—it was seen as an "inferior good"—but the higher price conveyed an impression of quality.

Sales of other products, such as Rolls Royce automobiles, have risen dramatically when the price was doubled. Of course the Rolls Royce is a quality automobile, but is it really twice as good as a Lincoln?

A popular price promotional feat heard through the marketing grapevine is the "half price jewelry sells double when priced double" story. Kotler and Armstrong (1990: 301) tell the tale well. They relate that Silverado Jewelry, located in Tempe, Arizona, had trouble moving mother-of-pearl jewelry priced at cost plus a moderate profit. The store owner left a note with the assistant manager to cut the mother-of-pearl price in half. Her manager misread the note as "times two" instead of "in half." Customers suddenly perceived the mother-of-pearl jewelry as valuable, and the product soon sold out. Just think, if diamonds were as common as cut glass, how valuable would they be?

Snake Oil for Just $35 a Bottle!

During our frontier past, small towns in the Midwest and West were visited by enthusiastic traveling salesmen in colorful wagons. Their wares? "Snake Oil! It'll cure what ails ye'. Only one dollar a bottle."

The salesmen sold lots of snake oil to customers who were often convinced that the liquid (often a distilled liquor augmented with a hodgepodge of more or less natural ingredients) was miraculous stuff. A dollar per unit was expensive back in the 1800s, yet people paid the price.

Nowadays, people pay a good deal of money for prestige health food products such as Km potassium mineral supplement. Km is a brown liquid composed of compressed herbs in a white, one-quart plastic bottle that costs $35 a quart. Km is promoted at New Age health fairs and distributed by neighbors in a multilevel marketing set-up. Matol Botanical International, which makes and markets Km, has sold lots of the miraculous stuff in the U.S. and Canada since the company began mass production in 1984. If Km were priced at $3.50 instead of $35, it is doubtful that the product would sell enough extra units to equal the revenue and profits with the present premium price. Natural food consumers consider a high price a small price to pay for the perception of healthiness.

Ice cream lovers believe that a premium price must reflect richness (Ingrassia 1988: B1). Hence, Haagen-Dazs ice cream (high priced) is perceived as richer than Breyer's (medium priced). A blind taste test I conducted at California State University, Hayward showed that college students ranked Lucerne ice milk (an economy brand) higher in taste preference than Haagen-Dazs.

I guess there's no accounting for taste—but how do we justify the price/quality correlation? Price is set by perception, and perception is set by price. Remember that as you work on differentiating the unique value of your product from your competitors'.

PLACE-CENTERED PROMOTIONAL FEATS

Can you name the Seven Wonders of the World? Most people cannot. But many can name seven natural wonders in the United States. (How do Old Faithful, Half Dome, Niagara Falls, the Grand Canyon, Big Sur, Mount St. Helens, and Lake Tahoe sound as contenders?) I bet you would have named at least three of these in your list. Once these natural wonders have been seen, they stick in the mind forever. The same is true of manmade structures.

What would you list as the seven manmade wonders in the United States? Your list might include the Statue of Liberty, the Pentagon, the World Trade Center, Epcot Center, Disneyland, the Golden Gate bridge, and perhaps the Transamerica pyramid.

Transamerica, a service corporation offering insurance, mutual funds, and loans, has established a monumental (literally) promotional feat in its building. All of its ads showcase the huge, beautiful structure. Transamerica's slogan: The power of the pyramid is working for you.

Tourists visiting San Francisco make the Transamerica tower one of the must-see items on their itineraries. The triangular skyscraper stands as a pinnacle of strength and stability—just what people who need financial services look for. Financial institutions have often used a strong building as a symbol of their fiscal fortitude. In hotelry, the restaurant market, and retailing (the world's largest industry), as well as in finance services, the building communicates a powerful message about what the customer can expect inside. Let's look at the promotional power of business buildings.

The Best Is Yet to Come

High-class department stores such as Macy's and Neiman Marcus may not boast distinctive architecture, but like banks, their buildings suggest quality construction. Consumers perceive these retailers as top line; whereas bottom drawer retail outlets such as Kmart, Price Club, and Liquor Barn are often housed in large, boxy buildings that resemble gussied-up warehouses. Both building types are very successful. As with premium versus bargain basement pricing, consumers tend to favor either the best or the cheapest in architecture. It's difficult to remember what lies between the two extremes.

One retail outlet, aptly called Best, embodies the best of premium and warehouse looks. Best sells electronics, jewelry, and other items at relatively low prices in a warehouse with style. The Best buildings are big, like a Kmart, but each Best outlet has very distinctive architecture that sticks in the mind. For instance, the Best store in Sacramento features an entrance that looks like a jagged crack in the wall when the store is closed. When the store is open, the entire entranceway extends out from the rest of the building. It looks as if the entrance corner fell away from the rest of the structure by accident. Once seen, it is not forgotten.

Best has won architectural design awards for their uniquely styled buildings. Whether style translates into profits remains to be seen. Best has been in business since the mid–1970s. The eye-catching exterior lures customers into the door; price, selection, and service keep them coming back.

Where the Action Is

Some say a woman's place is in the mall. Mall shopping and hopping has certainly become an American tradition for the entire family, especially during Christmas season. Whereas some malls are almost always jammed, others seem like ghost towns. On the surface, there seems to be little difference between mall offerings. The crowded mall features the same amount and type of stores and boutiques as the deserted mall. Why is one a success and the other a failure?

The answer is location, location, location—combined with correct architectural features and atmosphere. A fancy mall located in a ghetto will attract few browsers, especially at night. But even a nice mall may not make it at first if it is built near an established, successful mall.

For example, Hillsdale Mall is very popular. In Foster City, a few minutes from Hillsdale Mall, developers built Fashion Island Mall to compete. The mall is designed to look like a huge multilayered tent. In addition to the usual mall attractions (e.g., theaters, specialty shops, food outlets, and department stores), Fashion Island houses a nice ice skating rink and video arcade. Still, loyal Hillsdale shoppers sail right past Fashion Island.

From a consumers' point of view, Fashion Island is a godsend. Stores are so uncrowded that there is no waiting and a shopper is guaranteed good service from sales clerks. Fashion Island needs to coordinate big external promotions with their new buildings—perhaps a major fashion show will communicate that it is fashionable to shop for fashions at Fashion Island.

Arden Mall in Sacramento had a different problem. Arden is located in a good place and has been around for over 20 years, but shopping traffic declined in the '80s. Why? A newer mall across town called Sunrise was more fashionable to be seen at, so repeat customers checked out Sunrise and eventually shifted their loyalties away from tried and true but aged and outdated Arden.

Undaunted, Arden managers completely rebuilt, revamped, and restyled the mall. Old tenants who couldn't handle the new image were replaced by new boutiques. Major department stores, such as Sears and Weinstock's, participated in the refurbishing. New stores, including upscale Nordstrom's, moved into Arden. By 1990, curious customers left Sunrise and returned to Arden in droves. Arden's new mall was more popular than ever. As one shopper said, "Arden mall is so elegant. It makes you feel rich just to walk through it."

It's Just a Facade

Building facades communicate image just as well as structure and architecture of buildings and malls, and at a fraction of the price. A retail outlet can communicate volumes about what's inside by creating a promotional feat outside with facades and signage.

The question is, who creates the best facades? The franchises, of course. America is the world leader in franchising, and McDonald's is the king of America's franchises. Kids in cars crane their necks up at the towering golden arches on the freeway sign: "McDonald's—next exit." When the car leaves the off-ramp, the kids squeal as the golden arches come into view. Moments later, the kids revel in Ronald McDonald's playground and then munch a Happy Meal with McDonald's latest promotion printed on the box.

McDonald's golden arches symbolize Q. S. C. & V. That is, McDonald's marketing motto is quality, service, cleanliness, and value. Customers see it as cheap, fast, good food. As a reader of this book, you have a 99 out of 100 chance of being one of the 96 out of 100 people who eat at McDonald's at least once a year. You also have a 99.999 percent probability of recognizing the golden arches when you see them. McDonald's arches epitomize a continuous, international, planned promotional feat based upon place of sale.

Gas stations are also good at signage. When we see the yellow shell sign on the freeway, we know we are approaching a Shell gas station. Chevron's distinctive chevron cues consumers quite effectively. However, Mobil, Exxon, and Arco have an identification problem; they all look the same—red, white, and blue. USA gasoline stations also feature red, white, and blue, but sport a huge American flag above the station. Patriotic Americans know where to buy their gas.

Most corporate outlets, chain stores, restaurants, and national franchises feature excellent signage and storefronts that reassure customers that they have found the business that will reliably deliver what they want. Local retail businesses need to learn from franchisees how to communicate a store's personality to consumers with just a sign and simple exterior.

Walk into Electric Avenue

The inside of a store communicates as much as the building or outside decor. Sallie Hook (1989: 2) reports that in today's intensely competitive retail industry, store image is more important than location. She asserts that retailers need to focus on creative, powerful, well-defined images targeted to a specific market.

Hook cites Ralph Lauren's Madison Avenue store as an example of an implicit promotional feat. The store creates its image using singing canaries and other details to project a specific appeal.

Gump's, in San Francisco, features beautiful and interesting window displays that draw locals and tourists alike. The San Francisco Neiman Marcus store always has a grand and impeccable style that communicates elegance.

Montgomery Ward showcases a "store within a store" with its Electric Avenue department. Other department stores are also working on creating unique images for each department. Department stores get worthwhile implicit promotional mileage to the extent that atmosphere, displays, and merchandise selection and presentation attract and keep customers.

In-store image is not limited to major stores. Specialty stores, boutiques, and ma-and-pa corner stores must also create and maintain a store atmosphere that is congruent with their marketing philosophy. For instance, according to Wiggins (1990), a surf shop in Santa Cruz attracts more than surfers out to buy the latest surfboard or beach fashion wear. The Santa Cruz Surf Shop blends ocean ecology with surfer merchandise. Blow-ups of exciting surfing photos and Impressionist wave portraits line the walls. Books and monographs on the history of surfing and ocean-related topics are located in the shop library. Vintage surfboards hang from the ceiling. The shop has displays of prehistoric sharks and a 600-gallon aquarium housing local fish species. A visitor to the shop feels the aura of the ocean. The Santa Cruz Surf Shop is more than a store; it's an experience.

The Santa Cruz Surf Shop and Harrods in London have one thing in common: implicit promotional feats centered on *place*. The site, architecture, exterior, signs, landscaping, interior, lighting, types of merchandise, colors, window and merchandise displays, and even music contribute to an overall atmosphere that communicates a marketing gestalt subtly and overtly to the consumer.

CREATE AN IMPLICIT PROMOTIONAL FEAT

To fully capitalize on product invention and design, packaging, price, and place, promotion managers must work with everyone in the organization to make a product or service that consumers will go out of their way for. This is not easy, but it is necessary. With 25,000 new products on supermarket shelves since 1987, we marketers and promotion managers have our work cut out for us. Packaging and design expert John Blyth (1990: 8) states the problem succinctly:

> Because we live such jam-packed, visually overstimulated lives, one of the packaging industry's biggest challenges in the '90s will be to create packaging that makes consumers want to reach out and purchase a particular product.

In this chapter, we looked at some of these products. The American Marketing Association now recognizes new products that best meet consumers' needs for affordability, convenience, and ease of use (Schlossberg 1990b). The AMA gives out awards (called Edisons) to the top ten new products of the year. In 1989, Pepperidge Farm won the Grand Edison, the top award, for its innovative family of products.

Over the years, many new products have been developed that may have had consumers' best interests in mind, but perished for various reasons. (For example, the futuristic Tucker automobile died because of an investigation by the SEC.) Marketers want to make sure that a product doesn't die because it was poorly designed, packaged, priced, or placed. Let's look at the most outstanding example of a complete implicit promotion that not only survived, but thrived.

The Rest of the Hosestory

Earlier in this chapter, we were introduced to L'eggs, Hanes' snug-fitting hosiery packaged in plastic eggs. This product is the *sine qua non* of implicit promotion because everything about it was coordinated perfectly. L'eggs is more than just good product design and packaging innovation; the placement and pricing were also ingenious.

Hosiery was traditionally sold in specialty and department stores. Hanes decided to mass market L'eggs through supermarkets and drug stores using vans with the L'eggs logo on the side, rack jobbers to stock it, and special self-service racks to display all colors and sizes. The racks, used in at least 70,000 stores, take up just two square feet of traffic space. It's easy to buy a pair of L'eggs.

Hanes priced L'eggs at $1.39 a pair, which was more than cheapo stockings priced under a dollar that fit poorly and did not last, but substantially less than $3.00 hosiery sold in women's specialty outlets. Consumers perceived the price value in L'eggs.

Retailers receive L'eggs on a consignment basis, which saves them money and inventory problems (though they lose control of price).

Hanes serves its resellers by offering them a hefty margin (57 percent gross margin for its new product, Little L'eggs). The high margin, combined with Hanes' line of hosiery products dominating the market and phenomenal brand recognition (96 percent), makes for some happy retailers.

Hanes, a Sara Lee company, supports its product with top notch explicit promotional efforts. One of their first and best advertising headlines on television and in magazines was "Our L'eggs fit your legs." A mass mailing of 25-cent coupons encouraged consumer trial. True to form, L'eggs promotion snugly fits the product and its reusable package, fair price, and convenient placement in supermarkets and drug stores.

In addition to the success of L'eggs in the marketplace (annual sales regularly exceed $150 million), it is the most written about promotional feat in marketing communications/promotion management literature. It was used as a case study at the Harvard Business School in 1975 and later published in *Problems in Marketing* (Singer, et al. 1981: 341–357). Hartley wrote about L'eggs in *Marketing Successes* (1985: 126–139). Three promotional management texts devote a page or more to L'eggs (see Anderson & Rubin 1986, Dommermuth 1989, Govoni et al. 1986). L'eggs was also mentioned in Shimp's (1990) and Rossiter and Percy's (1987) promotion books and two of the leading marketing management texts, Kotler and Armstrong's (1990) *Marketing Management: An Introduction*, and Evans and Berman's (1990) *Marketing*. Hanes' promotional achievement has been noticed by marketing scholars and satisfied customers.

In this chapter we introduced the merits of implicit promotion, an area still underdeveloped by today's marketers. In the next chapter, we look at explicit promotional feats in the most popular of all marketing communication elements—advertising.

5

Outrageous Advertisements

"The difference between one advertisement and another, in terms
of sales, can be as much as nineteen to one."

—D. Ogilvy

MARKETING IS ADVERTISING! That's what many people believe. And
well they should, because businesses spend a lot of money on advertising. In 1988, the U.S. spent $126 billion on advertising; in 1990, the
total should exceed $132 billion. The United States comprises nearly half
of the total world advertising expenditures. Just think, if we applied
American advertising dollars to the savings and loan debt, we could pay
it off in five years and have money left over to feed and shelter the
homeless. Although this scenario is highly unlikely, it shows just how
much we spend on advertising.

Many of the dollars are spent on television advertising. According to
Advertising Age (Brown 1990: 4), in 1988, restaurants (ranked number
two in spending) accounted for $500 million of TV advertising, a 296.6
percent increase in spending since 1980. Of that, McDonald's alone
accounted for nearly half the total expenditures. So how can other restaurants hope to compete? They can't.

The fifth-ranked category in TV ad spending in 1988 was beer, which
accounted for $395 million (Anheuser-Busch spent $66 million just on
Budweiser). Cereal, ranked third, accounted for $504 million. Advertis-
ers spend considerable amounts of money to convince us to buy their
beer, cereal, and other capricious products. No wonder some people
believe that advertising is a social blight.

Media buying accounts for most ad spending, but not all; ad shops also earn good money. Endicott (1990a: S1) reported that 1989 ad agency revenues topped $85 billion—no small change by any accounting. With billions and billions of dollars being spent on advertising yearly, it's no wonder that laymen equate advertising with marketing. *Advertising Age*, the ad trade newspaper, calls itself "Crain's International Newspaper of Marketing." So it seems, to a significant degree, that advertising is marketing. But we want to know which ads in which mediums are promotional feats.

EFFECTIVE ADVERTISING

In this book, we showcase ads that have achieved promotional feat status; that is, have succeeded above and beyond expectations. *Beyond expectations* is operationalized as extra profit due to factors related to the ad campaign. Extra profit may be gained in the short run, long run, or both. It may result from a higher margin based on buyer perceptions of brand quality and uniqueness, from increased sales volume, or both. Longer run profit may come from a gradual build-up of brand recognition and loyalty which causes competitors to lose market share. It may also result from consumer knowledge of product benefits as a direct result of the ad (as in the case of direct marketing), or it may come from publicity generated from a very entertaining (new, shocking, funny, creative) or award-winning ad or ad campaign. Finally, extra profit may result from a multifaceted marketing communications program that combines various advertisements with sales promotions, personal sales efforts, publicity and public relations, and product design.

Bolstering Brand Image

Ad effectiveness defies easy description. Ogilvy (1963, 1988) believes that an ad is ineffective if it fails to build brand image and prod the buyer into using more of the advertised product than other brands, even if the ad is entertaining, award-winning, easily recalled, or expensive. Ogilvy's idea of an effective ad is any ad which establishes and maintains a strong brand image that results in profit for the producer and does not violate basic advertising principles derived from objective use of research and experience. He stresses that an ad campaign should sell the product's benefits to the consumer. Establishing and maintaining brand loyalty summarizes Ogilvy's goals for advertising.

Ogilvy has proven the effectiveness of building brand image through advertising. As he wrote in 1988 (p. xvii).

Good campaigns can run for many years without losing their selling power. My eyepatch campaign for Hathaway shirts ran for twenty-one years. My campaign for Dove soap has been running for thirty-one years, and Dove is now the best seller.

Clearly, these two campaigns have achieved promotional feat status and have established enduring brand images.

In *The Making of Effective Advertising* (1990), Patti and Moriarty address advertising principles of Ogilvy and Leo Burnett (his agency created Tony the Tiger and the Marlboro man), among others. Patti and Moriarty placed Burnett and Ogilvy's philosophies under the rubric of product focus. The authors placed the Foote, Cone & Belding agency and the Ted Bates agency in the selling proposition category. According to Patti and Moriarty, another agency philosophy includes the prospect-centered approach of BBDO. Each major advertising house espouses a unique philosophy, and they all produce effective ads—that is, they meet their objectives.

Entertaining Advertising

But there is yet another approach to advertising effectiveness: the artistic or *entertainment* approach. Patti and Moriarty write that Doyle Dane Bernbach agency focuses on artistry. They note that Bill Bernbach, founder of DDB and responsible for the Avis "We Try Harder" campaign, believed that effective advertising "was original, dramatic, and startled people into awareness. He believed in great ideas beautifully executed" (p. 7).

Similarly, Patti and Moriarty report that Hal Riney's agency, creator of the Bartles & Jaymes and Henry Weinhard campaigns, appeals to emotions over intellect. Aristotle would agree that pathos (emotional appeal) is as important as logos (logical appeal). In other words, both artistic and product/consumer benefit-based ads can work.

Here is another example of an "entertaining" ad that succeeded. Stan Freberg's Sunsweet Prunes campaign slogan, "Today the Pits, Tomorrow the Wrinkles," reportedly increased Sunsweet's sales volume an impressive 400 percent (Walley 1987: 60). Even conservative advertising professionals would have to admit that Freberg's zany campaign for Sunsweet was a promotional feat.

Do What Works

Who would you rather watch, a doctor in a lab coat or a beautiful model? Would you rather laugh or listen somberly? Would you rather be provoked or subjected to the same old formula? Consumers are sophisticated nowadays. They no longer are moved by tired old remakes of the same ads (unless they are entertaining, of course).

With the high cost of TV advertising, the numerous TV programs, and the huge increase in sales of remote controls, consumers will simply tune out or zap boring commercials. The same is true of advertising in other media. Clutter is a problem that will get worse before it gets better. Conservative, me-too advertisers will be zapped. Ashok Pahwa (1990: 8) says baby-boom viewers will stay tuned to quality ads. "The key may lie in creating commercials that more viewers would *want* to watch."

To achieve promotional feat status, an ad must work extraordinarily well. If it costs five times as much as competitive ads and is aired five times as often, then it must pay for itself in substantially increased profit margins for the product or service it is promoting. I believe the key is to expunge all ads and ad types that do not work and exploit that which works.

Here's what does not work. As Ogilvy points out, certain rules of advertising are immutable and should never be violated, lest an abomination of an ad is created. Any ad which violates basic principles or reliable and valid research findings is no good. These lousy ads which ignore established principles and findings are usually made in ignorance of what is readily available to all who pay attention. Here is an example from Ogilvy of an advertising principle based on findings that should not be violated: Don't show enlarged close-ups of the human face since they repel most people. Simple enough. Also, you must mention the product somewhere in an ad to make it effective, even if the ad entertains. (For instance, the initial Infiniti impressionist backdrops were nifty, but what the heck were they selling?)

In the 1980s, with the cola and hamburger wars, we saw the advent of comparative ads that usually attempted to disparage competitors' products while bolstering the subject. The result: consumers got confused and disgusted. I forgot who made the flame-broiled, hot n' juicy burger; I forgot which cola was sweeter.

Car ads often compare their brand with BMW or some other quality brand. What does the consumer think? Get the BMW (or Volvo). The problem with comparison ads is the fact that your competitor is mentioned. U.S. Sprint and MCI ads routinely compare themselves against AT&T. In effect, AT&T gets lots of free advertising. By the way, is there really a detectable difference between fiber optic sound and regular sound? I bet most people don't know or care. In short, don't compare yourself with another product to point out negligible benefits (like MCI's cost savings over AT&T).

Ogilvy says we should remember to promise the consumer a benefit. I agree with Ogilvy. Ads do not promote brand loyalty when they merely reflect a person's lifestyle category (Badge Theory) while not pointing out a brand's superiority over competitors. For example, an ad pitch centering only on self-esteem enhancement through use of the advertised brand is ineffective; brand superiority must be demonstrated.

So why not demonstrate brand superiority, promise benefits, center on consumer's problems, build a unique brand image based on product features, and entertain people in original ways that do not stupidly violate obvious and tested principles? And why not advertise cost effectively? Let's make our advertisements fit in with the rest of the marketing communications mix of a product. The rest of this chapter is devoted to advertisements or advertising campaigns that have made promotional feat status. Note that these campaigns are memorable (entertaining) and promise (and deliver) benefits.

We'll examine advertising feats by media. We'll begin, however, by looking at a marketing channel that Ogilvy studies closely—*direct marketing*, also called *direct response* marketing. Direct marketing, using a combination and variety of media, is the least discussed marketing method in traditional marketing texts (with the possible exception of multilevel marketing). Yet, it has grown from direct mail catalogs to electronic shopping by computer. Let's check it out. If your company still relies on several layers of channels to get to your customers, direct marketing may be in your future.

SHOP AT HOME

What could be more convenient than shopping, or at least obtaining information about products and services, from home? Nothing. Back in 1740, Benjamin Franklin started America's (and perhaps the world's) first mail-order catalog. Direct marketing was born. It has been booming ever since and is becoming one of the most popular ways to market products. According to Green (1984), over 30 percent of all sales in the late 1990s may be the result of nonstore retailing.

It makes sense that a manufacturer or distributor could make more money by eliminating middlemen and retailers from the distribution channel. A manufacturer must ship products to consumers one way or the other. Why not ship directly and pocket the 35-percent markup that retailers demand? Why let huge retailers such as Toys R Us dictate pricing policies to manufacturers? Why initiate, maintain, and pay for "push" marketing efforts to satisfy demanding retailers?

Here's a nightmare scenario. To introduce a new food product, a manufacturer must go through hell to get decent shelf space. If 10,000 new products vie for space every year, how do you ensure a decent spot for your food item? According to Beckett (1990b: A1), many supermarkets require food companies to pay "slotting allowances," or fees for shelf space. Sometimes these slotting allowances (called payola in the radio industry) cost millions for a national rollout. This may result in higher prices for consumers. In addition to the shelving fees, food companies often accompany a new product with free merchandise, coupons, and a "failure fee," should the product flop. To woo cautious retailers, manufacturers must convince them with market research, test marketing results, in-store demonstrations, and the like. Is it worth it? Some food companies are joining the exodus and are trying direct marketing approaches to sales.

If a food company can direct market, then just about anyone can. Let's begin our look at direct response by reading our mail.

Direct Mail Is Alive and Well

Direct marketing through catalog mailings has long been a workhorse marketing method for department stores such as Montgomery Ward, Spiegel, and Sears. It was a good way to tap into the rural market; these people wanted goods but seldom made it to a city to shop at the big stores. With the advent of two cars in every garage, a general and steady rise in population, and migration to suburbia, many believed direct mail was dead. But we consumers and the postal service know differently.

We still get major department store season catalogs, but sometimes we have to pay for them (fair enough). But now we can order catalogs and merchandise in just about any specialized market (e.g., kayaking supplies, survivalist gear, garden tools and plants, martial arts weapons, medieval clothing, comic books, etc.).

Catalogs and direct mail account for nearly half of all direct marketing sales. Americans receive an average of 50 catalogs a year. Many we use; some we even keep. About 10,000 companies mail out over 12 billion catalogs annually.

Some of the best catalogs appeal to the yuppie, baby-boomer market. Banana Republic offers expensive safari clothes for urban wear. Their interesting catalogs sell lots of khakis. Sharper Image made a big splash in the 1980s with their offbeat, expensive goodies that any image-conscious yuppie would want. They were successful for many years, due to their outstanding catalogs. Sharper Image was in the enviable position of having people call their store in downtown San Francisco to purchase their very own catalog—never mind the merchandise.

When people go out of their way just to buy a catalog, that constitutes a promotional feat. Now, if you add an 800 telephone number with friendly operators standing by 24 hours a day, take major credit cards, and deliver that day, you're in business. Say "yes" to customers; "no" to dealers.

With the advent of VCRs in every home, some companies (such as Neiman Marcus and Royal Silk) sell or give away video catalogs (video-logs) to target consumers, who are usually upscale. Videos allow customers to see products in action. Congbalay (1990: A1) reports that videos and other expensive gifts are now mailed to upscale consumers every year to get through clutter and stimulate purchase.

Toyota mailed 200,000 videos of their new Previa minivan to potential customers during the summer of 1990. Compaq Computers sent 40,000 floppy disks to targeted consumers to demonstrate their new $20,000 computers. These examples show that high-tech junk mail is on the rise, and it is effective—at least for now.

Traditional direct mail increases every year. Charities use the latest techniques (startling statements on the envelope, pseudo-surveys, free stickers or address labels) in direct mail to get a response out of us pennypinchers. And it works.

Banking on research which shows that cold cash is the best incentive, *USA Today* in 1990 mailed thousands of potential readers two quarters to buy a complimentary issue at the newsstand. To encourage subscription, they sweetened the deal with a 25 percent discount *and* a $15 rebate for a year's subscription. All the customer had to do was charge it when they dialed the easily remembered phone number, 1–800-USA–0001. That's a direct mail promotional feat.

An Infomercial by Any Other Name

Television advertising rates increase steadily every year, along with more channels and more clutter. How can a company effectively reach target consumers, persuade them to pay attention, and then buy? The answer may lie in *advertorials* or TV *infomercials*.

An advertorial is print advertising that looks like a news item. It works for print ads if consumers view it as credible (Elliott 1984). So why not extend the advertorial concept using the impact of TV? A House subcommittee asked the same question (Dart 1990) when investigating infomercials on TV. An infomercial is an advertising hybrid that hawks products or services in documentary style.

Infomercials are becoming more popular. In 1989, $450 million worth of goods and services were sold using infomercial promotion. Representative Ron Wyden predicted that merchandise sold through infomercials could reach $1.6 billion (Dart 1990: A3).

Infomercials are effective because they give consumers information. Often, athlete celebrities like Fran Tarkenton and Joe Namath, actors such as John Ritter and Ali McGraw, and diet/exercise gurus like Richard Simmons "star" in the program-length infomercials. According to Coffey (1990: E1), TV has-beens "peddle weight loss programs, hair-gain programs, skin-rejuvenating products, teeth-whitening products, cosmetics, sunglasses, real estate success, woks, credit-consulting courses, surface protectors, exercise aids, memory aids, study aids, etc., etc."

Sometime during the infomercial an 800 number or ordering address is provided, making the extended advertisement a direct marketing and TV advertising promotional feat. Infomercials are promotional feats for four reasons: they make the news, people watch them for 30 minutes (even though they zap a 30-second TV commercial), they successfully persuade consumers to buy, and with the steadily increasing number of specialized TV networks competing for time, they sell commercial space and fill deadtime programming slots.

However, there is a dark side to infomercials, just as with their print cousins. Consumers must believe the pitch is credible. Therefore, infomercial advertisers must be certain not to defraud or mislead consumers with program-length commercials that air under the guise of standard programming. Whereas Belch and Belch describe the infomercial in objective terms in their advertising and promotion book (1990: 358), popular press writers depict infomercials derogatorily. Tom Shales (1990b: E1), in the *Washington Post*, (a newspaper with a circulation of nearly a million that sells its articles to other major newspapers), railed against infomercials as "the new breed of program-length ads that have infested America's airwaves like killer bees at a picnic . . . replete with hired (or just infinitely pliable) studio audiences."

So, let the advertiser beware. What seems like a great promotional gimmick today could be a lawsuit and bad publicity tomorrow.

Now That's a Clever Cleaver

We have all seen TV direct response ads for records, books, and exercise products such as the Abdominizer. These ads lack sophistication, but they are inexpensive to produce and often make money. This makes them effective. Direct response commercials follow tested methods to sell products; this accounts for their success. A typical golden oldies music offer will show performers singing hits while a list of songs in the collection scrolls up screen. At the end of the ad an 800 number appears along with other ordering information. We are likely to see more direct response TV ads in the future because, in a predictably straightforward manner, they show how the product benefits the consumer, how much it costs, and how to get it. Whereas home shopping channels may not last forever (they show products too slowly—it's much quicker to thumb through a catalog), direct response is here to stay. Here's an example of why.

It's difficult to say which TV direct response ad is best, but certainly the Ginsu cutlery commercial is a classic. In the ad, the announcer voices over video of the knives in action. The viewer keeps thinking the ad is finished, but the announcer blurts, "Wait, there's more!" By the end, they offer a complete cutlery set with accessories and a clever cleaver for an almost unbelievably low price. According to Auchmute (1985: 18), the Ginsu ads sold 3 million knife sets for a total of $40 million over a 7-year period. It's amazing that millions of consumers would buy cutlery they have never seen thanks to a fast-talking voice and a fast-cutting knife demonstration. A question: do the knives cut through nails? Of course, but wait, there's always more!

ALL THE MAGAZINE ADS FIT TO PRINT

Since 1970, over 2,000 new magazines have appeared (many have since disappeared). Most new magazines specialize, which means print advertising dollars are spent only on targeted consumers. For example, in 1989, if you wanted to put a four-color, full-page ad for Gatorade in *Time*, it would have cost $120,000. The same ad in *Tennis* (circulation 531,000) would cost only $23,000. Targeting selectivity, along with the permanance factor (magazines are saved; newspapers are chucked), and quality reproduction (color), make magazines a good advertising medium for many products and services.

The trick is to get readers to pore over every word and then seek out your product over others. Ogilvy lists time-honored tips for print ads in his books. Research tests show which appeals work. Yet, often a successful magazine ad must *stand out* to get noticed.

Take a Stand

So how far must a magazine ad stand out to get noticed? Every year, car manufacturers run *gatefolds* (foldouts) when introducing new cars. Gatefolds (which are very expensive and must be reserved well in advance of publication) attract attention. Most people will unfold the extra page to look at the new auto. Using gatefolds is a promotional feat because they are so effective—yet so expensive. Also, jaded consumers no longer ooh and ah at gatefolds; they are now mere commonplace.

McDonald's created a premium print ad that outdid gatefolds. In 1988, McDonald's ran a two-page ad for the McD.L.T. burger. On one side of the magazine page were five finger holes accompanied by this message: "Hungry? Just insert the fingers and thumb of your left hand into the holes and turn the page." After readers inserted their fingers and turned the page, they found they were holding a four-color burger and reading "Get your hands on a McD.L.T." *Adweek* hailed the ad as one of the best of 1988.

To attract attention, cosmetic and deodorant companies use "scratch 'n' sniff" to appeal to the olfactory sense. Some companies offer product samples or 45-rpm records to grab us. Most unusual print ads cost big bucks. In 1990, Cutty Sark Scots whisky featured a metallic mirror in a print ad with the words, "you're looking at the image of a Cutty Sark drinker." This clever ad forced the reader to take notice. It was also relatively inexpensive.

Two of the most expensive and noteworthy print ads that literally stand out are the 3-D "pop-up" ads created for Honeywell and Transamerica that featured each company's architecture. Research by Starch INRA Hooper showed that these two ads outscored traditional four-color ads in the "noted" and "seen/associated" scores by two to one. These two ads are definite promotional feats. They had better be; they each cost over $1 million to produce and run just once.

What's Wrong with This Picture?

"Slice of Life" print advertising is usually not very memorable, but Benson & Hedges squeezed a promotional feat out of a ho-hum creation during their "For people who like to smoke" campaign in 1988. They ran a print ad showing a group of five yuppie women and one older man enjoying a formal brunch. Seemingly out of place is a thirty-something, bare-chested man wearing pajamas who walks in on the party and is greeted in a smaller photo by one of the women holding a cigarette.

We wonder, "What's happening here?" *Advertising Age* asked its ad trade readers the same question (see Dagnoli 1988, Skenazy 1988) and received over four hundred replies. Philip Morris, getting in on the fun, staged a contest among consumers to guess what was going on. Entrants received a Benson & Hedges coupon and "most original" winners received a pair of pajamas. Apparently, the contest and the hoopla helped boost Benson & Hedges' image among yuppies.

Absolut vodka's award-winning photos in their magazine ads pique readers' interest. Their "Absolut San Francisco" ad shows the top of an Absolut bottle with the rest obscured by fog. Their "Absolut L.A." may be their best. We look down at an inviting swimming pool shaped like an Absolut bottle, complete with label. Another great Absolut print ad, created by TBWA of New York, shows a martini glass bending toward the Absolut bottle. The caption reads "Absolut attraction."

Other image-building slogans under the Absolut bottle include "Absolut elegance" (the bottle sports a bowtie) and "Absolut treasure" (the bottle is at the bottom of an ocean reef with tropical fish swimming about). Once seen, Absolut ads are not easily forgotten. Continuity is the promotional feat for Absolut. However, the $100,000 prize and national publicity that Absolut got for winning the 1988 MPA Kelly Award for the "Absolut L.A." ad didn't hurt their image—or pocketbook.

The Executioner

Sometimes the ads themselves are nothing to write home about but their execution is. More and more we see advertisers inserting two or three ads in a publication to keep the reader occupied. In 1986, Carmichael Lynch created three half-page ads for Harley Davidson that were put in a series. First, the reader saw a close-up photo of the word *Classic*. The reader turned the page and was exposed to a medium close-up shot of the Electra Glide Classic cockpit as viewed from the air. Finally, the third half-page showed the entire motorcycle along with copy and the caption: "A Harley can take you places you never knew you had places."

Headline Ads

To capture readers' attention, advertisers must always be alert to what's new while avoiding the dreaded disease of me-tooism. Auto advertisers have turned en masse to safe sloganizing in print and TV ads (Garfield 1990a: S14). Here are some of the extremely dull, copycat, forgettable entries. Chevrolet: "The heartbeat of America." Toyota: "I love what you do for me." Chrysler: "There is no luxury without engineering." Nissan: "Built for the human race." Ford: "Have you driven a Ford . . . lately?" Lexus: "The relentless pursuit of excellence." There are more, but I'll spare you.

Suffice it to say, some of these slogans might work if all the other auto ads forsook sloganeering. Gutless slogans that all sound the same and are made of ticky-tacky don't sell cars or anything else. Something a little bolder is needed.

And here it is: Capitalize on headline news (spend five minutes a day watching Headline News to see what constitutes a headline). Levin (1990: 1) reports how advertisers capitalize (literally) on Mikhail Gorbachev's popularity. DOC Optique featured a print ad with Gorby wearing red tiger-stripe sunglasses under this headline: "Sunglassnost." A Smirnoff ad mentioned an old Beatles' tune title: "Back in the U.S.S.R." These headlines are clever and effective, if not overused or abused. The trick is to create a tasteful topical slogan that changes with the news and newsmakers and does not imitate competitors or irritate consumers.

Some advertisers are even bolder in using news events in ads. *Newsweek* ran a story on advertisers' use of the Iraqi war crisis to sell goods (Miller, et al. 1990b: 66). They reported that the Minneapolis bus company printed Saddam Hussein's face in an ad to promote ridership (and thus save gas). Their slogan: "Stop pumping him up."

The 1990 movie "Navy SEALS" was hyped as coming to the rescue in a "Middle East Mission." AT&T capitalized the most on the Mideast conflict by coming up with a great promotional feat: they made a public service offer to fax messages free to American troops stationed in the Persian Gulf. The two-page AT&T offer was published free by major magazines such as *Newsweek*. *USA Today* devoted an entire page to AT&T's fax service. AT&T engendered warm feelings from the public for their generous (and smart) offer.

Newspaper advertisers also benefited from the Gulf crisis in 1990. Advanced Automotive Technologies took out a full-page ad in the *San Francisco Chronicle* to push their gas-saving device called the PetroMizer. The headline read: "U.S. Car Owners Fight Iraq With New Economical Gas Saving Breakthrough!" The subheading read: "United States Army tests report gasoline savings of over 28%!!!" Very clever advertising. Let's look at other newspaper advertising feats.

NO SNOOZE IS GOOD NEWS

During the last couple of years, newspapers have had to struggle to bring in advertising dollars. Still, newspapers remain the number one vehicle for advertising in absolute dollar terms. For example, in 1988, over $31 billion was spent on newspaper advertising, according to the Newspaper Advertising Bureau.

Except for national newspapers (e.g., *Christian Science Monitor*, *Wall Street Journal*, *USA Today*), most newspapers serve local and regional advertisers. Thus, promotional feats on a major scale are hard to find. Yet, promotional feats (such as AT&T's and PetroMizer's) occurred, thanks to savvy copywriters. Let's look at more examples of superlative newspaper advertising.

National News Nuggets

Two days after the October 19, 1987 "Black Monday" stock market crash, Merrill Lynch responded with a full-page ad in major regional papers, the *Wall Street Journal*, and *USA Today*, which blared: "After October 19: A Perspective." The eye-catching, timely headline was followed with 600 words of copy that realistically but optimistically addressed what happened and what investors should do next. Merrill Lynch's quick and reassuring reaction, which involved their chairman and several department heads in the ad's creation, was used most effectively through the newspaper medium (Goldman 1988). According to Goldman, Merrill Lynch then followed up with a series of general financial advice ads over the next few months in international and local newspapers.

The Merrill Lynch story illustrates the impact that newspaper advertising can have when delivered in bold, innovative, and timely fashion. Also, Merrill Lynch utilized classic and simple print advertising maxims in the series. They showed that an interesting headline, followed by *newsworthy* copy, with simple black print on white paper and plenty of white space, works quite effectively.

On the Local Scene

Local newspapers have had trouble attracting national advertisers, but still fare well with the local advertisers (despite more inroads from direct mail, telemarketing, and the Yellow Pages). Typically, local newspapers advertise retail sales. Often, especially in Sunday editions, newspapers will deliver color inserts and supplements, including lengthy sale catalogs for department stores such as Macy's. Although effective, these are so common that they hardly count as promotional feats.

Airlines periodically engage in price wars and brag about the frequency of their flights to various cities. American Airlines scored a big hit in October 1990 with a full-page regional ad in the *San Francisco Chronicle* with the headline, "Read Our L.A. Times." Then a list of seventeen hourly nonstop flights from San Francisco to LAX followed. The ad was expensive, but let everyone know they could go to Los Angeles any time on American.

Kenneth Cole, a fancy shoe store located in New York and San Francisco, announces its semi-annual sales with clever plays on headlines. The store takes out large half-page or full-page ads, includes a picture or eye-catching phrase, and then simply mentions the semi-annual sale. No prices on specific shoes are listed in the ad.

One ad, which looked like a letter to the President, read: "If you choose to pardon Imelda, please do so in time for our Semi-Annual Sale." Another interesting Kenneth Cole ad showed a photo of Manuel Noriega with a quotation from Kenneth Cole: "One heel you definitely won't find at our Semi-Annual Sale."

A photo of a jungle accompanied this Kenneth Cole newspaper ad: "If our shoes were disappearing as quickly as the rain forest, we wouldn't need a Semi-Annual Sale." Another of their timely ads featured a picture of people climbing over the Berlin Wall. The caption: "Now there's nothing to keep anyone from coming to our Semi-Annual Sale."

In Kenneth Cole's June 1990 ad in the *San Francisco Chronicle*, all these entertaining ads were reduced and reprinted in a half-page ad, again featuring a clever quotation from Kenneth Cole. It read: "We know you may have seen these before, but recycling is in these days."

Even though newspapers typically deal with local merchants and products, are losing ground to direct mail and other marketing communications, and can't deliver high quality reproduction like magazines can, the medium is still number one in ad dollar volume and can still deliver promotional feats for its users. At least, this is what Kenneth Cole must think.

THE GREAT OUTDOORS

Outdoor advertising (signs and billboards) has been expanded to include transit advertising (on and in buses, cabs, and subway trains), wall murals, skywriting, and aerial displays (blimps, inflatable or floating icons), among others (including innovative new examples). Outdoor advertising expenditures in sports stadiums alone exceeded $200 million in 1989, due partially to the introduction of electronic billboards.

Although the outdoor advertising category comprises less than 2 percent of all advertising, the Institute of Outdoor Advertising estimated that $1.4 billion was spent on it in 1988. As the industry develops new outdoor media and government regulation curtails other forms of advertising (such as the abolishment of tobacco and hard liquor ads on television), outdoor advertising will continue to grow.

Billboards, still the primary form of outdoor advertising, have changed dramatically over the years. They can even be found on chair lifts at ski resorts. Nowadays, billboards are often three-dimensional, with figures extending above the sign or even sticking out from the sign. In the summer of 1990, a San Francisco television station rented a billboard that featured a sign painter mannequin sitting on a real scaffold watching a ballgame on TV. This billboard was definitely eye catching and entertaining.

Classic Billboards

The trend toward more innovative and entertaining billboard advertising is likely to continue, mainly because motorists get bored looking at the same old sign for a month. In California, drivers heading toward Nevada get inundated with glittery billboards pitching entertainers and "good odds" at innumerable and indistinguishable gambling establishments. I have seen hundreds of casino billboards, and they all look the same. Me-tooism simply adds to the roadside litter and does little to entice gamblers. Perhaps less glitz and more substance might shore up these feeble attempts to lure us big winners.

Why can't the casinos learn from Coca-Cola, the most recognized and remembered brand around the world? True, Coca-Cola has been around for a long time, but it is also around all the time. Most major cities have a conspicuous, permanent, electric billboard that spells C-O-C-A-C-O-L-A. Do you know where your local Coke billboard is? I bet you do. They're big, they're ubiquitous, they're simple, and they're memorable.

Where the Flavor Is

In 1988, the tobacco industry, the number one outdoor advertiser, spent $358 million. So, which cigarette ads on billboards do you remember? I polled 188 of my students in 1989, and 95 percent remembered the Marlboro Man. Virginia Slims came in a distant second with a 20 percent recall. The "Marlboro Country" theme, developed by the Leo Burnett agency 25 years ago, is one of the longest running and most successful advertising campaigns of all time. Marlboro, at one time positioned as a woman's cigarette, was repositioned as a real man's "outdoorsy" cigarette. Marlboro became the number one selling cigarette 20 years ago—and has been number one ever since. This classifies as a top drawer promotional feat.

Although the Marlboro cowboy often appears in print media, he has appeared on billboards around the world, standing as the rugged, American individualist working the land and enjoying a good smoke. Marv Gunderson, an artist who has created Marlboro billboards in his San Diego studio since 1974, was credited as "a kind of secret weapon for Philip Morris, Inc." (Revett 1983: M19).

The success of the Marlboro billboards shows that a classic approach, artistically executed, can consistently build and maintain a strong brand image. Billboard artists and advertising executives take note, and come to where the flavor is.

Blimp Out

The Goodyear blimp, which most youngsters know as the camera in the air at football and baseball games, is the quintessential flying logo. Since the Goodyear blimp is so successful, tire competitor B. F. Goodrich had to spend television advertising dollars to tell viewers that the two companies were different. The blimp concept proved irresistible to some companies, such as Fuji, so they got their own blimps in the 1980s, but they're still not Goodyear. Dommermuth (1989: 500) best summarized the promotional power of the Goodyear blimp: "As a platform for publicity, Goodyear's blimp creates a far more powerful and authoritative perception of the company's products than an equal amount of advertising would."

Blimps are not the only advertisements afloat. An innovative new way to advertise is through inflatables. The movie *King Kong* was promoted with an inflatable of the big ape. Universal Studios had an inflatable pirate commissioned to draw attention to *The Pirates of Penzance*. Budweiser had a huge six-pack of Bud blown up to pavilion size.

Outdoor advertising is one medium that has unlimited potential for promotional feats. Point-of-purchase advertising is popping up all

over—televisions in supermarkets and gas stations airing advertisements, or ATM screens pitching Carl's Jr. at Wells Fargo Bank.

What promotional feat may happen next in this creative medium?
Let's see. I read somewhere that a good feat might involve Transamerica
lighting up its pyramid like a Christmas tree. We could expand on that
and hire "Santa" to hang glide down from the top of the pyramid and
into the San Francisco streets. Santa could then give away pyramid
models plastered with a commercial message to kids (or adults) during
the holidays. Don't forget to alert the press. Who knows? Maybe you
could think up an even better idea.

RED HOT RADIO

Radio is red hot! So the Radio Advertising Bureau says, and it's probably true. After all, more than $7 billion is spent annually on radio
advertising. These dollars are divvied up among 10,000 FM and AM
stations across the U.S.

What does radio got that TV ain't got? *Low cost*! Radio commercials
are cheap to produce and inexpensive to air (about $5 per thousand
listeners reached). Also, radio is very flexible. If a company wants to
change its commercial at the last second (literally), radio can accom-
modate. No other medium can make that claim. Additionally, radio
commercials can complement TV or other media ads by "reminding"
listeners through jingles and catch phrases.

Local Yodels

Radio services the local market. Its primary advantage is in publicizing
or reporting on a client's local promotion. A station can send a DJ personality to a site and broadcast live. The DJ's presence stimulates listeners to go to where the DJ is. This feature is underutilized by most
advertisers. Radio stations need to promote themselves more through
sales force activities. Promotional feats are waiting to happen using radio
and sponsors.

Serving local merchants and manufacturers means that radio can make
a big deal about promoting retail establishments frequented by dedicated
listeners who would shop at a store that projects the image (and sells
the merchandise) they desire. Advertisers are learning to target their
commercial dollars to stations that service their market segments. For
example, in the San Francisco Bay area, businesses that cater to senior
citizens advertise more frequently on KFRC (Magic 61), a station that
specializes in big band and the softer music that many seniors prefer.

Companies save money by advertising on a specialty station that may
have a lower Arbitron rating (thus lower rates) but which reaches more

of their consumers. Is this a promotional feat? No, it's just smart allo-
cation of media dollars and avoidance of a marketing communications
mistake. So many marketers still operate under me-tooism when spending their media dollars. They blindly pay premium rates to the radio
station with the highest Arbitron ratings (which means more aggregate
listeners stratified by age and sex), and ignore stations that have low
Arbitron ratings but attract a specific type of consumer—the one who
would shop at their stores.

Worse, many media buyers eschew cheap radio and pay through the
nose for the high impact and glamor of TV when they don't need it.
The point is, just because a medium is popular, powerful, and com-
mands the most money for its use does not mean it should be considered
the best way to reach consumers. Perhaps it should not be used at all,
especially if your competitors frequent it.

As a marketing communicator using advertising, you should choose
media that will *cost effectively* reach targeted consumers best and induce
them to find, buy, use, and recommend your product or service.

Media management (including vehicle, reach, frequency, and other
variables) is the expensive part of creating and implementing a promotional feat using the controlled, nonpersonal, mass communication
called advertising. If an advertisement is decent and given ample exposure through an effective media mix, it will succeed, at least nominally.

And if an ad campaign is well thought out, matches the company's
objectives and image, is designed for maximum sales and communication impact, and is executed effectively, then a promotional feat may be
on its way. Radio is one medium that is just waiting for a local or national
advertiser to take advantage of its power. Let's look at one memorable
promotional feat using red hot radio.

Leave on the Lights, the Party's Still Goin'

Motel 6, the largest budget motel chain in America, lost 33 percent of
potential customers and $18 million in 1986. It was a very bad year. It
was time to upgrade and get competitive. Previously, the motel giant
had never had an organized advertising campaign. That would change.

Motel 6 began broadcasting national radio ads featuring the country
voice of Tom Bodett telling tuned in listeners about Motel 6's various
amenities, ending with the slogan, "We'll leave the light on for you."
Bodett's soft, slow, melodious drawl, accompanied by a meandering
fiddle tune, contrasts with the usual fast-talking, blaring announcers
who read most radio ads in the U.S. It's refreshing and relaxing to hear
ole' Tom talkin' on the voice box. He's so popular that he sports his
own fan club; many believe he's the president of Motel 6. At any rate,

Motel 6 is back in the black and still features Tom Bodett (through 1990) with his latest message to weary travelers.

The Motel 6 radio ads reign as the classic radio promotional feat by which all others are judged. Sure enough, other also-ran motel chains are copying the celebrity spokesperson approach. If they're smart, they'll think up something original and entertaining—something that tells people about their unique features and how these features will benefit travelers. We're waiting . . .

Radio advertising can be red hot. What radio needs to do is change with the times. It needs to find a way to entertain us once again, so listeners will tune in to radio instead of TV. With local TV cable companies charging ad fees comparable to radio, the FM/AM stations need to rethink their missions. In the San Francisco Bay area, a hundred stations compete with each other. Most offer the same boring formats: adult contemporary (elevator yuppie music), soft country, and golden oldies. How about Radio Theater? With a little ingenuity, radio can move from the backburner to the microwave—and truly be red hot.

TELEVISION IS KING

In the 1980s, the average American household watched TV for seven hours per day. With more channels offering more TV programs (super stations, new networks, more local channels, more specialty stations), household TV usage may even increase in the 1990s. Just about every household owns at least one color TV; over half own two or more. Someday soon, the average American will videotape one show while watching two or more others through the windows of a giant yet portable and affordable screen. Do you think TV advertising rates will continue to rise? You betcha.

The American Association of Advertising Agencies found in a survey that it costs an average of $156,000 to produce a 30-second national TV ad. In 1988, television advertising spending topped $24 billion dollars. With the move toward shorter commercials (15-second slots will soon become the norm), and over a thousand ads a day being shown on the tube, advertisers face a major problem with clutter.

As the clutter factor rises with rate increases, something has to be done just to get noticed. The answer is to think up cost-effective, powerful TV ads that get results. Let's look at a few TV commercials and ad campaigns that have achieved promotional feat status. In each case, we see that innovative, entertaining ads which extolled their products' benefits achieved the best results—sales!

Ring Around the Collar

"Those dirty rings." Wisk liquid laundry detergent used this frequent complaint of women as the theme for their product, which held a 2.8 percent share of the laundry detergent market. After the switch to the "Ring Around the Collar" campaign, Wisk's market share rose to a respectable 8 percent. This classic campaign toured for 20 years. In 1989, Wisk changed the theme to another catchy slogan, "Tsk, tsk, tsk, Wisk, Wisk, Wisk." This one may last 20 more years.

Some classic TV ads such as the Wisk commercial last a long time. Some famous ads are later revived and aired again. Hamm's beer brought back the popular Hamm's bear "from the land of sky blue waters." Ketchum Advertising brought back the "I want my Maypo" ads. Horovitz (1990: D1) reports that the cheap ad for Wendy's, created by Cliff Freeman & Partners, was reworked. Horovitz claims that some ad executives consider the Wendy's pitch the slogan of the decade: We'll always remember, "Where's the beef?"

During the Superbowl in January 1990, Coca-Cola held a reunion on the hill where the "I'd like to teach the world to sing" commercial was shot. According to Mabry (1990: 42), Coca-Cola hired Pinkerton detectives to find some of the original hilltop singers. The Coke ad reprise was a big hit. It was the real thing, man. Retro ads are back. Hopefully, only the good ones will be regurgitated. Plop, plop, fizz, fizz . . .

Beer Wars

For centuries, beer drinkers had to choose between lager, porter, stout, pilsner, and ale. Then came malt liquor. Over the last decade, we've seen the dubious creation of light beer, dry beer, and even non-alcoholic beer (mmmm, yum). With hundreds of national, international, and micro-breweries around, how is a beer drinker to choose what to drink to quench that couch potato thirst?

Anheuser-Busch at one time wanted beer aficionados to drink Budweiser, the King of Beers. Then, when Miller introduced Lite and started a new category of beer for the weight-conscious guzzler, Bud Light was formulated.

Miller Lite ran a series of TV ads for 15 years using has-been but humorous athletes such as Bob Uecker, retired sports greats, and comedians such as Rodney Dangerfield to fight it out over whether Lite "tastes great" or is "less filling." Many of these funny, memorable ads entertained us with ironic twists at the end. Some were cliffhangers, like the Halloween "Who stole the Miller Lite" contest with Micky Spillane, aired in 1989. The innovative ad campaign was replaced in 1990 with mundane comparison advertising, as if anyone could really tell the difference between one light beer and another.

Bud Light humorously compared itself to Miller Lite with its some-times clever "Give me a Light" series in which lots of lights were shown but no beer. Finally, the hapless beer drinker would order Bud Light and everything was rosy. Bud Light simultaneously ran its very popular Spuds MacKenzie celebrity/party dog featuring a pitbull terrier (actually a female) surrounded by gorgeous gals in various settings.

In 1989 and 1990, Anheuser-Busch ran its "Bud Bowls" during the Super Bowls. The cliffhanger ads pitted Bud against Bud Light in a football game. The audience had to watch every ad to see who won. Some people thought the Bud Bowls were more entertaining than the actual football games.

These beer war TV ad campaigns are good and qualify for promotional feat status. They had better. Miller Lite and Bud Light together spent over $120 million on TV advertising in 1988. A single 30-second spot during the 1990 Superbowl cost $700,000 (not counting production costs). One would have to sell a tremendous amount of beer to recoup costs for a single Super Bowl spot.

Brazen Little Raisins

Let's leave the world of ultra-expensive TV advertising and enter the world of simple, inexpensive, excellent advertising. The California Raisin Advisory Board hired Foote, Cone, and Belding to let everyone know about California raisins. They came up with the clay animated (clay-mation) dancing raisins who sing "I Heard It Through the Grapevine." Well, everyone loved it. The ads won first place in Video Storyboard popularity surveys in both 1987 and 1988. The $6 million dollar ad cam-paign was positively frugal compared with the spending of second-place Pepsi/Diet Pepsi ($106 million) and third-place McDonald's ($386 mil-lion).

The question is, does popularity produce sales of raisins? The answer is yes. Kotler and Armstrong (1990: 406), summarizing several sources, reported that raisin sales are up 5–6 percent per month. Also, the Cal-ifornia Raisins now endorse other products (such as Post Raisin Bran) and have become top-selling merchandise items. They adorn lunch-boxes, sheets, and t-shirts. You can buy the little critters and put them on your desk at work. These brazen raisins are hot commodities.

Animation in general and claymation in particular have found their niches in television advertising. We now have the Noid for Domino's Pizza—an ad that gets good recall. Here is another good example of claymation in action.

Marinucci (1990) reports that Ketchum Advertising created claymation dinosaur figures for Mini-Dinosaur Grahams, a Mother's Cake and Cookie product. The company already had a bestseller in their Dinosaur Grahams with no advertising, but wanted to totally dominate the kid cookie market. So they created claymation tyrannosaurus rexes and other cute dinosaurs. Only time will tell how successful the campaign will be, but it's getting off to a good start. We'll see how long it lasts before it becomes extinct.

Bo Knows Bonos

In the early 1960s, Converse basketball shoes were the choice of most teenagers trying to be cool. In the 1970s, Adidas reigned. In 1988, Reebok led the athletic shoe market with $3 billion in sales. But Nike took over in the late 1980s and has stayed on top in the deadly shoe wars. Now, Nike faces serious competition from Reebok and a smattering of other brands, including New Balance and L.A. Gear.

The shoe war ads have reached some exciting highs and lows. In 1990, Reebok came up with a bungie-jumping contest off a bridge in which the guy wearing the Nike brand shoes slipped out of the bungies and presumably fell to his death while the Reeboks held their jumper. The ad was dramatic but was pulled because it was considered too dirty and deadly. It's not nice to imply that if you wear your competitor's shoes you will die.

There seems to be ample room for heels in the $5 billion athletic shoe market, but Nike's Bo Jackson isn't one. In fact, he's the hero(es) of several great TV ads for Nike (who spends $60 million per year on ads to help stay number one). Nike's first award-winning ad showcasing Bo's multiple athletic abilities was shown during the 1989 baseball All-Star Game, in which Bo was playing.

We all remember the ad. A slew of athletes (such as cyclists and weightlifters) and other Nike celebrity athlete spokespersons such as baseball's Kirk Gibson and basketball's Michael Jordan all say "Bo knows" whatever sport he's playing. John McEnroe queries, "Bo knows tennis?" And Wayne Gretzky laughingly says "No" to Bo playing hockey. The funniest part happens at the end when Bo plays the guitar and world-famous guitarist Bo Diddley remarks: "Bo, you don't know Diddley."

The 60-second ad was later reduced to 30-second spots with clever variations. Finally, just before the 1989 Superbowl, we were treated to the climax of Bo's guitar playing dilemma. He makes some sweet-sounding moves on the gitbox and Bo Diddley admits: "Bo, you *do* know Diddley."

Everyone (except Nike's competitors) loves the Bo series. Bob Garfield, ad critic for *Advertising Age*, paid the highest compliment to the "Bo knows" commercials. He said the ads garnered "$16 trillion worth of publicity" for Nike (Garfield 1990b: 56).

Fortunately for us entertainment-craving ad watchers, Nike's ad agency (Wieden & Kennedy) didn't rest on their laurels. In 1990, they jazzed up the Bo cross-training idea even more. Magiera (1990b: 4) aptly describes the "Multiple Bos" ad, which is destined to become another classic for Nike. Magiera says the ad "is a special-effects-laden minute of hilarious confusion that cleverly weaves in elements of Nike's earlier cross-training commercials featuring Mr. Jackson."

The ad has L.A. Raider Jackson trying to place K.C. Royals' Jackson. Several images of Jackson depict him playing various sports from past ads. All the Jackson images together announce, "Bo don't *surf*."

"That's what you think, dudes," says Surfer Bo. Californians are already sporting "Bo don't surf" bumper stickers. I have one on my truck. My kayak company, Tsunami Products, is wondering whether Bo can kayak. Naaah.

As the topper to these shenanigans in the "Multiple Bos" commercial, Sonny Bono walks in among the multiple Bos and says, "I thought this was another Bono's commercial." The corny pun and the commercial end, but Nike's beat goes on.

I believe the Bo series of TV ads to be among the best ever invented. Hopefully, other ad agencies will end their me-too conservatism, get creative, take a risk . . . and Just Do It.

Energize Me

One of the most creative and fun ad series of all times has got to be Eveready's battery-powered pink bunny who bangs a big "Energizer" drum through the middle of boring fake ads (and through a few real ads from corporate parent Ralston). Rick Fizdale (1990: 3), CEO of the Leo Burnett agency, gave his impressions of the Energizer campaign.

> When I first saw it, I applauded the TV screen. I laughed so hard that these tired old couch potato eyes produced tears of joy. Not since Apple's "1984" had I seen anything so bold and fresh. Creative standards had risen to a new plateau.

These words of high praise came from the head of a rival agency (the Energizer campaign was created by Chiat/Day/Mojo).

The Energizer Bunny's ongoing drumming underscores the theme that Eveready batteries outlast others. The famous bunny made its last (or perhaps latest) appearance on *Cheers*, with the show's characters appearing in the commercial. Innovative use of marketing tie-ins is a promotional feat that others are likely to imitate. Meanwhile, Eveready's batteries and bunny keep on drumming. And the beat goes on, and on, and on . . .

The Ad of the Decade

Super Bowl Sunday is more than just the most popular thing on TV, it's also where the best and brightest new ads make their debut. It cost over a million bucks to air a 60-second ad during the Superbowl. Beer and cola makers will assuredly spend millions and millions in their wars to win our hearts and guts. What it all boils down to is advertising advertising for advertising. Tom Shales (1990: E1) says it more clearly. "The Super Bowl is the biggest ad for advertising ever."

So, if we see the "best" ads on Superbowl Sunday, then the best ad of all time is likely to be aired then. Correct? Maybe. The important thing about advertising during the Superbowl is that everyone watches your ads, then talks about it for weeks afterward. Hopefully, viewers buy whatever product or service the ad promoted. It is the generation of zillions of dollars of free publicity that makes it all worthwhile for advertisers. Each advertiser hopes to unleash a promotional feat on the public.

Only memorable, shocking, new, innovative, interesting, entertaining ads have a chance to be remembered. All others are dead in the water. As Butler (1985: F.C.7) pointed out, formula advertising is boring. He wrote, "Some advertisers may choose to ignore that fact. Some consumers may choose to ignore their advertising."

One Superbowl non-formula ad still clearly remembered nearly a decade later is Apple's "1984" ad which introduced the Macintosh. The director was Ridley Scott, who directed science fiction films such as "Bladerunner" and "Alien" and also directed ads for Chanel No. 5 and the Nissan 300ZX (in which the car races a jet).

We remember the plot of the "1984" ad. First, we were teased before the big day by short ad announcements which read, "On January 24th, Apple Computer will introduce Macintosh. And you'll see why 1984 won't be like '1984'." We all looked forward to the big media event.

Then, on Super Bowl Day, just as predicted, the ad happened. We saw a dimly lit theater, filled with "Brave New World" delta clones watching Big Brother (who was supposed to be IBM) on the giant screen. Suddenly, a woman, looking decidedly original in her cross training gear, rushes into the theater swinging a hammer. She hurls it at the screen and shatters the Big Brother image . . .

Big Brother is dead; long live Little Sister. We consumers loved the ad and Macs began selling like, well, Big Macs. Apple's nonformula ad became formula nouveau. Ad Impressionism was born. On cue, even though it took a few years, advertising copycats did their best impressions. Apple's 1985 "Lemmings" commercial was a cynical, infuriating impression of its previous great ad. We computer consumers may be clones and drones, but we sure as hell ain't lemmings. I went out and bought a Compaq. Little Sister was acting too much like Big Brother.

The Macintosh has had its ups and downs since 1984. After losing market share because of being way overpriced, it was revamped and sold for half price in 1990. That was more like it. Apple has regained some of its former polish.

Apple may never have another promotional feat like its "1984" ad, but for a moment, it was the best. Thanks to that ad, Chiat/Day/Mojo was named Agency of the Decade by *Advertising Age*. And, in 1990, Cleveland Horton made the following announcement (p. 12):

> Based on the commercial's numerous big elements—startling, creative, feature-film production values, brash media schedule and "event marketing" daring—the editors of *Advertising Age* have selected "1984" as the Commercial of the Decade.

The ad deserved it. It was an event, a happening. It was advertising's promotional feat of the decade.

Money Can't Buy It

The "1984" ad was good. But what made it extra good was that everyone talked about it—and still talks about it. We'll talk about "Bo knows" ads for years. These entertaining ads *sell* products. But what really sells products is the simplest, best form of advertising. It's so good that money alone can't buy it. It's called word-of-mouth.

The only way that word-of-mouth can work is when the product, its advertising, and all other promotional activities work in harmony. Then, people talk about the product, seek it out. And that is how promotional feats happen.

6

Promotion Gimmicks

"First, sales promotion involves some type of inducement that provides an extra incentive to buy."

—G. E. Belch and M. A. Belch

MARKETING IS SALES PROMOTION! That's what professionals in the burgeoning sales promotion industry claim. Consumer sales promotion (incentives designed to stimulate immediate purchase or use of a product) spending is second only to advertising in selling to consumers. A graph in the July 1989 *Marketing & Media Decisions* showed that 1988 spending on sales promotions was $124 billion, only $2 billion less than that of advertising. About 40 percent of sales promotion dollars were spent on consumer promotion (the rest was on trade promotion). Accounting of consumer-oriented sales promotions is hazy, since many companies report money spent on samples and other inducements as manufacturing rather than promotional costs. There seems to be a trend toward more sales promotions at the expense of advertising.

This move toward sales promotions is due to several factors. First, because of the proliferation of products that resemble each other to the point that consumers cannot differentiate them, buyers walk the aisles looking for quick bargains. In short, consumers are price- and promotion-sensitive when they can't tell the difference among competing products. We discussed this problem earlier. The conservative approach to product development that has dogged marketers over the past decade shows no signs of abating. Therefore, even great advertising can't fool the people all the time when no true difference between products exists.

Another reason for the surge in sales promotions is the specious notion that increased sales volume in the short run is good news, even if it costs the company millions and fails to obtain brand loyalty. I see marketers blindly copying each other in the incentives-based price wars. The prevailing thought seems to be, "If company X is offering a cents-off coupon then we'll match 'em." The result? At best, consumer confusion; at worst, savvy consumer purchasing at the expense of brand loyalty.

So, for a sales promotion to be a promotional feat, it must cost-effectively achieve its purpose—to encourage immediate trial. Additionally, it must enhance the brand image, shorten the purchase cycle, or at least increase usage at no significant cost to the producer. A final component—it must make the news, in effect, generate publicity. In this chapter, we'll begin with traditional promotional tools such as couponing and end with sensational "promotional events"—the future of sales promotions.

In this book, I focus on manufacturers' and retailers' promotion directly to consumers (pull strategy), rather than promotion pushed through trade channels (e.g., quantity price-offs, display and advertising allowances, push money, and trade shows) or the sales force. In this book three reasons account for why I steer clear of trade promotions.

First, most trade promotions are either confidential or at least don't make the papers. thus, no one knows about them and they could hardly be called promotional feats, even though they effectively push products through layers of middlemen.

Second, as a manufacturer competing with 40 others in my industry for limited shelf space, I am dismayed at the power retailers possess. I hate to have to offer them all kinds of deals just to give them the privilege of displaying our superior products which enhance their image, satisfying customers with a product with an excellent warranty, and making a hefty profit. Because of the overall inefficiency of middlemen and retailers (in general), I advocate direct marketing approaches to targeting consumers.

Third, the thrust of this book has been promotional feats aimed at the consumer. So, even though over half of all sales promotions are aimed at channels (Kessler 1986: 83), we will concentrate on consumer sales promotions, an area ripe for promotional feats.

SALES PROMOTION SUCCESSES

Consumer sales promotions come in many traditional forms: coupons, rebates, price packs, premiums, samples, and in-store displays. I would not consider any of these prime candidates for promotional feat status, but they can be quite effective if tied in with advertising and trade promotion, and if they match consumers' needs and are well-timed. We'll begin by examining the ubiquitous coupon and its cousins, rebates and price packs.

Billions and Billions of Coupons

Coupons have been around for generations. They appear on print ads in magazines and especially newspapers. They can be mailed, inserted inside a product package, or picked up from a point-of-purchase (POP) display. Many coupons are now generated by scanners at the checkout stand and placed in customers' shopping bags. In this case, the cashier scan computer is programmed to flag certain products and issue cents-off coupons for competing products.

The cashier coupon is a promotional feat because it targets consumers based on their immediate purchase behavior. Cashier coupons, which usually offer a substantial cash discount, signal the consumer that she's made a mistake in buying a certain brand of coffee, and next time she can get money off her next purchase of Yuban.

According to Meyer (1981: 66), coupons accounted for 63 percent of consumer promotions in 1980. By 1988 (according to Donnelley Marketing surveys), coupons were still the number one form of consumer promotion used by firms with under $1 billion in annual sales volume. In 1988, 88 percent of larger firms (over $1 billion annual sales) used direct consumer couponing.

In the 1990s we see that coupons are still flourishing everywhere. In October 1990, I received a coupon book chockfull of good deals on various pantry items from Thrifty Drug Stores. Not only did they offer $589 worth of savings, but they featured a "Fall Into Wealth" sweepstakes worth $50,000, including a grand prize of $10,000. They offered 300 coupons on representative items from their entire store selection. All coupons were dated, and a few were tied into manufacturers' coupons or rebates which saved customers even more. One Thrifty coupon priced Efidac/24 nasal decongestant (perfect for autumn colds) at just $2.99. The coupon stated that with the manufacturer's mail-in rebate of $2.99, the price was *zero*! This is one way to guarantee immediate purchase, or sample trial in this case.

Thrifty even offered a few 50 percent direct savings off specially marked popular items such as Kodak videotape. These specials were printed with four colors on high-gloss heavy stock. This got our attention. The three-hundred coupons were printed on cheap black-and-white newsprint so the booklet was cost-effective. It was bulk mailed early enough so all customers would receive it by the first day of the promotion. The central office developed and handled the coupon book promotion; all outlets had to do was ensure adequate stock.

Thrifty made sure they followed all legal requirements regarding raincheck policies, quantities, and availability of merchandise. Store managers briefed employees on the promotion, and it generated a good deal more traffic than normal. Thrifty executed an effective, retail-oriented sales promotion feat centered on coupons. The promotion was nothing fancy; it was just well conceived and executed. This kind of promotional feat based on couponing with a sweepstakes sweetener doesn't make the news or win awards, but it's a cost-effective inducement. It stimulates immediate purchase behavior. Who could ask for more?

Though couponing is still used, it is fraught with problems. Retailers have increased handling fees for manufacturers' coupons. And they should; it's a hassle to deal with coupons. Many coupons are redeemed fraudulently—perhaps a million a year. To top it off, because of coupon clutter (over 220 billion coupons are distributed in America each year), most are ignored by consumers. In fact, less than 4 percent are redeemed (Kotler and Armstrong 1990: 422).

Some manufacturers have switched to rebates, where the consumer gets the price reduction by mailing some proof of purchase back to the manufacturer who then mails a check back to the consumer who then must go to the bank and deposit the check. As you can see, this saves on retailer handling fees but does not reduce energy expenditures on the part of the manufacturer. Alas, the poor consumer must go through major hoops and barrels to receive cash back from a rebate offer.

Telzer (1987) reports that the good news is rebates stimulate purchases but not redemption, hence are more efficient than coupons, which are redeemed at purchase. The bad news is that consumers don't like the extra hassle and may avoid a rebate deal unless it gives them substantial cash back (such as rebates for automobile purchases). Coupon redemption alone is complicated enough for customers. Remember, in these hectic times, consumers are very busy. If nothing else, manufacturers and retailers would be wise to do everything possible to make purchasing as easy as possible.

Here are six tips for using coupons and rebates. First, do it sparingly and only to encourage trial of new products in a zoo of competitors, or to stimulate repurchase and use of a slipping cash cow. Otherwise, you may find that your current users comprise the bulk of your coupon redeemers—and they will be pleased that you are such a willing sap.

Second, don't just give the product away by slashing the price so much that you lose money and merely move merchandise temporarily. Also, a major price slash signals the consumer that the product isn't worth much (or it would cost more, much more). Regaining or defending market share is a make-work, expensive, brand-demeaning excuse for a huge rebate, coupon, or cents-off deal.

Retailers join in the coupon wars and lose lots of money trying to out-coupon each other. Supermarket chains such as Ralph's (Graves 1987) sometimes reel out "Unlimited Double Coupons!" promotions to lure consumers back from other stores offering—you got it—unlimited double coupons! The winner in this kind of war? Quick-footed shoppers.

Here's a scenario. You decide to offer 25-cents-off coupons on your $2 pantry item. This is fair. Your competitor retaliates by offering 50 cents off his brand. How should you respond? Raise your price 30 cents and find another incentive to stimulate purchase. I'll describe more traditional incentives in a moment and outlandish sales promotions later in this chapter.

Third, put your coupon (properly worded, priced, and dated) in a print ad or direct mail piece which bolsters brand image. Also, you may wish to combine the coupon with a refund offer or even a sweepstakes. The goal is to make your advertising and promotional incentives complement each other and present a reasonable value to the consumer.

Fourth, a price pack (cents-off deal) beats a coupon or refund any day because it is *convenient* for both the retailer and consumer. Incidentally, it's also easier for the producer.

Fifth, as in tip number two, don't take so many cents off that regular users stock up for hibernation leaving no stock for new users or users of competing brands. Grocers don't like dealing with disgruntled customers demanding rainchecks.

Sixth, avoid taking so few cents off (like 4 cents off a $2 item) that consumers scoff at the offer and harbor disdain for you and your product. Instead, carefully calculate the minimum cents-off needed to stimulate an immediate purchase, preferably at the expense of competing brands, and go for it.

My research shows that 25 cents off an item under $5 will stimulate trial for most people looking for a bargain. Here's why. Most people think in round numbers and significant cut-off points. In chapter 2, I discussed test pilot trivia. We all know that Yeager was first to break Mach 1. Mach 1 is a significant number; Mach 1.8 is not, even though it is nearly twice as fast. A quarter is a significant amount of money; just like Mach 1.8, 38 cents is not. In conclusion, significant price packs such as a dime, quarter, half-dollar, or dollar are eye-catching and stimulate purchase, whereas numbers that sound like log-linear transformations turn buyers off.

Sample This Premium

Let's examine the promotional utility of two related incentives, the sample ("trial offer") and premium (free or reduced-price good that accompanies purchased good or service). The similarity between the two is that the consumer gets something for nothing, or nearly nothing.

Small "free" samples are used to introduce a new product or a "new and improved" mature product. Samples are sometimes sent directly to consumers through the mail. Often, a coupon or refund offer accompanies the freebie. Sampling via mail or door-to-door dropoff is very expensive, so only big companies with big promotion budgets can afford this kind of product introduction, but it delights consumers. Here's an example of expensive sampling. Kotler and Armstrong (1990: 422) reported that Lever Brothers spent $43 million when it distributed free samples of its Surf detergent to most American households.

Samples are also attached to packages of other products, given out, or even featured in an ad (e.g., a scratch-and-sniff perfume ad). The potential promotional feat aspect of samples is that they induce *trial*, which is very important to packaged-goods items that have a short purchase cycle.

The problem is that samples cost too much money, even though they feature relatively low unit value. The solution is to offer self-liquidating samples, that is, samples that are sold (cheaply), near or slightly below manufacturer's cost. That way, the consumer gets to try a bit of the product, but it doesn't cost much. Most people are willing to shell out coins for a sample of something they might like. The best example is travel-size samples of shampoos and lotions that sell for under a buck. Shoppers buy them for travel kits, and if they like them, purchase the larger quantities next time.

The sample-for-a-shilling technique could work for many other products (like food items). Everyone benefits from this kind of sampling promotion. It's cost effective and could be a promotional feat if handled correctly.

Big ticket items can be sampled. Car dealers and Apple Computers offer "test-drives." Apple's 24-hour Macintosh sample period was a good trial inducement coupled with a print ad campaign of a gloved hand driving a Mac mouse. McElnea and Enzer (1986: 42) reported that the initial Mac test drive promotion resulted in 200,000 trials and a significant increase in sales.

Service-oriented companies can also offer samples. AT&T offered to connect potential or past customers for AT&T for free—and reconnect them to another long distance carrier if they were not satisfied with AT&T's service. This kind of inducement is definitely a promotional feat; it entices customers to choose AT&T, yet costs AT&T peanuts.

Premiums are similar to samples and are often included in- or on-package. Kids' cereal premiums serve as the best example of this successful technique. The trick is offering a premium that is related to the purchased product (like offering a WD–40 sample with a Wagner Power Painter), is something that consumers really want and probably can't get other ways (like junior astronaut certificates from Safeway's Frosted

Flakes), and/or is a self-liquidating premium of a t-shirt, hat, seat cushion, cup, pen, or other item with a company's brandmarks emblazoned on the item (such as Budweiser t-shirts and other "specialty advertising" merchandise) and sold at very low prices. Any variation on these themes could provide a cost-effective way to serve customers better and reward you not only with immediate purchase but perhaps brand loyalty as well.

In 1990, Duracell offered a unique premium that is sure to attract customers and may keep them. To combat Eveready's bunny campaign, Duracell battery ads touted a batter tester as part of the Duracell package. Their particular package premium exemplifies a new kind of cheap yet useful accessory to the purchased product.

The "package premium" idea is not new. Bailey's Irish Cream and Tia Maria coffee liqueur are sometimes packaged in reusable, attractive tins at no extra cost. In 1990, Freixenet appended gold markers on their Cordon Negro champagne so users could write personal messages right on the bottle. These kinds of package-related premiums often induce trial and are worth considering when looking for a unique way to get people to buy your product.

Displays are POPcorny

Point-of-purchase (POP) promotions (usually displays or demos next to a product) remind shoppers to pick up the displayed item. Some POPs are simply convenient product holders that highlight a particular brand. Some companies supply these holders to aid merchants who stock impulse items such as cigarettes. Due to the competition for shelf space, this is one successful way to get a display.

Another display idea offers shoppers expensive items such as silverware or china at good deals. All shoppers need do to participate is either buy a certain amount of goods from the store or just enter the store. Safeway sponsors these promotional displays periodically.

In late 1990, Safeway offered a high-quality aluminum cookware set at reduced prices if the shopper made a certain amount of purchases at Safeway. Each week, a different pan or skillet was featured. In a couple of months, eager shoppers could obtain all the pots and pans. Shoppers were given the option of buying a pan at normal prices on off-sale weeks. Unfortunately, the promotion company selling the cookware neglected to train Safeway personnel on how to run the promotion. Cashiers had no idea what week they were in since no actual dates were stated on the huge end-of-aisle display. Result: wasted money and space, and confused, disgruntled customers.

This display promotion could have been successful if the rules were kept simple. Displays should be eye-catching and should encourage an immediate sale or trial. Unless the display is part of a game, contest, or sweepstakes, keep the detective work out of the POP.

The pot-and-pan promoter could have learned successful display techniques by studying past masters. The editors of *Sales Promotion Handbook* (Riso 1979: 898) described an outrageous display created back in the early 1960s for Sea & Ski tanning lotion. The dramatic display was an 11-foot lifeguard tower layered with "Tanfastic" Sea & Ski lotions and oils. At the top were life-size figures of a tanned male lifeguard ogling a shapely, tanned woman preparing to dive off a diving board. This display was built before marketers tested the effectiveness of promotional efforts and tied in sales increases to specific promotional activities. But the fact that the Sea & Ski display is included in a book in its seventh edition shows that it was a classic promotional feat.

Here is a more recent dramatic demonstration display. When Du Pont was pulling its Stainmaster carpet through distribution channels, it complemented its TV ads of "great saves" of food spills on its carpets with a POP demonstration center set up in 10,000 stores. The POP involved customers. They dipped a swizzle stick with Stainmaster and a competing carpet into red fruit drink and then stirred clear water with the sticks. The fruit juice disappeared from the Stainmaster carpet—but not from the competitor's. Du Pont's use of dramatic demonstration (tied in with its other promotional efforts) helped make Stainmaster a best-selling carpet in a commodity market. Demonstrations, if simple and dramatic, will draw crowds. Just ask any extra-strong glue company.

One of the best POPs ever made was Pepsi's "tipping can" display. Here's how it worked. The battery-operated display (either two six-packs or a one-liter bottle) would suddenly lurch partway off the shelf every 30 seconds. Shoppers' eyes would be drawn toward it and they would be amused—and reminded to pick up the Pepsi. Merchants were encouraged to set up multiple displays so an entire shelf would appear to tip. Kids lined up just to see the display. Kotler and Armstrong (1990: 423) reported that the award-winning display "helped get more trade support and greatly increased Pepsi sales" in test market stores.

The tipping Pepsi POP is a promotional feat. It garnered trade support (very difficult these days) and encouraged sales. Plus, it won a promotions award, which shows industry acknowledgment of a superior promotions project. The Pepsi display typifies the kind of POP that will make it in the 1990s. It moved (static displays are boring), ran by itself for weeks and took up hardly any space (no hassle for merchants), increased store traffic (benefitted merchants), entertained customers, and increased sales volume for Pepsi. Considering that it was a dynamic display, it was also relatively inexpensive.

POP spending is on the rise. Shimp (1990: 471) reports that POP spending has increased 12 percent per year since 1983. Because of the big enemy—clutter—promotions professionals must carefully select displays that tie in with overall marketing communications objectives and won't have to compete with forty other POPs in an aisle. (If you create an expensive display, you wouldn't set it up on the Las Vegas strip. No one would notice it.) The key is to always be looking for new opportunities to exploit. And don't forget to test a display before rolling it out nationwide. If it proves a dud, you can bury it quietly before setting up at the end of the aisle at Safeway.

Win a Game or Contest in Our Sweepstakes

Games, contests, and sweepstakes are American marketing phenomena that are here to stay. Many states feature lotteries to increase state revenues and put a little pizzazz in everyone's life. The California lottery, fourth largest in the world, has raked in $11 billion between 1986 and 1990. On average, Florida, Maryland, New Jersey, and Ohio residents buy $150 worth of lottery tickets a year. Americans love to gamble.

Marketers have taken advantage of our desire to win by luck by offering us cash, trips, and goodies to participate in games, contests, and sweepstakes. A *game* gives consumers pieces to a puzzle each time they come in the store or buy. McDonald's or one of the other fast-food franchises has a game of some sort going all the time—to the point where many consumers are fed up with the whole enchilada, especially if the game is complicated or hard to win.

A *contest* requires entrants to guess trivia questions or submit something that is judged by someone. As you read this, at least one radio station in your local area is staging a contest on the air. Many listeners tune out when the DJ announces "Be our thirteenth caller to answer correctly and win."

Sweepstakes involve entering your name for a chance at big prizes. Belch and Belch (1990: 534) favor sweepstakes: because they are easy to enter and administer, they are superior to contests. They note that sweepstakes generate interest in a brand. "In an increasingly cluttered media environment, sweepstakes can provide consumers with an extra incentive for attending to an advertisement."

I agree that sweepstakes make it easy for everyone and can tie in with advertising to build brand image. But even sweepstakes contribute to the clutter facing consumers and should be used sparingly. To sweeten a sweepstakes, make big cash awards the primary prize. Why? Everyone loves $20,000, but not everyone may be inspired by the two-week, expenses-paid cruise for two to Antarctica to see the penguin IceCapades. (Of course, if the sweepstakes sponsor is *National Geographic*, then Antarctica may be the perfect prize.)

The object is to make the prize something that potential or actual users of your product or service would lust after, but nonusers wouldn't. Also, always set up your sweepstakes so people can enter only once, otherwise, some people with nothing better to do may sign up a zillion times and win.

Tie in Cross Promotions

Promotional activities can be more cost effective by using *cross promotion*, where a coupon or other incentive for one product is distributed or promoted by another product or service. Cross promotions are especially useful for small businesses who can help each other and better serve their joint customers.

In his book *Streetfighting*, Jeff Slutsky (1984) describes clever cross promotions that work. In one of Slutsky's examples, Russell's formal wear store printed a special coupon offering a free tuxedo for the groom, free shoes for everyone, and ten percent off an entire outfit for a member of the wedding party—a good incentive offer. But here's the clincher. On the bottom of the coupon, Russell's printed "Courtesy of Armstrong's Diamond Center," a local jewelry store that catered to newlyweds. Armstrong's gave Russell's coupons to ring buyers who trusted their jeweler's judgment and were thankful for the tip.

This is a promotional feat. To make this cross promotion even better, Russell's could distribute some kind of offer for Armstrong's—to return the favor and better serve customers. Slutsky calls this a two-way cross promotion. I envision a whole group of merchants in complementary businesses routinely offering n-way cross promotions. For example, in the Russell's/Armstrong's example, the cross promotion could extend to a bridal wear shop, a florist, a baker who specializes in wedding cakes, a portrait photographer, a landlord who rents special events space, and so on.

Cross promotions are also good for large businesses. In 1990, American Savings Bank and Continental Airlines offered a cross promotion where a customer who got a CD from American Savings would get a free companion ticket or reduced fare from Continental. There is nothing special about this cross promotion except that it shows that large service companies can work together to encourage trade and satisfy customers. Cross promotion is an area that has yet to be fully exploited by companies with complementary products or services.

Tie-ins, similar to cross promotions, occur when several services or products pool their promotion resources to increase sales, promote new use, or broaden user base. Sometimes, advertising tie-ins are used (e.g., when mall merchants share expenses for a 60-second cable TV spot highlighting each business and their mall).

Sometimes one company will sell merchandise or services for another, usually related, product or service. For example, Burger King sold Teenage Mutant Ninja Turtle videos and merchandise to get young people into their restaurants. Later in 1990, Burger King sold Simpsons Family merchandise and plugged the new time slot for the popular TV show. Again, Burger King was selling Simpsons to attract younger (and older) customers to their franchises. Both of these merchandise tie-ins delighted Burger King and its many customers.

Here's another good tie-in. In 1989, Ralston put $10 rebates for HBO or Cinemax subscriptions in their Chex Snack Mix boxes. They also gave people a chance to instantly win a portable Casio TV. Ralston was capitalizing on the fact that people often watch cable TV while eating Chex snacks. This was a natural tie-in for complementary, non-competing products.

Walt Disney Productions regularly participates in various tie-ins and cross promotions with a multitude of products (e.g., Lipton tea) and services (such as airlines, hotels, other vacation offerings) with great success. By tieing in with Disney, a company can make a lot of money because everyone wants to go to Disneyland and Disney World.

The biggest cross promotion deals may be movie tie-ins. Magiera (1990a: 1) contends that marketing tie-ins with companies like McDonald's "can add $20 million to $30 million to a studio's $8 million to $10 million marketing budget."

For example, Paramount's *Days of Thunder*, released in summer 1990, featured a Chevy stock car named after Coca-Cola's Mello Yello drink. Chevrolet advertised their car (a Lumina) and the movie during the Indianapolis 500 race and through much of the summer. Chevrolet also promoted the film in magazine print ads and in auto displays in malls around the nation. Coca-Cola also cross promoted the film and offered a sweepstakes with their Mello Yello soft drink featuring a Chevy Lumina as a prize.

Cross promotions and tie-ins have the potential for promotional feat status because they appeal to customers on many levels. If cleverly done, such as with movie tie-ins, plenty of money can be made (or saved) by all. Like other classic sales promotions, most effective cross promotions will fail to make the news, but they are still promotional feats if they exceed promotional objectives and contribute to the overall marketing communications mix for a product or service.

Cross promoters must be wary of making stupid blunders which hurt one of the companies involved. For example, in 1984 TWA and Polaroid teamed up to increase sales of Polaroid cameras and film and encourage use of TWA during the slow season. The offer was simple. If a customer bought a Polaroid camera, she received a 25 percent discount on TWA flights. Everyone thought this was a good tie-in promotion for both companies.

TWA made one small boo-boo—they forgot to limit the offer to "one per customer." Sure enough, Polaroid cameras sold like hotcakes. Travel agencies and departments bought thousands of cameras. According to Shimp (1990: 595), over 150,000 coupons were redeemed, many for expensive international flights. For TWA, the promotion was a multimillion-dollar nightmare; for Polaroid, it was a simply marvelous promotional feat.

PROMOTIONAL EVENTS

Let's leave traditional promotional activities and describe some extraordinary promotions that not only make or save money and encourage immediate purchase or more consumption, but make the news as well. The following "events" begin to merge sales promotion with crowd-pleasing publicity stunts. In Chapter 3 we discussed publicity stunts associated with entertainment events. Now we will look at a few entertaining promotional events.

Just Country Pumpkins

In the old days, tedious ribbon-cutting ceremonies epitomized promotional events. Since then, some companies have managed to make a modest event out of a new product announcement and have garnered some media attention by employing spotlights and a band. This typifies the twentieth century promotional "event" and is boring beyond belief.

What possible news interest can there be in unveiling a new computer? Absolutely none. Yet a few reporters do cover the story and we get to see a picture of Steve Jobs or John Sculley smiling next to a personal computer that looks remarkably similar to existing models but differs in the placement of bells and whistles. These expensive curtain-raisers accomplish a purpose but do not qualify as promotional feats. Carefully placed new product releases would probably accomplish the same goals at a fraction of the cost.

Sometimes a shopping center or store will sponsor a fashion show and feature a famous designer such as Bill Blass or Calvin Klein. Hosting a famous person like Pierre Cardin can help promote licensed products bearing his name that are sold at a major retail outlet. Fashion shows and famous names help move merchandise, but usually don't achieve promotional feat status.

Similar to fashion shows are celebrity appearances. Professional athletes, beauty contest winners, entertainers, and even comic characters such as Spiderman visit malls and boost attendance at anniversaries, special sales, and other retail events. These activities contribute to promotional objectives, yet typically are not promotional feats. After all, it's highly unlikely that a person playing Spiderman could emulate a Harry Houdini stunt and attract several thousand people at once.

The best bet for common happenings such as grand openings and new product unveilings is to include an array of special events such as those just described. Perhaps each thing will attract a certain person, one at a time, until the halls in the malls are full. Here is an example of how a small town 25 miles south of San Francisco packed in paying people by offering a parade of pumpkins.

Mid-October is a slow month for most businesses. Merchants in the farm town by the sea called Half Moon Bay have found a way to attract 20,000 extra customers. They sponsor a Pumpkin Festival. The festival includes a parade, art festival, and sidewalk displays of sundry merchandise. In 1990, the Pumpkin Festival was so successful that Highway 92, a two-lane road connecting Half Moon Bay with the greater San Francisco Bay area, was backed up for eight miles for the entire weekend. Motorists waited on the road for two hours for the opportunity to check out Half Moon Bay's culture and purchase a Halloween pumpkin from one of the many roadside pumpkin patches.

Though the Pumpkin Festival is fun, it is really no big deal. Yet the little town bursts with the overflow of tourists and city folks straining to see the sights and wading through row after row of orange pumpkins until they find the right one. These people could have purchased a quality pumpkin for a comparable price at their local supermarkets yet chose to make the drive anyway. Why?

The Half Moon Bay Pumpkin Festival works for five reasons. First, merchants, farmers, artisans, and city leaders cooperate to make the festival happen with a minimum of red tape and bickering. Second, the festival has earned a reputation through word-of-mouth over the past few years as a fun activity. So Bay area media, merchants, and friends announce the festival before it happens and everyone is reminded about it.

Third, the town builds the event around its natural strength—agriculture, and specifically pumpkins! Fourth, the festival features a variety of activities to attract patrons on several levels. These activities tie in with each other.

Finally, the festival's timing is right. There is nothing better to do in mid-October, so why not check out the Pumpkin Festival? Besides, the kids love it. Thus, a small town successfully draws people away from the bustling city and into the rustic life by the Pacific. This is a promotional feat.

Hole-in-One Event Marketing

No big corporations underwrite the Pumpkin Festival in Half Moon Bay, but event sponsorship has increased dramatically over the past few years. *Event marketing* is sponsorship or brand identification with a public event—social cause, athletic, or cultural. According to Freeman (1988: 48–S), $1.35 billion was spent on event marketing in 1988.

Sponsoring an event gives a company a chance to garner publicity while still controlling its exposure to consumers. Ideally, a company should sponsor an event that is naturally associated with its product or service. For example, it makes sense that Budweiser would sponsor auto races and monster truck events because many fans drink beer. It seems reasonable that Volvo would sponsor tennis tournaments since Sweden has good tennis players and many tennis aficionados can afford Volvos.

Why Virginia Slims would sponsor a tennis tournament is unclear. Most people don't associate athletic games with women's cigarettes, even if the Slims tournament is a women's event. Nevertheless, nearly 75 percent of college students in my classes named it when asked to provide a list of professional tennis tournaments. Outrageous as it may seem, Virginia Slims may have achieved promotional feat status from the *negative* publicity it has received over its sponsorship.

Cigarette and alcohol products sponsor many events, and even brand-marks of common household products now adorn race cars. Procter & Gamble sponsors race cars with Crisco and Tide plastered on doors and hoods. Who would believe it? Shimp (1990: 507) notes that P&G also sponsors Cinco de Mayo in the Los Angeles basin and reaches 4 million Hispanics in the process. All told, P&G spends over $30 million a year on event marketing (Freeman 1987: 41).

P&G uses event marketing effectively and maximizes the impact of promotional dollars spent by targeting specific events that will reach desired consumers in a positive way (e.g., Cinco de Mayo). In this age of advertising expense and clutter, event marketing may provide an underused avenue to tie your company's brand in with an appropriate event. The trick is to find an inexpensive yet high publicity value event that you can sponsor alone. The Chinese New Year is in; the Olympics are out.

But to really make the most of event marketing, you must find a way to dominate an event in a positive way. Jeff Slutsky (1984: 72–73) describes a small business event marketing promotional feat in his book *Streetfighting*. Here's the story.

A retailer was approached to contribute $750 to a charity pro-amateur golf tournament. In return, he would get his name on a placard with two dozen other sponsors. The local media covered the tournament and he wanted that positive exposure. So, instead of cash, he offered a $10,000 check to anyone who could get a hole-in-one on the ninth hole. Half would go to the golfer, half to charity.

The retailer had a huge check blown up and displayed at the ninth hole. Every time the cameras focused on the ninth hole, the retailer's name was broadcast on TV. He received lots of publicity and community goodwill.

The idea of small businesses offering great prizes or cash for a charity cause is sure to get positive publicity, yet it seldom happens. If you worry about having to fork up the prize or $10,000, do like the retailer in this story did—insure the risk.

A Calculated Wisk

If your company is big, or you have lots of money to spend on promotional activities, sponsor an event you create. Belch and Belch (1990: 505) showcased a scintillating promotional feat developed by Lever Brothers in 1987 to promote Wisk at the expense of new entrants in the liquid detergent market.

Lever Brothers decided to celebrate 30 years of Wisk success, encourage retail support in displaying and shelving New Improved Wisk, and gain community goodwill around the nation by sponsoring "Lighting up the Sky" fireworks celebrations.

Each fireworks show was tied in to local celebrations. The fireworks display lasted 24 minutes and was set to a medley of rock 'n' roll songs— 30 years of music for 30 years of Wisk. How romantic. The climax of each show was a "ring around the sky" pyrotechnical burst that represented the familiar "ring around the collar" line. Lever Brothers made the twenty-three-city stunt complete by offering coupons, a sweepstakes, VIP parties for retail buyers, and trade allowances.

The event promotion was expensive but scored big on all counts. Three million people watched the fireworks and most Americans were aware of the event. Wisk set new sales records, maintained market leadership, and won a Promotional Marketing Association of America "Reggie" award for outstanding promotions.

It seems that with coordinated promotional effort, just about any company could light off some fireworks about its product or service. So what are you waiting for, the Fourth of July? Let everyone celebrate your brand.

The Red Baron Rides Again

Red Baron Pizza knows how to celebrate its brand. They took to the skies—no fireworks, just vintage WWI planes decked out to look like something the Red Baron would fly. The planes barnstormed thirteen key markets. Costumed Richtofens gave out coupons and asked customers to "fly with the Red Baron."

The inexpensive ($1 million) promotion lasted only four weeks, but sales jumped 100 percent wherever a fly-by took place. Over the next three months, some Red Baron Pizzas experienced four times normal sales volume (Kotler and Armstrong: 426). Additionally, the fly-in was rated one of the best sales promotions of the year. The lesson: the public loves entertainment. So, find something fun about your product or service and whoop it up in an original way. Who knows, maybe you could win a "Reggie."

Challenging Pepsi for the Championship of the World

Commonly, advertisements claim that "four out of five doctors/dentists/mothers surveyed preferred the advertised brand over others." Car manufacturers regularly show how their cars outperform competitors in certain categories and thus are better.

People like to hear about and watch product comparisons but they would rather participate in competitions. Pepsi-Cola decided back in 1980 to challenge market leader Coca-Cola in a national taste test competition to find out once and for all which taste people preferred when they didn't know which cola they were drinking. This time, people didn't have to rely on the word of an announcer; they could take the taste test themselves. And they did.

Belch and Belch (p. 518) reported that Pepsi (after pilot testing) conducted 3,000 in-home blind taste tests across one-hundred cities. Most people preferred Pepsi over Coke. So Pepsi initiated the Pepsi Challenge in which booths were set up in malls and large stores where consumers could find out for themselves which was better. And most people found that the sweeter Pepsi tasted better than its rival.

Pepsi sweetened the deal with price-off coupons and advertised that it tasted better. The promotion paid off for Pepsi and they used it successfully for a number of years. Eventually, Pepsi surpassed Coke in supermarket sales. This long-running promotional event achieved feat status for Pepsi.

In 1990, Pepsi was still urging cola drinkers to take the Pepsi challenge. Joe Montana and Ray Charles took the challenge together in a TV ad first broadcast during the Superbowl while Believable Joe was throwing touchdown passes between commercial breaks.

Here's the rest of the story. When Pepsi surged forward with its successful challenge promotion, Coca-Cola retrenched and did its homework. Coca-Cola tested colas and reformulated and eventually came up with new Coke, which was sweeter and rivaled Pepsi in taste preference. We all know that loyal Coke drinkers revolted and demanded old Coke. Coca-Cola capitulated and then offered two competing colas—Coke "Classic" and the new Coke with the blue stripe down the can (to make it look more like Pepsi perhaps?). All the hullabaloo is over. What's to excite the crowd? Here's what.

I suggest that Coca-Cola initiate a new promotional campaign: the "Coke Heavyweight Championship of the World," starring the new Coke against Pepsi. Coke's research (and mine) already shows that a small but significant number of people in blind taste tests prefer new Coke over Pepsi. Why not challenge Pepsi drinkers to the Cola Championship? Pepsi has been running this challenge thing into the ground. It is time for Coke to strike back. Do you think the public would respond to such a challenge? They would.

The Great Doll Adoption Promotion

If challenges don't strike your fancy, then try something really unique. Coleco did and a mass panic began. This event was the most outstanding example of a promotional feat that I have found. The Cabbage Patch Doll phenomenon represents the perfect marriage of promotion and publicity.

Back in 1983, Coleco Industries marketed the Cabbage Patch Kids, which were some of the homeliest dolls ever created since Raggedy Ann. Rather than take the usual route of begging Toys R Us to shelve the dolls next to dozens of other dolls, Coleco took the dolls directly to the consumers. Here's how they did it.

First, Coleco staged a mass adoption ceremony in Boston with a bunch of school kids. This made the local news, then the national news, the *Today Show* with Jane Pauley, the *Tonight Show* with Johnny Carson, and Dr. Joyce Brothers' column. Child psychologists declared that the dolls were great gifts. Women's magazines suggested them as good Christmas presents. Coleco gave away the dolls to kids in hospitals. Radio stations gave the Kids away as prizes.

The seeds were planted, they sprouted, they grew like weeds . . . er, cabbages. Demand increased geometrically. Retailers were giving the dolls away as premiums. At the height of the Christmas shopping season, demand exceeded supply.

Merchants ordered shipments via next-day service. Cabbage Patch Kids Adoption Center displays were set up at prime locations in stores. The displays consisted of a sign announcing the Adoption, some helium-filled balloons to signal the location, and shelves of the dolls. Quite simple, but effective.

Girls and their parents mobbed the adoption sites to get their very own doll and authentic adoption certificate to show to their friends. Stores ran short of supplies. The "Cabbage Patch Panic" began. Kids (and parents) fought each other to get the last dolls on shelves. Mothers and daughters flew from store to store, mall to mall to find the quickly disappearing doll. Scalpers sold the dolls for exorbitant prices. The Cabbage Patch frenzy was updated every night on local TV stations around the country.

After a while, supplies returned and the craze simmered down. Then, during the 1984 Christmas season, the mad rush to obtain the Kids occurred again. Only this time, copycat manufacturers flooded stores with imitations that undersold Cabbage Patch Kids. The young consumers were too wise; they ignored emulators and fought like banshees for their Cabbage Patch Kids.

Coleco scored a major hit with the Kids. It was the number one selling big doll. Coleco realized an amazing return on their investment. How amazing? They spent just $500,000 on the entire campaign in 1983! A simple adoption promotion skyrocketed into the publicity coup of the 1980s. Kids said, "Build the dolls, and we will come." Apparently so, because sales finally leveled off at $600 million in 1985—and that's a lot of cabbage!

And it's not over yet for the Cabbage Patch Kids. Fitzgerald (1990b: 10) reported that giant Hasbro (who bought the Kids from Coleco in 1989) revived the doll and expect to milk at least another $100 million in sales from this cash cow. Let's see, if one of the kids could be adopted by Barbie, then we'd witness the cross promotion of the century. According to Miller (1989: 10), $450 million was spent on Barbie in 1988 and nine out of ten girls own at least one. But a Barbie/Cabbage Patch Kid joint promotion would require cooperation from rivals Hasbro and Mattel. Nah, couldn't happen. Or could it? A promotional feat lies in wait there somewhere.

PUBLICITY IS BACK

Public relations, which used to be called *publicity* and was at one time *the* way to build brand image, has been downgraded to "marketing's stepchild" (Merims 1972) and has become the least used of all marketing communication tools. But public relations (getting positive media coverage and developing a squeaky-clean positive company image) is bouncing back. Although most press releases are routinely ignored by editors, publicity stunts (pardon me, promotional feats), if properly planned and executed, must be noticed. In 1988, the Department of Commerce predicted a 20 percent rise in PR. I believe we are seeing this prediction come true.

It is time for publicity to take its rightful place beside its siblings in the marketing communications mix. Alone or in concert with its fellow promotion tools, publicity will be used to build brand image and encourage immediate purchase. Let me show you examples of building (or saving) image and stimulating sales.

The Return of the PR Man

We are beginning to see the resurrection of the once extinct "PR Man" (and woman). To whom does a beleaguered Donald Trump turn to fix up his image? Or hotelier Leona Helmsley? Or Victor Kiam, the Remington shaver icon and owner of the New England Patriots, whose team sexually harassed reporter Lisa Olson in their locker room after a football game in 1990? They all turn to the dean of damage control—Howard J. Rubenstein.

In the case of Kiam, Rubenstein set up a public apology to Olson by Kiam. Then, according to Hammer (1990: 54), Rubenstein sent out a print ad in which Kiam admitted "no excuse" for his players, but said, "I never called Lisa Olson a b---h," and signed his name under it.

Not only public figures can benefit from image enhancement by PR professionals. Companies can as well. Perrier and Koala Springs mineral water corporations were both blasted by benzene contamination and had to remove product from stores. They both could have used some professional PR help to bring back their "pure" images. Exxon and chemical companies who suffer from image problems due to leaks, spills, and other mishaps should seek out a Rubenstein. Leona Helmsley got her money's worth from Rubenstein—the "Queen of Mean" received 10,000 fan letters after Rubenstein helped her.

Get Your Earthship Now (Before It's Too Late)

Of course, you can stand in as your own PR man if you own a small business. Michael Reynolds, who hails from Taos, New Mexico, constructs unique houses—they're made with tires and cans retrieved from the dump. He's figured out a way to make self-sustaining houses that can be built by anyone for a pittance. No joke.

Reynolds represents his construction company, Solar Survival Architecture, as the icon for the movement toward inexpensive homes that free owners from depending upon the power grid and natural gas. (See chapter 7 for more company icons.) He gives talks about his product, homes called "Earthships." His talks proclaim his message about independent living through ecologically sound housing.

He receives lots of positive publicity in Taos. The local papers feature articles about him, his book (Reynolds 1990), his planet-saving homes, and his planned Rural Earthship Alternative Community Habitat (REACH).

Actor and Great Western Bank spokesman Dennis Weaver had a beautiful Earthship built for him. Now Keith Carradine wants an Earthship. Perhaps a Cabbage Patch Craze will develop if enough stars purchase these homes. The publicity certainly helps Reynolds get the word out.

In fact, the Cousteau Society's magazine, *The Calypso Log*, ran a five-page feature on Reynolds and his homes (Knipe 1990), and thoughtfully included Reynolds' address.

Many Cousteau Society readers contacted Reynolds and he was deluged with mail requesting more information. His company responds to queries with newspaper articles about him and an Earthship information sheet which includes an order form for his $25 book and $300 seminars. If a person purchases a book, an order form insert offers detailed Earthship construction drawings for $350 to $500.

Reynolds' low-key promotional efforts fill seminars and sell a lot of books, a substantial number of construction plans, and an occasional home. Clearly, Reynolds' good product coupled with his promotional feats are making his business quite successful. Reynolds relies on word-of-mouth advertising to sell his products and services; with each bit of exposure he receives, a new network of advertising is created. In time, most everyone will have heard of and want to know more about his Earthships. His steady and ever-increasing use of publicity is paying off. But wait, there's more.

In the *Calypso Log* article, the author recounts how Reynolds once tested the structural soundness of one of his Earthships by driving a filled cement mixer up one of the sloped walls. Knipe (p. 16) reported that "The exposed tires did not even compress under the weight."

Too bad Reynolds didn't get the *60 Minutes* film crew to verify the stunt and broadcast the feat to the world. If that had happened, undoubtedly Reynolds would have appeared as one of Johnny Carson's guests the next night. As it is, Reynolds is enjoying plenty of business drummed up by his publicity efforts.

Volvo is Crushed

There's nothing like driving a cement mixer on your house to prove how tough it is. That's just what Volvo must have thought. In a 1990 print and TV ad, we saw a monster truck called Bear Foot drive over a line of cars, including a Volvo sedan. As we might expect from "a car you can believe in," the Volvo was the only car left that didn't crush in.

Unfortunately for Volvo, the word leaked out that the demonstration was rigged (Serafin and Levin 1990). Essentially, the other autos' pillars had been cut and the Volvo (actually, three Volvos) had been reinforced. After being caught red-handed, Volvo said "no foul intended" and immediately ran corrective ads that claimed that Volvo's actions were for "safety." Now there's "an ad you can believe in."

But Volvo really made headlines (front page of *USA Today*) when the United States Hot Rod Association announced it would rerun the publicity stunt—right over the Volvos. This time, the Volvos would not be reinforced. Elliott (1990: 1) reported that the USHRA would run the monster trucks over Volvos at a couple of its sanctioned events.

According to Loro (1990: 77), the Volvos held up pretty well at the monster truck exhibition in Philadelphia. Three monster trucks had to run over five old Volvos several times to crunch in the cars. All in all, the Volvo automobiles held up under pressure. Volvo serendipitously ended up with some good publicity because their cars really are strong.

The Wave of the Feature

Volvo may be wise to enlist the crisis management services of Mr. Rubenstein. If they plan another stunt, they should try to make it a promotional feat. Perhaps Volvo should employ Wave Promotions of Washington, D.C. to demonstrate their cars in a street stunt.

Wave Promotions specializes in ambush sampling and other guerrilla marketing techniques to get a product out to potential consumers. *Ambush sampling* entails employing a squad of gaudily dressed free-sample distributors who leap out of vans and give everyone samples of the current product in a very noticeable way.

According to Miller (1990: 2), Wave's ambush sampling tactics work. Stolichnaya Vodka experienced a sales increase of 20 percent after using Wave. Bacardi Breezers retained Wave in 1989 and rose from forty-ninth in distilled spirit sales to sixth by 1990. Here is a description of one of Wave's best promotional feats.

Have you heard of Smartfood, the natural popcorn? Wave worked for the popcorn maker distributing samples about town. But Wave didn't use the common supermarket demonstration booth. They put together a SWAT team (Smartfood Whacky-Attacky Team) consisting of a bunch of college students dressed in Smartfood popcorn packets that were bigger than a doorway. The costumed students stormed through parks and malls and distributed samples to everyone, then vanished into thin air.

Miller describes the activities that Wave committed for Smartfood:

> The company pulled just about every stunt in the book: human billboards frolicking on overpasses, a bike and billboard brigade that appears at parks and special events and windsurfers landing on the beach to hand out Smartfood samples (p. 5).

Smartfood has a troupe of Comedy Cruisers complete with jugglers and fire-eaters to attract a crowd. It seems as if ambush marketing is here to stay.

Smartfood has now gone in-house with its wacky promotions since being bought by Frito-Lay. The parent company encourages Smartfood's shenanigans, and they keep on a-comin'.

In 1990, Smartfood put a coupon on a billboard for $500 off a purchase of Smartfood popcorn. The billboard featured a picture of the Smartfood popcorn bag and this headline surrounded by coupon border: "Bring this to your grocery and save big on Smartfood."

Sure enough, the temptation was too great for a spunky shopper named Diane Sullivan who climbed the billboard and clipped the giant coupon, then redeemed it at a local store. The store people didn't know what to do, so they called Smartfood. Before you knew it, Ken Meyers, president of Smartfood, gave Sullivan $500 worth of popcorn for her herculean effort. The stunt was a big success. If you want to know how big, read page 5 of the October 16, 1990 *National Enquirer* (Mullins) and find out. Every food company could use this kind of free advertising.

Make Your Big Event a Promotional Feat

Crazy but crowd-pleasing publicity stunts garner positive product awareness *and* encourage immediate purchase. I believe we'll see more marketing stunts in the future. To make them work, carefully plan them, just as you would an advertising or typical promotional campaign. Think: what do political candidates do to get media attention? They stage an event. Your products deserve an event in their honor, don't you think?

Some advertisers worry that publicity is neither controllable nor measurable. But as a marketing researcher, I totally disagree. Like any field experiment, conditions can be controlled, manipulated, and monitored. And the results can be measured in two ways. First, by counting articles or column inches and determining the exposure rate by looking at circulation figures, or by counting seconds of air time on radio and TV. Second, by looking at sales figures after the promotional stunt. One could even resort to conducting an awareness/intention pretest before the stunt, and then administering a posttest to calculate the percentage of change after the promotional feat.

The point is that publicity, tied in with other promotional mix variables, is what is needed to cut through the mountains of clutter that consumers ignore. Good publicity will compel consumers to seek you out. Be creative, think up your own promotional feat, then call in the media!

7

Company Icons

"Nobody survives in the business world who isn't selling."
—Malcolm Forbes

MARKETING IS SELLING! This is the marketer's oldest trade secret. Just ask David Ogilvy, Ed McMahon, or Malcolm Forbes. We know that selling, the oldest form of marketing, has been around since the Bronze Age. Mercury, the cunning god of communication, was established by the Romans as the icon of merchants and traders.

Commodity bartering and selling has occurred all over the world throughout recorded history. In the United States, peddlers traveled about in wagons selling spices, wares, and cure-all remedies of dubious quality. These Yankee peddlers migrated west and sold settlers ammunition, precision instruments (e.g., clocks), and furniture. They traded with frontiersmen and native Americans, and thus were able to sell furs back east and earn profit everywhere they went.

As America expanded, the traveling sales force grew in proportion. In 1850, there were fewer than a thousand traveling salesmen; 50 years later there were nearly 100,000. Nowadays, hundreds of thousands of people engage in the art of selling. Whereas advertising, promotions, and publicity all pull the consumer to the product or service, modern sales people still push products from manufacturer to consumer.

Personal selling takes many forms. We have order-takers, who answer telephones, deliver ordered goods, or ring up sales in stores. These "salespeople" rarely achieve promotional feat status, since their jobs are

passive and functionary by nature. They do not make the news or typically reap huge profits for their companies.

The other form of salesperson is active by nature. These people we
call order-getters, who solicit by telephone, traveling, or in-store contact.
These people can achieve promotional feat status because they have the
potential to earn big money for their companies, although most will not
make the news.

David Ogilvy spent his formative years as a door-to-door salesman—
an order-getter. It was there he learned that the primary business of all
marketers was selling. He carried the "selling is everything" philosophy
with him when he entered the advertising profession. Because active
selling is an integral part of all business in one way or another, we will
take a look at what it takes to be a super sales agent who earns extraordinary profit for his or her company.

Then we'll join Ed McMahon and other famous celebrity spokespersons who not only earn big profits for the organizations they represent
but make headlines as well. Finally, we'll explore the promotional feats
of chief executives such as Malcolm Forbes, who publicly represent their
companies as top salespersons, as company icons.

SUPER SALES AGENTS

Personal selling may be America's number one promotional activity.
According to Futrell (1989: 7), "American firms spend over $100 billion
on their salespeople, which equals the amount spent on sales promotion
and advertising."

Over 10 million people are employed in the sales profession. The need
for sales professionals will increase in the 1990s. Experienced sales agents
earn over $40,000 per year. We can see that selling is very important
and that good salespeople are the lifeblood of successful sales operations.
But what makes an ordinary salesperson a super sales agent?

First, super sales agents have already mastered the basics of selling.
They know their own and their competition's products and services,
their customers, and the market in general. They understand people
and are experts in listening, expressing, and persuading. They are pro-
ficient in the steps involved in all selling: prospecting, planning the sales
call, approaching, presenting, meeting objections, closing, and offering
follow-up support and service.

Additionally, super sales agents possess certain traits that aid in their
selling success. They possess a lot of energy, love people and selling,
have a high need to achieve, are optimistic and persistent, believe in
themselves and their product, are good at analyzing and problem-solv-
ing, are willing to take calculated risks, manage time wisely, mentally
rehearse, and are adaptive and creative. These people also possess per-

sonal integrity, unlike the stereotypical slick con artist that salespeople are often compared to.

Finally, super sales agents are savvy. They are courteous, respect customers' traditions and values, dress and groom appropriately, are punctual and reliable, and are interpersonally competent.

I would add one more thing to the list of super sales agent qualities. This person understands and helps coordinate the entire marketing communications mix. This person knows and fosters the corporate culture and mission. All IBM salespeople wear white shirts, not just to make everyone uniform, but to consistently communicate professionalism across the workforce. Army Green Berets wear the green beret to build esprit de corps and communicate to others that they are an effective, elite unit.

Super sales agents and managers understand their part in the push-pull promotion strategy of a business or business unit. By comprehending and furthering the strategy of the whole company, not just their unit, salespeople transcend the trained monkey role that so many people in modern organizations assume without a second thought. In short, super sales agents follow the company line but also empower themselves to lead. On this note, let's look at leaders in the sales field—leaders who have achieved promotional feat status.

Joe Gandolfo and Friends

Sales agents who make many more sales and thus more money than their compatriots are automatically placed in the Personal Selling Promotional Feats Hall of Fame, assuming their sales successes were directly attributed to their efforts and the costs associated with each close were reasonable.

One salesman who qualifies for admission is Joe Gandolfo, the wizard of insurance sales, who works for John Hancock Mutual Life Insurance Corporation. Futrell (1989: 42) reports that Gandolfo has allegedly sold more life insurance than anyone else. He averages over $800 million per year; he sold $1 billion in 1975. Gandolfo, who knows the insurance underwriting business thoroughly, claims that 98 percent of his success is due to understanding human beings. That makes sense, Joe, and underscores the greatest strength of personal selling—direct contact with buyers.

Another Hall of Famer is Vikki Morrison, who is a real estate agent for FirstTeam Walk-In Realty in Huntington Beach, California. Futrell (p. 155) reported that Morrison sold $48 million of real estate between 1981 and 1985. One of her secrets: extensive prospecting. Morrison knocks on four hundred doors a month. Who says personal selling doesn't have the reach of advertising?

Network marketers can achieve the Hall of Fame if they work hard. We often hear of Amway and other multilevel distributors making big bucks. Futrell (p. 409) described the sales success of a Tupperware team from St. Louis, the Fingerhuts. They began by hosting two Tupperware parties a week. A few years later they were ranked number four in all-time sales for Tupperware and managed a sales force of 50 managers and 480 dealers. They close $4 million in sales a year for Tupperware. They made it big through effective time and territory management.

See Zig Ziglar at the Top

Clearly, the Sales Hall of Famers succeeded for more than one reason. They did everything right. More than likely their sales achievements were due to inherent factors combined with learning. That is, these super sellers were made *and* born. In a survey of sales and marketing professionals ($n = 10,000$), 85 percent felt that effective sales personnel were *made* (Bragg 1988). This means that salespeople can definitely be trained to sell effectively.

Zig Ziglar, spokesman for sales champions, would agree. Ziglar, author of the "sensational nationwide bestseller" entitled *Zig Ziglar's Secrets of Closing the Sale* (1984), is quite the consummate champeen seller. Mary Kay Ash, founder and president of Mary Kay Cosmetics, said that Ziglar "will undoubtedly go down in history as the number one salesman of our time." He has sold countless audio and video programs on persuasion. Before he achieved fame as a motivational writer and speaker, he was a highly successful salesman of many products and services—from cookware to insurance to sales-training. He spent 18 years in the real world of direct selling.

From his experience and the eclectic wisdom of others, Ziglar presents scintillating bits of solid advice for potential sales champions in his book. Here are a few of Zig's more useful sayings for all of us in the marketing profession to ponder.

"People buy what they want when they want it more than they want the money it costs."

"When you convince the prospect that your product scratches where he itches, he will buy. When you make him *itch* for ownership, he will *scratch* around until he comes up with the money."

"I'm personally convinced our divorce rate would be reduced 90 percent if men and women *delivered* in marriage what they *sold* while courting. I'm also convinced *your* sales career will be even more rewarding if you deliver what you sell."

"I'm convinced that many sales are missed not because of poor technique but because of *no* technique. *Ask for the order.*"

And here's my favorite Ziglar response to a prospect who complains that the price is too high. "I don't think there's any question about the price being high, Mr. Prospect, but when you add the benefits of quality, subtract the disappointments of cheapness, multiply the pleasure of buying something good, and divide the cost over a period of time, the arithmetic comes out in your favor."

Ziglar was not the first super salesman to disseminate words of wisdom to potential sales winners. Dale Carnegie, the original sales trainer, wrote the highly motivating best-selling book *How to Win Friends and Influence People*. Ever hear of it? Of course you have. Dale Carnegie sales seminars remain one of the most popular in the land.

In addition to Ziglar's and Carnegie's books, I count twenty-eight other super sales or related books by past or present sales champions. There are also about twelve selling texts available today. Finally, there seems to be an abundance of inspirational "you can do it" books in bookstores and libraries by famous authors, speakers, and sales mentors such as Norman Vincent Peale, Robert Schuller, and Napoleon Hill. These three people have championed the cause of interpersonal persuasion, which may be less efficient than mass communication but is more effective.

Dr. Chester L. Karrass may be the sales guru for the 1990s. His seminar, "Effective Negotiating," is offered over a hundred times a year in over sixty cities at a cost of around $600 per participant. The Karrass organization conducts training seminars with nine of the top fifteen American companies. As of 1991, over 400,000 people have attended his company's seminars. Karrass is a super salesman who teaches others how to be super sellers. His success, like that of Ziglar, Carnegie, and other selling sages places him in the Sales Hall of Fame.

CELEBRITY SELLERS

Often, companies use celebrities in advertising to represent their image. Usually, they choose celebrities with high credibility (e.g., John Houseman for Smith Barney), likability (Bill Cosby for Jello), or just plain star appeal (Michael Jackson and Michael J. Fox for Pepsi).

These celebrities act as spokespersons for a product with varying degrees of success. Houseman and Cosby represent two very successful company spokespeople. But in both cases, they have been overexposed—that is they have been used for too many different products, thereby losing some of their effectiveness. I related to Houseman when he told us that Smith Barney "makes money the old-fashioned way—

we earn it," but thought his credibility was wasted on McDonald's burg-
ers. Lovable comedian Cosby was perfect for Jello and Coke but unbe-
lievable as a spokesman for E. F. Hutton.

The Best Athlete

Back in Chapter 3 we asked who was the greatest athlete. The public
is fickle on this point. If we judged by endorsements, basketball star
Michael Jordan might take the cake. As Nike's "Air Jordan" icon, he
earned $4 million a year in the late 1980s. He was later joined by Bo
Jackson. That we know.

In Chapter 3 I said that Joe Montana was reported to be the greatest
athlete ever by 290 San Francisco Bay area college students. Of course,
this was the day after the Super Bowl in 1990. Joe has been a slow starter
in the endorsement world but he is rapidly picking up steam. He now
endorses Pepsi, Power Burst, L. A. Gear, Genesis, and other fine products.

Not just the best athletes serve as celebrity spokespeople. William
"Refrigerator" Perry rocketed to fame in 1985 when he switched from
350-pound tackle to bullish running back to score a touchdown for the
Bears. He then scored really big with some $2 million in endorsements.
But his fame and celebrity athlete status were meteoric. Soon, he was
back on the line—just another major appliance.

I Must Be in the Front Row

Sometimes the worst athletes successfully serve as celebrity spokespersons. Take the case of mediocre baseball catcher Bob Uecker. Somehow, he parlayed his ho-hum baseball career into Has-Been Hall of Fame
with his hilarious hijinks for Miller Lite. His success with Miller helped
him secure other endorsement contracts. Then he wrote a successful
book about his unsuccessful career. Finally, he landed a spot on a TV
sitcom. If this guy gets anymore "unsuccessful," he'll end up one of the
richest celebrity athletes in America. We could all use that kind of dis-
appointment.

There's plenty of room for athletes good and bad to endorse products.
My ocean adventure kayaking team, the Tsunami Rangers, are available
real cheap for celebrity endorsements. We'd like to endorse Old Crow
whiskey or Blackjack cigars. Would you believe Beeman's gum?

America's Most Celebrated Pilot

Back in Chapter 3 we discussed adventurers such as Mountain Man
Messner, a big celebrity endorser in Europe. In Chapter 2 we described

achievements of aviators who broke world records. Probably the only pilot alive today to attain and maintain celebrity status is Chuck Yeager. Once again, what is he famous for?

If you answered he's famous for AC-Delco auto parts you are correct. He's also featured in Rolex watch print ads, where they discuss his aviation exploits and dub him "America's Most Celebrated Pilot." As with celebrity athletes, there is untapped opportunity for companies to use adventurers as spokespersons. These people are promotional feats waiting to happen—and at a good price!

He-e-e-ere's Ed McMahon!

Some entertainers do more than entertain and then appear in ads as spokesperson. They actually sell. Art Linkletter is an example. But who's the greatest celebrity super sales agent of all time? It's hard to say, but Ed McMahon, Johnny Carson's sidekick, is certainly one of the contenders.

McMahon began his selling career at sixteen as a bingo caller for a migrating carnival. Later he sold pens, pots, and pans. He's been selling for 50 years. Because of his selling experience and TV fame, he's a perfect candidate to hawk all kinds of merchandise on TV and radio—and that's just what he does.

Ed has been so successful that he wrote a super-selling "how-to" book called—you guessed it—*Ed McMahon's Superselling* (1989). Being an entertainer, what unique advice does McMahon give that Ziglar and other supersellers don't? He says that selling is a lot like entertainment. "There's no better route to sales success," he claims, "than incorporating Johnny Carson's performance techniques into your basic methods" (p. xiii).

McMahon claims that selling is acting—creating illusion. He notes: "One business that's a lot like show business is sales. Selling is acting, pure and simple, and the more showmanship you put into your salesmanship, the more money you'll make" (p. 2).

I agree with McMahon. An effective sales agent is an excellent performer—an entertainer. The celebrity athletes I discussed are all good performers, both on the field and on camera. Tennis pro Ivan Lendl may be too tight-lipped to sell, but John McEnroe is a ham and Andre Agassi makes big bucks with the revelation, "Image is everything." Image is not everything, but these examples show that the common salesperson and celebrity spokesperson must both entertain when promoting products.

The Party Animal

Some companies choose to use animals as entertaining (maybe even persuasive) "celebrities." Some animals are real, others are cartoons. Morris the Cat is real; Garfield the Cat is not. Some animals portray themselves while others play characters. Budweiser Clydesdales and the Merrill Lynch bull are real animals acting like themselves who represent the spirit of their brands. Tony the Tiger and Spuds McKenzie, cartoon and real animal, respectively, both play characters. They represent the anthropomorphic personality of their brands.

Without a doubt, Tony the Tiger is Gr-r-r-eat! Everyone knows Tony. Everyone also knows Spuds, that sexy, fun-loving guy of a dog (who's really a b---h).

Spuds is the official spokesanimal for Bud Light and made his first appearance during the 1987 Super Bowl. Since then he's either starred in or played cameo roles in numerous Bud Light commercials. When his gender was questioned, Spuds received a great deal of publicity (as any star would). He's been on TV, he's made the tabloids, he's been merchandised, he's been accused of being a bad influence. Truly, Spuds is an American legend.

Spuds was not the first TV dog, and he won't be the last. But he is one of the most famous brand icons to be an animal. Using animals as symbols is an interesting way to capture consumers' attention. Famous people and animals attract us. We go out of our way to watch them. If we identify the celebrity personality with the brand, that's effective. The use of Spuds McKenzie as icon for Bud Light is a promotional feat.

CHIEF EXECUTIVES AS SALES REPS

The founder or president of a company is symbolically very crucial to consumers' perceptions of a company and what it stands for. Military, political, and expedition leaders understand the importance of playing a role so their compatriots not only follow them but honor them as well. As we saw in Chapter 2, Alexander the Great, Cortez, Lawrence of Arabia, and Chief Joseph all displayed a charismatic persona that captivated the hearts and minds of their people.

If marketing is war, then put your great general in front of the troops, not just to beat the competition but to symbolize what your country stands for. A nation's leader is the figurehead, the icon of the country. A company's leader is also an icon—an image or figure that represents the spirit, personality, and integrity of a brand.

Some leaders of American companies—and of America—have achieved promotional feat status by authentically representing themselves and their companies; each serves as the number one salesperson for the organization.

The rest of this chapter is devoted to company icons, those individuals who spearhead their organization's image campaign to win the elusive prize of consumer loyalty. We begin our discussion of the promotional feats of these Free Enterprise Heroes by highlighting the career of the Icon of America, the father of American advertising, diplomat, patriot, inventor, philanthropist, free thinker, civic leader, printer, writer, editor, and face on the $100 bill—Benjamin Franklin.

Ben Franklin—Icon of America

I chose Ben Franklin as America's icon because he epitomizes what people can become in this country if they put their minds, hearts, and sweat behind it. Franklin died at eighty-four in 1790. He lived a full life the true American way. Here's his inspirational story.

He grew up dirt poor and became an apprentice to his brother at twelve. His abusive older brother taught him the printing trade. Everything else Ben learned on his own. He never attended a university because he couldn't afford it. State colleges and scholarships were unheard of in the colonies. By age twenty-one, Franklin had just mastered the trade of printer and was flat broke. But he was ready to devote a lifetime to hard work to get done what must be done.

In contrast, many affluent Americans today are still mooching off their parents by age twenty-one. They're graduating from the best colleges and are looking for the easiest way to make megabucks. Some even consider crooks such as Ivan Boesky and Michael Milken to be heroes.

We know that Franklin must have been a genius. He discovered the Gulf Stream and principles of electricity. He invented bifocals and the Franklin stove (which he never patented). He invented a musical instrument that Mozart and Beethoven wrote music for and played the harp, guitar, and violin. As a swimmer, he could not be beaten (except by Tarzan and every twelve-year-old swimmer in America today).

He made a modest fortune as printer, writer, editor, and publisher. He drew America's first political cartoon. He designed the first mail-order catalog. And, according to two best-selling marketing texts (Kotler & Armstrong 1990; Evans & Berman 1990), Franklin is a major historical figure in American marketing and advertising.

Franklin was very civic-minded. The first militia and subscription library in America were started by Franklin. He organized the nation's first volunteer fire brigade. He was Pennsylvania's first governor, America's first postmaster general, and the diplomat responsible for enlisting France's military support during the American Revolution. He also set up a trust fund for poor people to learn trades (now worth several million

dollars) and established a public university (the University of Pennsylvania).

His detractors claim he was a womanizer, but there is no evidence
that he was unfaithful to his wife. It is not a crime to love all women
and have all women love him. Franklin was a Renaissance man, a prag-
matist, the "philosopher of dissent" (Hall 1975). He is the grandfather
of our nation—an industrious man who solved problems and knew how
to enlist the support of others for his cause.

Franklin accomplished many things. The one thing he did not do was
fly a kite in a thunderstorm, although he did invent the lightning rod.
The year 1990 marked the bicentennial of Franklin's death. When he
died in 1790, 20,000 people (the most ever assembled in America at that
time) attended his funeral in Philadelphia. That was his final promotional
feat.

But Franklin-based promotional feats still happen in America, especially in Philadelphia, where he is regarded as a patron saint. Michael
Kilian (1990) detailed all the two-hundredth-anniversary celebrations
Philadelphia planned in Franklin's honor. The city already features the
Benjamin Franklin National Memorial to pay tribute to their hero. But
on the anniversary of his death, Franklin scholars from around the world
reappraised the scholarship of the great man, and all sorts of celebrations, music festivals, and parades were held in his honor—for a year!
Now that's a long-lived promotional feat.

His legacy lives on in over thirty cities and towns which bear his name
in the United States. His trust fund for the poor still thrives. Articles
are still written about him (e.g., Lord 1990: "The Truths and Myths
About Ben Franklin"). Successful companies are named after him (e.g.,
the Franklin Mint and the $43 billion Franklin Group of Funds).

Franklin is also famous for his clever sayings. One of his sayings
appropriate for us in business is: "Keep thy shop, and thy shop will
keep thee." One that best captures the independent spirit that beats in
the hearts of free Americans is: "Our cause is the cause of all mankind."

Some critics of Franklin charge that he was able to accomplish so much
because he lived in a frontier country with lots of problems and opportunities. This is true, but the world has as many or more opportunities
and problems than it did two hundred years ago. Why, in just the San
Francisco Bay area alone we face major problems such as AIDS, homelessness, earthquakes, other natural and manmade disasters, traffic
congestion, substance abuse, illiteracy, drought, violence, and more.

If Franklin were here today, he might grapple with these problems
and turn them into opportunities to serve his fellow humans. He'd
probably do it like this. Say the problem was illiteracy (common in the
1700s as it is today). He'd debate the issues with a philosophical group
of folks such as his Junto club. In a Socratic fashion, he'd listen and help

fellow thinkers discard chaff and identify wheat. Then, in a series of articles and cartoons, he'd let the public know about it, both in his own publications and in others. He'd advertise and use direct mail to ensure that everyone got informative and persuasive missives. His published (and nowadays, broadcast) messages would not only elucidate the problem, but would detail the fair, far-reaching, and fiscally sound solution that avoided pork barrelism yet encouraged civic involvement (with monetary penalties for abstainers).

To make sure his plan worked, he's probably think up some new invention or a novel way to encourage reading (like sponsoring a mobile subscription library or a university with free tuition for poor people). He'd let anyone interested in helping use his patents and the problem would be solved. It would probably make money and go down in the history books—as a promotional feat!

Why can't we come up with innovative ways to solve our country's problems and take advantage of opportunities, communicate our ideas to the proper publics in an effective yet efficient way, make a profit to boot, and then brag about it? We can. Our next icon, Malcolm Forbes, did it and had fun in the process.

Malcolm Forbes—Lived While Alive

Whereas many Americans fail to live up to Franklin's standards of industry and independence, some live life to the fullest, make an honest fortune, and contribute to the common good. One of those people was Malcolm Forbes.

The late Malcolm S. Forbes, icon for *Forbes* magazine, lived for 70 years then died—in the headlines, as usual. *Advertising Age* gave him a full-page photo memorial and his magazine featured a commemorative portrait of him on its cover after his death.

A great chief executive, Forbes devoted his life to promoting American business and focusing on chief executives (company icons) in his magazine. An annual *Forbes* feature was the "Executive Compensation Survey" issue in which hundreds of top executives' pay, performance, and personalities were highlighted. Forbes was himself a company icon and the advocate of other company icons—hence, the magazine's focus is always on the top person. His son wrote "the chief executive officer makes or breaks a company" (Forbes 1990: 19).

He was a big advocate of the capitalist system, and told everyone about it. His corporate jet, "Capitalist Tool," was a perfect photo-op backdrop for the flamboyant Forbes. His balloon (he was also a world-class balloonist) had his name emblazoned on it and managed to make it into the media on more than one occasion. His balloon/motorcycle trip to China in 1985 not only made headlines but was the subject of a PBS documentary.

Although Forbes inherited his money and magazine, he never rested on his laurels. According to James Michaels (1990: 116), who Forbes hired in 1954, Forbes was fond of making fun of his success. A favorite Forbes quip: "I owe my commanding position at the magazine to sheer ability, spelled i-n-h-e-r-i-t-a-n-c-e."

Forbes did lead an interesting life, one that Franklin would have wished to live. As an Army machine-gunner in WWII, he was severely wounded and spent years recovering. He was a cancer victor. He almost died trying to cross the Atlantic in a balloon and suffered a few motor-cycle wrecks. Some of his initial publishing ventures were flops, as was his bid for governor of New Jersey in 1957. "I was nosed out by a landslide," he commented.

Forbes was undaunted by failure or human shortcomings. He liked to have fun. In 1976, he posed for a print ad for Harley-Davidson and was a regular at the summer motorcyclists' celebration in Sturgess, South Dakota. He was a regulation socialite. His big seventieth birthday bash in Tangier cost him $2 million, and he didn't write off a penny of it. Gossip columnist Liz Smith (1989: E1), described Forbes' unrepentant attitude about the glitzy party. He figured the $2 million was well-spent and gave his magazine $100 million of TV and press coverage.

He hung out with Liz Taylor (Ben Franklin would have approved), and this made the tabloids for months. Like Ben, Malcolm never worried about his detractors; he was too busy making honest money. As *Forbes* publisher Caspar Weinberger wrote: "The things that impressed me most were his kindness, his consideration for others, his unfailing po-liteness and his genuine love of people" (1990: 37).

Forbes was a kind and fun-loving man with excellent business acu-men. He successfully combined his skill in business with his flair for the spotlight. Wherever Malcolm went, a promotional feat was sure to follow.

Captain Outrageous

Forbes is not the only media kingpin to make headlines. CNN's "Ter-rible Ted" Turner also knows how to turn his every move in business into a promotional feat. Ted Turner's story is simply amazing. He lives not just the American dream, but the world vision. He wouldn't run for President when he can help the whole planet by masterminding the Communication Age.

He worked for his father's billboard company in Georgia for a while after college. But his career and fortune didn't blossom until he bought Channel 17 in Atlanta back in 1970. Then came his TBS Superstation in

1976. In 1980, his top-rated news station CNN was born. In 1990, he merrily celebrated CNN's tenth anniversary with actress Jane Fonda on his arm and his success heralded across the land in every news source, including a four-page spread in *Newsweek* (Alter 1990).

The 1977 America's Cup winner worked hard to compete against the established networks, and succeeded—no, superseded—the Big Three. He was belittled by the press during his hard years when he was hundreds of millions in the hole. Typical magazine headlines read, "Turner's Windless Sails" (Powell, et al. 1987), "A $1.6-Billion Credibility Gap" (Flanagan 1987), and "TV's Boldest Gambler Bets the Plantation" (Sherman 1987).

The press was also kind to Turner. When he started turning a hefty profit in 1989, the media were his fine-feathered friends again. He made the cover of *Business Week* with a feature story on him aptly titled "Captain Comeback" (Ticer, et al. 1989).

But even the bad press was good news for Ted Turner; he seemed to crave adversity. He made and lost all kinds of deals. The bottom line: Ted Turner and his quiver of TV stations are profitable, powerful, and here to stay. Carman (1990: 3) reported that CNN and Headline News "are valued at more than $1.5 billion. There are 1,700 employees and 23 news bureaus, 14 of them abroad. CNN is on 9,400 cable systems, reaching 54 million American households." Impressive.

Here are some more figures. Melissa Turner (no relation) noted that TNT (Turner Network Television) "was the biggest launch in basic cable history, reaching 17 million homes. Now only 17 months old, TNT has more than doubled its reach to 41 million homes" (1990: 1). Apparently, everyone wants to watch old, sometimes colorized, movies.

His cable network stations (TBS, TNT, Headline News, and CNN) made so much money that in 1989 their combined profits beat out CBS and ABC (Whittemore 1990: 11).

Turner has received more press than any other media mogul over the past ten years. One of the reasons? His stations reach just about every person in the world who has access to TV. To Turner, the world is truly a global village. He has used his influence to help sponsor (and of course broadcast) the Goodwill Games. He's donated over a million dollars for projects that help the world and was a leader in making "environment" documentaries.

Ted loves the press he receives from his wild and controversial business and humanitarian moves. He went duck hunting with Fidel Castro back in 1982. When Woody Allen said he didn't like the colorizing of old movies, Ted told him and other critics "to turn the color knob down."

Turner shared the media business and media spotlight with Forbes. He is an unofficial statesman when he speaks out on and tries to solve world problems, just like Benjamin Franklin. Who knows, maybe Ted

Turner will be drafted as President, although he'd probably prefer the title Ambassador to the World. See his coronation soon on your local cable station!

Lee Iacocca—King of the Road

Industrialists have been key figures in shaping America's economy, values, and image. Andrew Carnegie created the modern U.S. steel industry. His achievements made the Industrial Age flower and opened the door for machinist-turned-auto-magnate Henry Ford, who made a car in every garage a reality for Americans, thanks to his assembly line.

Fortune magazine polled CEOs and found that their choice of the most effective leader was Ford Motor Company's Donald E. Petersen (see Ballon 1988). But if you were to ask the American people who's number one, Chrysler's Lee Iacocca would win hands down. Iacocca, of all CEOs, took best advantage of a trend that began in the 1980s of consumers admiring the risk-taking individualism of "executive celebrities" like Iacocca and Remington's Victor Kiam (Dobrzynski and Davies 1986).

Iacocca, son of Italian immigrants, was an engineer and salesman for Ford. He helped create the famous Mustang, which sold over 400,000 its first year. (Talk about business successes.) Personality conflicts with some of the top folks at Ford got him fired from his position as president. But he avenged his termination by helping Chrysler rise up from the gutter. He's a decisive, straight-shootin' CEO who pleaded with President Carter for a loan (he got it) and then told union laborers to take a $3 per hour pay cut. (He also got that!) To put his lack of money where his mouth was, he docked his own pay to $1. An hour? Nope, a year!

His leadership in saving Chrysler remains one of the top examples of what corporate generals can do when they put themselves in front of their troops. Alexander the Great would be proud of Lee Iacocca.

Iacocca's real promotional feat status occurred when he began starring in Chrysler TV and print commercials. He asked the American public to try his cars: "If you can find a better car—buy it."

Although he said he was retiring from advertisements because he was worried about overexposure, he's managed to appear in about fifty commercials and is still a strong media figure in 1991.

Iacocca's popularity is not due just to his communication savvy. He chaired both fundraising and fundspending campaigns for refurbishing the Statue of Liberty. Not only did he receive deserved public credit for the fine fix-up, but he got all kinds of sympathetic response from the public for again getting fired (this time because he was too effective as a volunteer chairman for two related projects—next time he'll charge the government a million bucks a day for his executive services).

When he wrote his best-selling autobiography in 1984, he accomplished three things: 1) He donated his royalties to the Joslin Diabetes Center in Boston. 2) He set the record straight about his professional achievements which will serve as examples for young people thinking about a career in big business. 3) And he catapulted off the fame he garnered from his Chrysler ads to position himself as the top icon of American industry.

Iacocca's autobiography sold over 6.5 million copies. He will be happy to note that I waited until it was marked down 25 percent to $14.95 before I bought it. I bought his second book, *Talking Straight*, when it was released in paperback for a mere $5.50.

He talks straight in both books, but is much more pessimistic in the second. He talks about Japan's protectionist trade practices in the first book. In the second book he predicts hard times for the U.S. in the '90s as we face the next century in debt, polarized, with homelessness a growing problem. He fears the banks may fail or war may begin. If we read the news, it looks like both may happen before dawn's light.

In 1990, he wrote an essay in *Newsweek* on the "congenital $3 trillion" national debt and offered a straightforward solution to overspending, a major cause of the debt: "I'd decree passage of an automatic income-tax surcharge that every year would equal the deficit figure." He figured this might make politicians more accountable.

Iacocca is a modern-day Franklin. And like Franklin, he not only recognizes problems, he actively seeks ways to fix them. Franklin never wanted to be President—he probably thought he would be too constrained to effectively act as he thought best. Iacocca probably thinks the same thing about himself, but he may yet be called to the duty.

Iacocca's a popular media figure, an exemplary company icon for Chrysler, and much more. He's a respected modern industrialist, one who is not only mentioned but featured in the top marketing texts (e.g., Evans and Berman 1990; Kotler and Armstrong 1990). No other extant chief executive gets as much press in college textbooks.

Finally, not only is he famous for the Mustang, fifty TV commercials, civic deeds, his written works and speeches, and textbook sidebars, but he and Chrysler were immortalized by the funniest yet most hardhearted judges of all—the political cartoonists. You know you have become a promotional feat maestro when you get humorously lambasted by cartoonists for several years.

And His Dog Spot

There are many big-time corporate icons whose promotional exploits have been discussed in this chapter. Franklin started young and worked until he had freed his country from tyranny and amassed a fortune for the benefit of others. Forbes carried on and expanded his family tradition of fostering commerce. Turner created his own media empire against all odds. Iacocca rescued one of America's Big Three automakers from a shallow and early grave.

Other successful corporate stars know how to play the promotional feat game. Steve Jobs and John Sculley have both bitten the same apple in the computer business. Ray Kroc, Colonel Sanders, Famous Amos, and Dave Thomas exemplify successful company icons in the Eat Food industry.

In this chapter we have described successful salespersons like Zig Ziglar and super pitchmen like Ed McMahon, but who is the local-boy-makes-good who became a super car salesman who is also a great celebrity pitch man who happens to be one of America's foremost company icons? Read on and find out.

He was born one of nine children in Osage County, Oklahoma, where everything was not okay—his family was dirt poor. Cal still had a fun childhood swinging on the local playground bars (also known as oil derricks). He worked all his life, including mastering a paper route back in 1928 at age seven. Like Ben Franklin and many other poor people in the 1930s, Cal never finished high school. He worked for the CCC instead.

He sold his way into the Army Air Corps and became a B–17 pilot without a college education. He flew twenty-nine bomber missions over Germany in the war and was awarded the Distinguished Flying Cross, Air Medal, and the President's Citation. After the war, like many vets before and after him, he returned home and found he had no job, no job skills, and no college education. That meant he couldn't pilot airplanes for the airlines. He tried to go back into the Air Force, but they wanted only college-educated pilots, not the experience that comes with twenty-nine harrowing missions. Chuck Yeager, who also lacked the college education, was lucky he stayed in the service after the war, or he might never have broken the sound barrier.

With no marketable skills, Cal was in a quandary. He sold a car to get money to buy a gas station. The gas station was a flop, but Cal found he could sell a car, then another car, then another—and make a good profit. He started his own little dealership in Corpus Christi and started making good money. In 1948 he bought a Hudson dealership in California and soon became the number one Hudson dealer.

He became a Dodge dealer in the Los Angeles area and quickly zoomed to number one. Eighteen years later (in 1974), Cal became a Ford dealer. He now operates three large dealerships in Anchorage, Seattle, and Long Beach.

Cal then became a Chevrolet dealer in 1982 and now runs three large Chevy dealerships in Sacramento (his headquarters), Cupertino, and Houston. In total, he owns nineteen automobile franchises and realizes sales in excess of $200 million a year—and he's never had a partner or stockholder!

Have you guessed who the celebrity executive is? Yes, It's Cal Worthington and his dog Spot.

Cal is number one sales agent, company icon, and corporate spokesperson who not only appears in TV commercials (the corniest but the best) but writes, directs, and produces them. His commercials usually involve him, a dog named Spot (more on that later), a daring stunt of some kind, a funny jingle, and always, "A better deal."

During the commercials, Cal wears his relaxed Western garb. According to his biographer, Bob Cox (1975), and a good memory of hundreds of his commercials that I have watched with a big smile, Cal's pitch usually goes something like this:

> *Announcer*: "Here's Cal Worthington and his dog Spot."
>
> *Cal*: "If you'll just come on down and let me make you a deal I'll give you this (insert tinny electronic item) for just listening to the deal. We even have free tickets for the kids at (insert fun place for kids). I'll stand on my head to make you a better deal (insert of Cal standing on the wings of a biplane 10,000 feet up as it does a loop). And if that isn't good enough, I'll eat a bug (he smiles). Now you wouldn't want me to do that, would you? (He then rattles off a few of his great deals.) So come on down and make a deal. If you're on the lot, better watch out for old Spot." (He smiles and pets Spot—a lion).
>
> *Jingle*:
>
> "If you're looking for a better set of wheels,
> I will stand upon my head to beat all deals,
> I will stand upon my head until my ears are turning red,
> Go see Cal, Go see Cal, Go see Cal."

This ad jingle has twenty-six verses (at least). Once you've heard it, it is stuck in your mind forever. The jingle, Spot, and Cal's stunts have put him in the news.

Cal's dog Spot is definitely not a dog. Over the years, it's been a gorilla, monkey, various birds, a flea, pig, skunk, llama, iguana, camel, bull, and a raccoon. And of course we can't forget the lion, tiger, and bear, oh my.

His biggest and most difficult "Spot" stunt was with the king of the food chain, Shamu the killer whale. When he filmed his Shamu/Spot spot, he was the only person other than the trainer who had ridden Shamu. I think it would be great if Cal would bring back a montage of some of his best "Spots" and put them in his car ads today. I guarantee people would watch it. I would.

The reason I always watched Cal is I thought he was daring. I wouldn't stand next to a foamy-mouthed gorilla trying to tear my head off and laughingly say what Cal said: "Speak Spot. Well, he doesn't speak much, but when he does, you better pay attention. . . . I can beat or match any deal that guy out in the Valley can offer you, and what's more, my dog can whip his dog" (Cox 1975: 102–103).

I asked what his greatest stunt was and he admitted it was probably the eight loops he did while strapped by his feet to the biplane. Worthington told me, "I did all my own stunts; I never used a stand-in."

My ocean adventure kayaking company and my kayaking stunt team (the Tsunami Rangers) talked Cal into doing a head stand stunt with us for his seventieth birthday. We look forward to the publicity of being seen with Cal.

His TV ads and trustworthington personality make him a TV personality who has been a guest on various talk shows. He's been on Johnny Carson's *Tonight Show* several times and has also appeared on the *Today Show*, *Real People*, *Good Morning America*, *Merv Griffin*, and *Johnny Carson's Greatest Commercials*, among others. Being Johnny's guest certainly is going to give a person and his business excellent publicity, and that's just what Cal got.

He's also been a big promotional hit in print. He's been featured in most newspapers in Los Angeles, Sacramento, and Anchorage. Additionally, he made the *National Enquirer*, no small feat. In short, Cal Worthington's honest, straightforward, country manner combined with his corny but compelling stunts have made him a company icon worthy of emulation by all aspiring salespeople just entering the field.

Cal went from nothing to becoming the most successful auto dealer in history. This can only happen in America. Cal spends a lot of time helping others learn the sales trade. He speaks at colleges, conventions, and to civic groups.

Like Franklin, Forbes, Iacocca, and Turner, he has sound ideas to improve our country. Many folks have tried to get Cal to run for senator or governor, but he refuses to compromise his ideals. Would he run for President if duty called? Nah. He likes the job he has now. "I wouldn't want to take the cut in pay."

I have admired Cal Worthington for 20 years. Two years ago I was asked by my university (Cal State) to participate in a "Faculty Follies" to help raise money for a new faculty lunchroom. Guess what I did. I put on my best business suit, stood on my head on the hood of my car and sang, "If you want to eat some lunch, and you want to eat a bunch, Go see Cal, Go see Cal, Go see Cal." The video presentation of my Cal commercial brought the house down, we got several thousand dollars donated, and now we eat in a new lunchroom.

Cal Worthington's success shows that small businesses can also use the key executive to be the primary public spokesperson for the company, its products, and services. If you don't believe me, or think you can make a better deal, then don't take my word for it, Go see Cal!

8

Designing
Promotional Feats

"Promotion strategy is the art of combining all promotional elements into a unified effort that provides mutual satisfaction of buyers and sellers."

—William G. Nickels

MARKETING IS PROMOTIONAL FEATS! Walt Disney, the "Showman of the World," knew that his product, imagination, could only make it through well-coordinated efforts, from product concept to promotional celebrations. Disney's theme parks were featured in the best-selling book *In Search of Excellence* because they are managed so well. The corporate culture at Disney theme parks revolves around "cast members" (all employees) playing their characters at all times. They are one big family that makes fantasy real to their zillions of customers. (Disney World alone satisfies over 25 million people annually.)

In the early 1950s, company icon Walt Disney was disgusted with the trash and filthy restrooms at a local amusement park, and he was bored with the same old rides. He wished he could go to a clean amusement park that would entertain adults as well as children. Walt decided to create his own playground. So, he recruited his Disney Imagineers and in 1955, Disneyland became a reality.

Walt was clever enough to invite the press in and they had a publicity field day. Ronald Reagan was one of the TV broadcasters who introduced the world to the greatest amusement park ever created. The publicity about Walt Disney himself gleefully enjoying all the exhibits and rides signalled TV viewers that Disneyland was a family place.

One at a time, people started taking their kids to Disneyland. Eventually, through word-of-mouth and publicity, Disneyland became a popular place. It was Nikita Krushchev's favorite place—his vision of America at its finest.

We know the rest of the story. The TV show *The Wonderful World of Disney* always featured Tinker Bell flying over the minarets of Sleeping Beauty Castle while fireworks lit up the sky. Soon, every kid in the land, including me, blew out their birthday candles while wishing for a trip to Disneyland. I dare say that ninety-five out of a hundred Americans over the age of thirty have been to Disneyland at least once. My daughter, who enjoyed Disneyland, now wants to vacation at Disney World. I believe she's not alone in desiring to experience both Disney theme parks.

The Tokyo Disneyland is also a moneymaker. By 1992, a European Disney park will open outside of Paris. No doubt it will also thrive. Disney executives are now toying with opening yet another theme park and resort near Los Angeles with an ocean theme, tentatively called DisneySea. This $2 billion enterprise will feature the world's biggest aquarium.

Just how successful are Disney's three theme parks? I calculated that as of 1991, about a billion people have been served. At this rate, the entire world population could tour Disney theme parks over the next ten years.

Here's a fact most people don't know. Disney is the world's biggest moneymaking movie factory. In 1988, Disney led all studios in box office revenue. *Who Framed Roger Rabbit* grossed $322 million worldwide in 1988. Disney owns Touchstone Pictures, which produced smash successes such as *Three Men and a Baby* and its sequel *Three Men and a Little Lady*, among others.

Since the creation of Mickey Mouse, who turned sixty in 1988, Disney has been a giant in the animation business. Its wonderful animated film features (e.g., *Snow White*, *Sleeping Beauty*, and *Fantasia*) have been cash cows over the years in theater re-releases. Now they are available in video format and sell (and rent) like crazy. Recent releases such as *The Little Mermaid* also sell well in videocassette.

Then, there's TV channels and programs. The Disney Channel is quite successful, along with several of their TV programs. And then, they sell or license merchandise, lots of it. They even have Disney stores which sell their merchandise in malls.

Since Disney's products are entertainment-oriented, in effect they cross-promote each other. You may see Mickey Mouse in *Fantasia*, seek him out at Disney World for a photo op, buy a bunch of Mickey memorabilia at the souvenir shop, then buy a licensed Mickey Mouse watch made by Seiko.

Disney theme parks cross-promote with companies such as Delta, AT&T, National Car Rentals, and various hotels and food services. This gives Disney more exposure at lower cost. Additionally, the Disney conglomerate spends a good chunk of money for advertising (over $249 million in 1987). Disney enjoys a comprehensive marketing communications system.

But they still rely on word-of-mouth advertising as their number one sales tool. Kids want to go to Disney World because their friends went and told them it was great. Also, Disney entertainment products continue to receive a disproportionate share of positive publicity. For example, *Time* (Koepp 1988: 67–73) and *Newsweek* (Leerhsen 1989: 48–54) each devoted seven-page spreads and a cover shot to Disney. Publicity doesn't come any better than that.

Disney, now headed by Michael Eisner, reigns as the world's number one entertainer. In 1988, Disney earned $3.4 billion and reported a profit of $522 million. I bet most big companies would love to be in their shoes. In my opinion, Disney represents the quintessential promotional feat system in the world. Their level of exposure and bottom line (business and consumer satisfaction) prove it every day.

What does Disney do that other companies don't? They always strive to improve, to satisfy customers even more. They take calculated risks. And they entertain, entertain, entertain.

In this chapter, we will put together what we have learned from our preceding stories on consumer-based promotional feats and focus on creating an effective *marketing communication system*. First, we'll discuss management aspects, then budget, and then promotion evaluation. Afterward, we'll examine outstanding marketing communication systems of four companies. We'll close this chapter with ways to become and develop a promotion executive, and leave you with ten tips for creating promotional feats.

THE MARKETING COMMUNICATION SYSTEM

Kotler and Armstrong (1990: 4) state that "*marketing* must be understood not in the old sense of making a sale—'selling'—but rather in the new sense of *satisfying customers' needs*." That is, marketing is an exchange process that meets people's needs and wants. The information exchange between seller and buyer is what marketing communication and promotion management is all about. Marketing communication, in my opinion, stands as the most important element of the art and science of marketing. To make it work, certain managerial factors such as chain-of-command, budget, and evaluation must be considered in addition to the actual implementation of all these promotional feats described thus far. Let's examine these factors, beginning with chain-of-command.

Promotion Management Chain-of-Command

Who's in charge of promotion around here? That is a good question. In many organizations, as mentioned before, various promotion functions fight each other for dollars. In-house promotion staff compete with outside agencies. The result is haphazard planning, implementation, and control of promotional efforts. The bad news is that many companies fail to establish an executive position with real clout to make sense out of the mishmash of promotion activities (personal selling and sales management, sales promotions, advertising and its media, display, and PR and publicity). The very bad news is that mismanaged marketing communication and promotion can waste money or even destroy a brand.

Confusion and loss of time and money can be avoided, or at least minimized by establishing a position in charge of all promotional activities for the company, division, product line, or even brand, depending upon a company's circumstances. The position might be titled vice president of promotion.

The promotion VP assists in setting overall marketing objectives, has a hand in product development and production decisions, keeps in constant contact with the marketing research/competitive intelligence director, coordinates the marketing communication aspects of the three nonpromotional elements of the four P's (price, place, product), and directs all promotion activities. The promotion VP leads, inspires, encourages, and empowers subordinates under the general promotion umbrella to create coordinated promotional feats in their respective areas.

The promotion VP ensures that each promotion function works within budget to achieve specific goals. Any person who cannot do this, or fears change or suffers from misoneism (hatred of innovation or change), is re-educated or given the pink slip and replaced by someone more concerned with creating promotional feats that benefit consumers and the company than in protecting his turf.

Dissent among departments fomented by ego-based agendas must be nipped in the bud. Executives, managers, and workers in many organizations I have consulted for tell me that ineffective norms and procedures continue because "that is the way it is (has been) done." As in the military, leaders must lead their team forward, undaunted by the status quo in their company or industry.

Marketing Communications Budget

Budgeting is similar to and different from pricing. They are similar in that a given department's budget is determined partly by operating costs and partly by perceived value to the company. They differ in that the budget for marketing does not usually earn a profit for the company, whereas a properly priced and positioned product does.

There are many approaches to setting budgets: the affordable method, percentage-of-sales method, competitive-parity method, and objective-and-task method. (See Kotler and Armstrong 1990: 392–394.) Various companies use these methods or some combination of these. Here's what I think is best. Study serious competitors to find out how much they spend on promotion. Do not imitate them or try to compete against them in a promotion/price war unless you are the market leader with lots of resources (e.g., AT&T).

Instead, set your promotion objectives, look at past sales and project future sales, then set your budget based on what you can afford. Nowadays, many big companies throw money at advertising and/or sales promotion figuring more money equals more profit. On the other hand, small businesses often rely on word-of-mouth advertising alone to promote their products or services.

A happy balance between committing too much money and no money needs to be established. This seems obvious on the surface but is difficult to do in practice. Promotion managers should always seek out the most cost-effective ways of achieving promotion excellence.

Implementing Promotion Campaigns

To execute marketing communications plans and strategies most effectively, promotion VPs must integrate human and material resources with the allocated budget and achieve measurable objectives. The key is to keep promotional activities simple and do them in order and concurrently—like a theater production or a play in a football game.

Notice that most professional football plays are simple but executed very well, compared with college razzle-dazzle plays that are complicated and exciting but less effective. The high school marching band does best when it plays a simple song well rather than screeching through something complex. The same principle works with promotion. Keep promotions simple, within or below budget, and execute them with the finesse of a symphony conductor.

Evaluating Promotions

Quantifiable objectives must be set for all planned promotion activities. Objectives should be based on past performance of the same or similar promotion (to act as a baseline) combined with a pilot test experiment conducted with target consumers in a focus group setting.

Promotion concepts should be discussed and rated by groups of consumers who are exposed to different promotion variations (conditions) and then asked to complete a questionnaire with rating scales. The scales contain items that compare promotion activities with others and measure consumer likes, preferences, and intentions.

Data from pilot experiments will help promotion managers forecast success of a promotion activity or campaign. See my book *Cost-Effective Marketing Research* for more details on how to efficiently conduct focus groups, set up structured observation and rating scales, and administer experiments.

The most important part of forecasting "promotion success" is operationalizing a dependent variable (a measurement). The typical measurement used is "sales." It is imperative that "sales" be defined and operationalized precisely. Past sales figures must be available to compare. Sales units and sales revenues over a set time can constitute a dependent variable (DV). Profit margin by unit sales is a good DV.

A short period (a day, week, or quarter) may not be long enough to adequately measure a promotion's effect on sales. For example, an advertising campaign may need time to build brand loyalty. The Infiniti car ads were considered artistic duds at first. But the advertisers had a plan. The early ads created a mood and a personality for the luxury brand. Eventually, they unleashed more detailed ads that showed the cars and told us more about them. A look at sales two weeks after the ad wouldn't reveal anything noteworthy. However, a year later, sales were up.

Sales promotions, which stimulate immediate purchase, are easier to measure. If customers redeem coupons, you know how many were motivated to buy based on the coupon promotion. This is great for coupons, but rarely works for anything else. If you plan to look at sales as a DV, you must ask people what made them buy the product.

For durables and luxury items, a simple questionnaire printed on the warranty can find that out. For services or other products, a scientifically designed telephone survey can help determine what factors contributed to the purchase.

Sales are caused by many things in addition to promotion. If a given brand is available and a competitor's products aren't, then that brand will sell if there is demand. Seasonal fluctuations, an unexpected endorsement of your product by the President of the United States, or retail promotion may cause sales of your product to jump—all at the same time as your big promotion campaign. So, how much credit can you give those ads or press releases?

Since it is difficult to separate contributing or instrumental factors in purchase behavior, simply ask your customers what factors influenced their decision to buy. You may have spent $100 million on advertising yet customers hated your ads so much that they tuned them out. But they liked the label on your nifty package so they bought it. Or maybe their best friend Mabel (who tried your brand because of the cents-off deal and the sweepstakes) recommended your product. Or, the feature story on you in *Life* magazine prompted them to give your goods a try when the friendly sales agent stopped by. Who knows? Ask, and ye shall receive data.

COMPANIES WITH SUCCESSFUL MARKETING COMMUNICATION SYSTEMS

America's Big Three automakers spent $866 million on advertising in the first half of 1990, yet still posted losses or meager profits. Obviously, not enough consumers believed their mediated messages. Americans apparently found a "better" car and bought it, or simply nursed their old cars along for a while. It seems, in the case of the car companies, that promotional efforts did not cause more sales or even enough sales. Yet it probably would have been worse if the Big Three had not advertised at all. A big promotional effort is not always a successful promotional effort, unfortunately. So what does a feature marketing communication system look like? Let's find out.

In this section, we look at four companies whose marketing communication systems work for them—that is, they are profitable. Whether their success depends on their promotional efforts is very debatable, yet these companies no doubt achieved extra sales from their coordinated promotional activities.

First we check out AT&T, the long distance telephone pioneer and giant, and its overall marketing communication system. Then we look at a specific division of megacorporation Time Warner and examine one "brand" and its marketing communication and merchandising success. Wall Drug, a very successful one-store retail outfit, is the subject of our third marketing communication system, based on clever offers on long distance billboards. Finally, we look at the promotional successes of my company, Tsunami Products—a small manufacturer of the world's finest kayaks.

AT&T—The Right Choices

After AT&T was broken up in 1984 for being too good of a monopoly, it went from being the telephone company to a communications company. Actually, AT&T has always been a communications company ever since Alexander Graham Bell invented the telephone back in 1876. In 1877, Bell and two friends (the three founders of AT&T) decided to introduce the telephone commercially, and the rest is history.

After divestiture in 1984, AT&T did two things. They trimmed their staff (by 1990 they had cut their staff by nearly 100,000), and they offered a dazzling array of remarkable new products and services.

They still made telephones (they lost their patent on that in 1977) and peripherals, but they also began to manufacture microcomputers that were clones of IBM personal computers and electronic networking solutions.

Where they really went for it was in service to their home and business long distance telephone customers. They made it their business to offer long distance telephone service to more places than anyone else. They have a Reach Out World Plan which cuts international phone call rates by 20 percent. AT&T's PRO WATS business telephone system was "another AT&T advantage" to save businesses more money than they could with MCI Execunet or Sprint Dial–1. AT&T offered to switch customers for free to AT&T—and then switch them back for free after 90 days if they were not satisfied. AT&T sent out press releases for all these new products and services and followed that up with great advertising. We'll discuss their advertising and public relations efforts a bit more later. On with the services.

Then AT&T offered their easy-to-use "Calling Card" for free to AT&T subscribers. Then came the biggie—the AT&T Universal Card, a MasterCard or Visa that doubles as a calling card with discounts for long distance calling with no annual fee—for loyal AT&T customers. All we pay for is interest on our monthly balance. Fair enough.

Corporate spokesman Cliff Robertson (the most believable guy on TV) calmly announced that the card was free if you signed up in 1990. AT&T took out full-page newspaper print ads that announced: "First things first, it's free. Forever."

The response was overwhelming. Kate Fitzgerald (1990a: 12) reported on the success of the card in an article in *Advertising Age*. "Launched in a March TV ad blitz, Universal has grown faster than any other credit card in history, snaring more than 1 million accounts in less than three months." That's some card!

This unprecedented service garnered AT&T lots of publicity and forced the banks to start thinking about providing customers with a little service instead of lip service. MCI copycatted and struck up a deal with other credit card companies but it was too late. The Universal Card had already saturated the market and customers were turning in their old bank credit cards when the pay-up notices arrived in the mail.

The rivalry between AT&T and the pretenders to the throne (MCI and US Sprint and their various mergers), continues in a free-wheeling brawl. The contenders charge AT&T with all kinds of nefarious crimes, and AT&T comes back hard with yet more service for their customers and more challenging comparative advertising. The struggle for the crown of communications makes the news all the time.

MCI and US Sprint both claim "more savings" as their prime value. No problem there. AT&T counters with ads that show consumers dissatisfied with the details of MCI and Sprint and not really saving money. AT&T says, "Get it in writing." MCI and Sprint both react defensively in print and TV ads and say they *will* put it in writing. To consumers, it sounds like they are admitting guilt.

MCI and Sprint gave AT&T free advertising by mentioning AT&T more than their own company. One MCI print headline in 1990 read: "Since when do AT&T and savings go together?" I don't know; all I remember from the ad is "AT&T and savings go together." Guess who wins the Total Recall Award?

AT&T featured a series of print and TV comparative ads contrasting service and price savings. To cause confusion as to which company gave the best money value, AT&T imitated MCI's spinning money counter to show cost comparisons. A typical ad shows two yuppie executives driving convertible sports cars down the street and talking on cellular phones while the money counter adds up the totals. In this instance, the AT&T call was a couple of cents cheaper. The caption in the print ad reads, "Are one of these long distance companies taking you for a ride?"

The war between AT&T (who enjoyed a 68 percent share of the market in 1990) and its rivals is a promotional feat for the entire industry. The winners in this marketing war are customers.

We can learn a great deal from the moves that AT&T makes to get and retain customers. What does AT&T offer that the others don't? They offer service as their prime value coupled with overall monetary value, rather than just slightly cheaper rates. MCI and US Sprint could try to offer consumers something unique and worthwhile, instead of trying to copy AT&T's every move.

Be original, guys! And remember a lesson the banks haven't figured out yet—show you care about your customers—you know, the average American from a suburb of Indianapolis. All you older executives who are reading this, think back. Remember when lending rates were under 10 percent? Remember when you didn't have to pay the bank to make money off your money? Remember when banks used to beg to give you a credit card instead of doing a two-month FBI check on your family history? Remember when tellers knew who you were? Remember when banks were solvent?

The lesson here is that AT&T is tuned in to what Americans want—both in communications services and in the credit arena. AT&T deserves their success. And they go after it aggressively, with the most brand advertising (according to Endicott 1990b, AT&T spent $253 million in the first half of 1990).

Their ads are not all comparative. Many are dramatic. In 1988, AT&T

featured their "slice of death" ads in which executives face the wrath of their superiors by making mistakes in choosing obsolete business phone systems instead of an AT&T system.

Other print and TV ads show people "reaching out" and calling loved ones from afar. The focus is on sentimentality. During football games, AT&T offers viewers a quiz in which they guess which of three football scenarios is "the right choice." This approach is entertaining.

AT&T has an extensive direct mail program and uses telephone solicitation to introduce customers to new services. In addition to advertising, AT&T gets name recognition and positive public support by supporting the arts (from their classic radio show *The Telephone Hour* to their sponsorship of *The MacNeil/Lehrer NewsHour* and *AT&T PRESENTS*).

They also pull publicity coups such as offering free calls for troops stationed in Saudi Arabia in October 1990, and in dropping their international rates 37 percent to celebrate the re-opening of Ellis Island. And to really clinch a place in our hearts, AT&T was the lucky recipient of a tribute by *Mad* magazine which featured a portion of the Sistine Chapel mural of God touching hands with man. The caption says: "Reach out and touch someone. AT&T. Our Creation is divine" (Jacobs 1991: 78).

Without a doubt, AT&T has made the right marketing communication choices and will probably continue to do so. Here's a homework assignment. Count the number of times a week you are exposed to AT&T, whether it be from TV or print ads, telephone solicitation, a newspaper article, whatever. I think you'll find that you get touched by AT&T just about every day! AT&T's marketing communication and promotion management system is an ongoing, comprehensive promotional feat.

Promoting Batman

A glance at Time Warner's 1989 annual report showed me that this is one company that is taking full advantage of the Communication Age, not to help people converse as AT&T does, but to inform and entertain. Time Warner earned $7.6 billion in 1989. Their businesses encompass several industries: magazines, filmed entertainment, recorded music and music publishing, cable television, HBO programming, and books. Their information and entertainment capabilities dovetail nicely as the joint venture looks toward dominating the global market in the 1990s with this philosophy: "Feeding the appetite for information and entertainment doesn't satisfy the hunger . . . it increases it."

I believe this statement is correct. It is hard to conceive that the little company called Warner Brothers, who created a cartoon rabbit named Bugs Bunny over 50 years ago, would emerge as the titan that it is today.

One little company that Warner acquired along the way was DC Comics, creator of two of the World's Finest Superheroes—Superman and Batman. Both super dudes have emerged from the cramped little writer's and inker's studio as major moneymakers. Let's focus on one of these characters who has been in the news of late—Batman!

I dare say there is not a single person in the U.S. who does not know of Batman. I swear I learned to read at a young age thanks to Bob Kane, creator of Batman.

The Batman phenomenon has been around for over 50 years, ever since he appeared on the cover of *Detective Comics*. Batman has had his ups and downs over the years, as has the comics industry. But in the early 1980s, the comics industry resurged, and comics specialty boutiques prove it.

In the 1980s, DC Comics produced a new "Prestige Format" of Batman, luring former readers back with beautiful illustrations and a penetrating look into the dark side of the Caped Crusader. Frank Miller's *Dark Knight* (1986), now a Batman classic, has made more money than any other single comic in history.

In response to a readers' poll, DC killed off Robin, Batman's sidekick. (This is responding to consumer demand at its best!) Warner Books also published several bestseller Batman illustrated books and paperbacks (e.g., Gardner 1990, *The Batman Murders*).

The *Batman* movie, released in 1989 on Batman's fiftieth anniversary, zoomed to the top of the summer releases and instantly became the biggest box office draw ever—about $250 million worth. Then the video was released a few months later at various penetration prices (some as low as $12.89) and made another $200 million for Warner.

Months before the film's release, Warner's advance publicity and promotional merchandise prepared the public for the new wave of Batmania. After the film, Topps started making Batman movie cards that were sold at drug and convenience stores.

By Christmas 1989, three hundred licensed Batman merchandise items had sold to the tune of $250 million. By Christmas of 1989, Batman fans could watch reruns of the campy Batman television series, wear an official (and expensive) Batman costume for parties, pay outrageous prices for antique Batman comics, play the Batman Role-playing Game available in game and hobby shops or by mail, obtain Batman logo merchandise from movie theaters and record stores, join Batman in Data East's software for Commodore and Atari computers, or purchase a myriad of Batman toys and models at toy stores everywhere.

Batman made the news several times in 1989. He made the covers of *Reader's Digest* and *Mad*. *Premiere*, the movie magazine, put Michael Keaton on their cover and devoted a six-page feature to Keaton and Batman (Minsky 1989). *Newsweek* headlined Batman on one of their covers and ran a five-page feature aptly called "Batmania" (Barol 1990).

Even *Business Week* got into the fun by writing about Batman merchandise counterfeiting (Jacobson 1989).

All the publicity sold lots of Batman comics, videos, books and merchandise. I calculate that Warner earned nearly $1 billion from Batman in 1989/1990. But Warner's success with Batman is due to more than a great cartoon character portrayed well in print and on the silver screen—it is also the result of a multidimensional, creative, strategic, and decisively executed marketing communications program.

Batman's fantastic popularity is the masterpiece of unknown promotion executives and their staffs who proficiently coordinate publicity, advertising, merchandising, and display. Speaking of display, I show off a life-size cardboard cutout of Batman in my office window at Cal State University, Hayward. All students know where my office is. I am still a Batman fan 30 years after reading my first comic.

Except for fans, who now enjoy the new *Robin* series of comics from DC which debuted in January 1991, who cares about the future of Batman? Warner does. As of this writing, a Batman movie sequel is in the works. This time, I think Warner should pull out all the stops and create some truly spectacular promotional feats to announce the opening of the movie.

On opening night I would love to see an acrobat dressed as Batman swing from a building on a Batrope and crash through a window above the marquee. Why not? Or perhaps the sequel could open in New York with searchlights filling the sky with the Batsignal. Maybe the Joker or some other archvillain could commit some publicity "crime" just before the movie opens.

All these publicity stunts could occur and I guarantee they would attract positive attention if done competently. For Batman and Time Warner, now is the time to feed our entertainment appetite and increase our hunger for more.

Where Is Wall Drug?

Let's leave the communications and entertainment industries and examine an area in which many of you work—retail. Through the story of Wall Drug, we will see that entertainment works in the retail environment.

Here's a question. Do you know where Wall Drug is? If you guessed the desolate Badlands in South Dakota, you guessed correctly. Realistically, no one should know where Wall Drug is, yet many of us do. Let's find out why.

A pharmacist named Ted Hustead and his wife Dorothy bought Wall Drug in 1931 and the town of Wall has never been the same. Back in '31 there were only 326 very poor people living in this prairie town. The

Husteads barely got by for five years. It seems the local people just didn't give the drug store enough business. The Husteads were getting desperate.

One hot July day, Dorothy suggested they put up a sign on the highway to attract passing motorists on their way to see the new Mt. Rushmore monument. So they set up a series of signs that drivers could read as they puttered by. The signs said "Get a soda . . . Get root beer . . . Turn next corner . . . Just as near . . . to Highway 16 & 14 . . . Free Ice Water . . . Wall Drug."

Motorists were amused by the sign arrangement, but what caught their attention were the words free ice water! That brought them in droves. By 1982, Wall Drug was drawing up to 20,000 people a day in the summer. I know, for I was their customer during the hot summer of 1989.

My wife and I were touring the Badlands and kept seeing these billboards here, there, and everywhere which said "Free Coffee and Donuts for Veterans!" or "Bikers Welcome!" We saw bumper stickers that read "Have you dug Wall Drug?" We hadn't dug Wall Drug so we decided to check it out.

When we arrived in Wall one early August morning, we saw that Wall Drug was actually a rustic, Western-style mall full of amazing items from the West and around the world. Most of the stuff is useful cowboy gear—hats, boots, whips, oiled raincoats, and nifty memorabilia of cowboy and Indian days, Badlands geology, and the like. There is also a cafe inside that seats 520. Various exhibits keep your attention. Their displays are country-looking but quite appealing and professional. They do good business. I found out that they grossed $6 million in 1988. Pretty good for a drug store on the Dakota prairie.

They attract tourists not just because of free ice water and a good stock of merchandise. They feature several free exhibits including an 80-foot dinosaur next to their playground and picnic area. They have two animated cowboy orchestras that the kids like. In the backyard they have a replica of Mt. Rushmore that tourists can photograph with themselves in the foreground. Another feature is the life-size "jackalope" replica, official animal of the northern plains states. A good time is had by all in their friendly mall.

To attract customers, they put up billboards all over the world. That is a promotional feat. Customers report seeing the signs all over Europe and Asia, but believe it or not, they have a billboard in Antarctica that reads "Wall Drug—10,645 miles." Next time you're way down under, check out the sign. And don't forget to ask for the free ice water.

Their billboards and simple word-of-mouth advertising keep their store full, but they also get a lot of publicity. They have been featured in *Time*, *People*, and *USA Today*. According to author Dana Close Jennings

(1969), who wrote a book about Wall Drug, the Wall Drug mileage signs started popping up in Europe during WWII, thanks to a GI who liked free ice water. Jennings (p. 43) reports that there were over 3,000 Wall Drug highway signs along roads in the U.S., and there may be as many across the world—Shanghai, Pakistan, Paris, Copenhagen, Korea, Rome, Vietnam, India, Gabon, and 143 miles from the Arctic Circle, to name a few. I guess Wall Drug's comprehensive (but low key) promotion strategy is a sign of the times.

The Tidal Wave of the Future

Small businesses are the backbone of America. I do the promotion for a small manufacturing firm called Tsunami Products, the tidal wave of the future. Our shops, located in Berkeley and Redding, California, make the world's finest sea kayaks out of DuPont's Kevlar 49, the material used to make tank armor and flak jackets. We don't earn billions like Time Warner, and we can't claim to be the world's largest drug store like Wall Drug, but we have made a modest profit since we began R & D and production back in 1985.

My cohorts in the business, builder Jim Kakuk and boat designer Glenn Gilchrist, were looking to build a small one-person boat that could handle anything the mighty sea threw at it and not just survive, but thrive. We figured we could contribute to the betterment of humanity by making a kayak that a person could live off if need be. We decided that unlike conventional kayaks, our boat must not fill up with water *when* (not if) the paddler falls out. Glenn and Jim devised a molded-impression cockpit that the boater sits on instead of in.

The prime value of our boat is that it is "built tough to be played with rough." It's priced at the top end. We introduced it at $2001 back in 1986—"a futuristic boat at a futuristic price." Our price through 1991 is less futuristic but more realistic at $2222.

By mid–1985, the Tsunami X–1 Rocket kayak was born. We called the boat the X–1 because we "break the wave barrier" (one of our print ad slogans). We made a boat for the ocean adventurer. Now all we had to do was sell it.

Our promotion consisted of new product press releases sent to all paddling and outdoor magazines. Almost all of them published our release and potential consumers got wind of our boat. Then we advertised in *Sea Kayaker*, a respected journal that many kayakers read. So far, our promotion was fairly mundane.

Then we decided to get famous. We sponsored the world's most gruelling 8-mile kayaking race called "The Golden Gate Kayaking Invitational," beginning in 1986. We have been sole sponsor of the race every June. It's a good deal for us because our boats are displayed and opinion leaders can see and try them. Additionally, our races get press in local and national publications.

Kakuk and I designed a series of informative and entertaining slide shows on ocean adventure kayaking which featured the X–1 and our world famous kayaking stunt team the Tsunami Rangers, Wave Warriors Extraordinaire. These slide shows (which featured me as the speaker and Kakuk as the multimedia wizard) proved to be crowd-pleasers at major kayaking symposia around the nation. We always displayed our latest model (usually painted in custom colors to showcase the crafts-manship put into each boat). The goods news is that conference planners paid us an honorarium for appearing and showing off our stuff to hundreds of people. All you trade-show enthusiasts note: we got paid to display our boats as the center attraction! That alone is a promotional feat for a little boatbuilder.

I have written twenty kayaking articles that have been published over the past six years. This helped spread our fame. Then several articles were written about us. The best article was written by Tim Cahill (1988), gonzo sports writer for *Outside* magazine, who had the piece published in *Pursuits*, a Whittle Communications publication that focused on "re-markable people, uncommon endeavors." Merrill Lynch is the sole ad-vertiser in *Pursuits*. After the article was published, I had stockbrokers from San Francisco calling me up to make sure I was real. Cahill's story on me was titled "Wave Warrior." A few weeks after his story was published, we were featured on the news on our local NBC affiliate. The Wave Warrior surfs the tube—TV tube, that is.

In 1989 the Tsunami Rangers produced a 20-minute entertainment video called "The Adventures of the Tsunami Rangers." The video won "Best of Show—Professional" in the 1990 National Paddling Film Festival held in Lexington, Kentucky. I showed the video to John Hagner, curator of the Stuntmen's Hall of Fame in Moab, Utah, and he arranged a Tsunami Ranger exhibit at the Hall, featuring my personal X–1 (named Black-and-Blue Bruiser) and some of my kayaking body armor. Mr. Hag-ner shows the video in his Hall of Fame theater. If you happen to be in Moab, check out our exhibit.

All this publicity has helped us sell boats. But we are not resting on our laurels. We are now working on an instructional video with an accompanying book called "The Tsunami Ranger Guide to Ocean Ad-venture Kayaking." We plan to market our videos and book through our direct mail catalog (which features our other products—the X–1, X–2 Starship tandem kayak, and our new Tsunami line of custom paddles). We currently sell goods back-of-room at our seminars and push our products through our dealer and agent network dispersed in key geo-graphical locations in the U.S. and Japan, Puerto Rico, and New Zealand, as well as coastal cities in California, our primary market.

Including fixed and variable costs, our videos cost $8 each to produce. We sell "The Adventures of the Tsunami Rangers" for $20 ($12 each to dealers or agents). We make a profit every time someone pays to look at us and our boats in action. We consider this a promotional feat. Our distributor in Japan paid us to dub our video into Japanese and sell it in Japan.

We often give the video to kayaking and canoe clubs and allow their members to copy it for free. They spread the gospel for us. When a canoeist from Virginia said the Tsunami Rangers were legends there, I was flabbergasted—not a single Tsunami Ranger has ever been to Virginia.

I broadcast the video on our local community cable station and encourage local surfers to pirate the video. (I live on the northern California coast near San Francisco). I give free seminars and demonstrations to locals who come to my beach house to try out our kayaks. I give away frameable, signed, $100 gift certificates for a "day with the Rangers."

We encourage our dealers and agents to do whatever is necessary to sell our boats other than cut the price. We never, ever cut our throats with rebates or price deals. We are top of the line. However, to best serve our customers, we offer "0 percent" financing and sell used X–1s and X–2s to folks who don't have much disposable income. Being a small business, we are also open to barter. We once traded an X–2, which normally sells for $2525, for a used Citroen automobile.

Like AT&T, we offer our customers service. We give every buyer a fifteen-page owner's manual, a ninety-page "Eric Soares Kayaking Articles Reprints," a signed copy of "The Adventures of the Tsunami Rangers," a five-year or five-thousand-wave warranty, and $100 worth of lessons with a Tsunami Ranger officer. Future buyers will receive our latest videos and books for free.

We maintain a list with the personal name of every boat we have ever made. Many of our boat buyers have become our personal friends and our best agents. Of course, they work on commission only. No one gets a salary at Tsunami Products. Our slogan: Salaries encourage sloth.

You won't find Tsunami Products in the Fortune 50,000, but we keep afloat in a market clogged with over forty competitors. We believe our high quality/high price product, combined with our commitment to service and our zeal for the limelight, will keep us swimming in profits in the years ahead.

I included the Tsunami Products story to show that new ventures can also develop effective, even exemplary, marketing communication programs if they know their market and are clever and resourceful. I suggest that start-up businesses use every opportunity to promote themselves. By the way, if you want more information on Tsunami Products, write me at P.O. Box 339, Moss Beach, CA 94038. I will be happy to serve you.

PREPARING FOR A CAREER IN PROMOTION MANAGEMENT

I hope that many readers of this book are already happily ensconced in the marketing profession, promotion field, or their own venture. For those who are already employed in positions that utilize your skills, you realize how important both education and experience are. And for those who are still seeking their proper niche, you may need to know what is and will be expected of promotion executives.

In Chapter 1 I noted that a promotion officer should be a generalist; that is, adaptable and skilled in many areas. In a paper I presented to the Association of Business Communication in 1989, I detailed comprehensive education and experience plans to develop a promotion professional. Here, requisite education and experience are summarized to familiarize you with the ideal career path for marketing communication generals. Let's begin with formal education.

A Degree in Marketing Communication

If Cal Worthington thought it was tough to get a good job without a college education in the 1940s, it is a fact that it's even tougher in the 1990s. Here's the education path I recommend.

Get a B.S. in business administration with an option in marketing, new ventures, or advertising. Minor in mass communication or organizational communication. In addition to core business classes (e.g., finance, production, accounting, economics, human resource management, marketing, business communication) take some of these courses for your option and minor: personal selling, sales management, advertising management and production, direct marketing, public relations, organizational communication, and broadcast production, newswriting, or graphic arts. Your capstone course should be promotion management.

If you already have your college degree, these courses can be taken as an undeclared graduate student. Or, you could take workshops and seminars offered by the American Marketing Association or other reputable organizations that teach these concepts.

Go out and get good experience in the work world before even considering an MBA. If your company will underwrite a graduate degree and/or you already have five or more years experience in the promotion field, it may be worthwhile to pursue an MBA.

If you go for the MBA, major in marketing. In addition to the required courses, make sure you take marketing research, consumer behavior, and seminars in marketing communication theory and issues.

That is all you have to do to maximize your time and money in college. No matter what, never get horizontal degrees (e.g., second bachelors or masters degrees, credentials, and the like). One MBA beats five BA degrees any time.

Work Experience in Promotion

The degree is important but it is not the meal ticket. People with an MBA and no job experience will be lucky to get a file clerk job at an ad agency. They are qualified for little else.

Experience is the passport to success and sales experience is the best form of experience for people in the promotion field. Remember, David Ogilvy, Ed McMahon, Zig Ziglar, Lee Iacocca, Malcolm Forbes, and Cal Worthington were all salespeople first and foremost. So, no matter what, get sales experience as soon as possible. If nothing else, you need sales experience to sell yourself.

In addition to sales experience, get a job or even an internship in public relations (for a club on campus perhaps), advertising (maybe an account executive), display (retail sales), and sales promotion (even if you have to promote dances at the university).

Put your education and experience together in a resume, put extra copies in your portfolio (which shows all your promotion achievements), and hit the pavement running. Join Toastmasters to get extra experience in public speaking, and you are on your way. There is no way you cannot succeed if you are a generalist—if you can sell.

The future of marketing and of promotion in particular belongs to those individuals who are willing to gain the necessary skills to succeed. All it takes is brains and hard work. We finish this chapter and the book by providing current and future promotion executives with a few tips to ensure success when communicating with the public about your product.

TEN TIPS FOR CREATING PROMOTIONAL FEATS

Each tip provides 10 percent of a successful marketing communication/promotion program or campaign. Each tip depends upon its antecedents to work most effectively. So follow these tips in order when creating a campaign, and you may produce a promotional feat or series of feats, and astound Alexander the Great, Harry Houdini, David Ogilvy, Cal Worthington, or your stockholders.

However, if something goes awry with your promotional efforts, work backward from tip number 10 until you find where you or your organization blew it. Fix it, regroup and restart, or retreat.

1. *Carefully craft products that maximize life quality.* Create new products that make life better. Dump, replace, or remake old products that fail to contribute to the common good. With quality supplies efficiently make a quality product.

2. *Produce and promote your product's prime value as highest quality or lowest price.* Everyone who counts must know that your product is *first* in something important; it must never be an also-ran brand. People remember first, most recent, or most potent; best or cheapest; that which satisfies their demands. They forget everything else.

3. *Coordinate pricing, placing, and packaging to communicate the product's prime value.* Properly positioned brands consistently symbolize organizational beliefs, reinforce product benefits and features, and imprint lasting identity in the minds of targeted consumers.

4. *Set highest promotion campaign goals based on lowest realistic budget.* Ignore how much the competition spends; you are trying to reach your goal, not win. You can't spend more than you have to spend (no deficits). The trick is to use allocated promotion money cost-effectively for the most powerful communication impact on marketing goals which should always be: many sales, repeat sales, and referred sales = long term profit and mutually satisfied exchange participants. To realize many sales, deliver what you promise.

5. *Design promotional activities to complement each other for additive or even multiplicative effect on heightened consumer awareness, preference, intention, and action regarding purchase of your brand.* All promotional activities further the brand in a cooperative, brand-building way. No ad, sales promotion, company spokesperson, or goodwill gesture stands alone; they all have necessary and sufficient roles to play to stimulate and reward exchange between you and your consumers.

6. *Make every promotional activity an event to be remembered.* Each promotional activity alone and in concert with others compels consumers to notice and seek out your brand because the promotion was powerful, dramatic, entertaining (not fluffy or flashy). A promotional feat in any promotion function must persuade on several levels—emotional, ethical, intellectual, and sensual.

7. *Execute promotional campaigns like a theater production—all operations go on linearly yet concurrently.* Promotional executives lead and oversee all promotion project teams (not "groups") to ensure the show goes on—to a full house, standing ovation, favorable critical reviews, and

a long run. Timely and cost-effective implementation of promotional campaigns is essential.

8. *Be flexible enough to change tactics at the last second to react to a new threat or capitalize on a new opportunity.* In short, be jazzy. Play the song list your band rehearsed, but be ready to honor requests from the audience. Some promotional feat opportunities are serendipitous and require hustle to execute effectively. Some company disasters call for immediate and effective PR feats. The key is to act quickly and decisively. And keep your last-second efforts simple.

9. *Evaluate promotional results against quantified objectives.* Everything planned and implemented must be controlled. Set up a cost-effective evaluation system that scores your promotional activities in ratio numbers that can be compared against estimates. Use evaluation as feedback for the next campaign cycle.

10. *Keep customers happy, loyal, and vocal about you, your company, and your product by providing excellent after-sale service.* Sell a promise; deliver what you promise; service what you deliver; promise service; sell a promise. Always pay keen attention to your customers' demands, continually monitor the competition and the business environment, and rapidly but smoothly adjust your goals, products, and promotions to feedback and new stimuli.

In conclusion, if you pay attention and do what is right well, you will sell. Continually refine your company's mission, product, and promotion to best serve humanity and your organization's mission will be completed. Learn from the past, but ensure that you look to the present and the future for worthwhile marketing opportunities.

Make all your promotional efforts harmonize with your company culture. Make them cost-effective, original, entertaining, and persuasive. Make them promotional feats. One final tip: Have fun.

References

Alden, J. D. (1987). Tomorrow's fleet. *U.S. Naval Institute Proceedings*, May, 177–186.

Alter, J. (1990). Ted's global village. *Newsweek*, June 11, 48–52.

Anderson, P. M., Rubin, L. G. (1986). *Marketing communications*. Englewood Cliffs, NJ: Prentice Hall.

Ansen, D. (1989). Boffo box office big boost to biz. *Newsweek*, July 31, 60–62.

Arpad, J. J., Lincoln, K. R. (1971). *Buffalo Bill's wild west*. Palmer Lake, CO: Filter Press.

Arrian (1971). *The campaigns of Alexander*. New York: Dorset Press.

Auchmute, J. (1985). But wait there's more! *Advertising Age*, October 17, 18.

Axthelm, P. (1974). The roots of Evel. *Newsweek*, August 26, 78.

Ballon, K. (1988). The no. 1 leader is Petersen of Ford. *Fortune*, October 24, 69–70.

Barlas, S. (1990). Bill poses threat to cigarette ads. *Marketing News*, February 19, 1–2.

Barol, B. (1989). Batmania. *Newsweek*, June 26, 70–74.

Beckett, J. (1990a). Behind the zeal for seals. *San Francisco Chronicle*, August 6, C1, C9.

———. (1990b). How supermarkets sell shelf space. *San Francisco Chronicle*, September 13, A1, A18.

Belch, G. E., Belch, M. A. (1990). *Introduction to advertising and promotion management*. Homewood, IL: Irwin.

Biebuyck, D. (1971). Evel Knievel. *New Yorker*, July 24, 22–26.

Blakeslee, S. (1986). Voyager succeeds in historic flight. *New York Times*, December 24, A1, A10.

Blumenthal, H. (1990). Your next TV: A screen 100 inches wide. *Peninsula Mid-Week*, March 12, 1, 9.

Blyth, J. (1990). Overstimulated consumers challenge designers, retailers. *Marketing News*, August 6, 8, 19.

Bourdon, D. (1971). Warhol as filmmaker. *Art in America*, May–June, 48–53.

Boxer, C. R. (1969). *The Portuguese seaborne empire*. New York: Knopf.

Bragg, A. (1988). Are good salespeople born or made? *Sales & Marketing Management*, September, 74–78.

Broder, J. (1990). Pentagon fights for survival. *San Francisco Chronicle*, January 24, Briefing 1, 5.

Brown, K. (1990). Ad spending on the tube since 1980. *Advertising Age*, January 1, 4.

Brown, M. W. (1986). Futuristic-primitive plane is a blend of brave dreams and improvisation. *New York Times*, December 26, A10.

Butler, E. (1985). Formula advertising just died a well-deserved death. *AdWeek*, April, F.C.7.

Cahill, T. (1988). Wave warrior. *Pursuits*, Spring, 10–16.

Carman, J. (1990). "Chicken Noodle" hits 10. *TV Week*, May 27–June 2, 3.

Carnegie, D. (1982). *How to win friends and influence people* (rev. ed.). New York: Pocket Books.

Christopher, M. (1969). *Houdini: The untold story*. New York: Crowell.

Clifton, T. (1990). Cosmetics with a conscience: The vision of Body Shop. *Newsweek*, February 12, 65–66.

Clouse, R. (1989). *Bruce Lee: The biography*. Burbank, CA: Unique.

Coffey, J. (1990). "Infomercials" provide work for pitchmen. *San Francisco Chronicle*, July 19, E1.

Cole, T. (1989). Irresistible force. *Popular Mechanics*, October, 59–62.

Congbalay, D. (1990). Better junk in new junk mail. *San Francisco Chronicle*, September 20, A1, A20.

Conover, J. N. (1989). Consumer behavior foundations for pricing. In D. T. Seymour (ed.), *The pricing decision: A strategic planner for marketing professionals*. Chicago: Probus.

Cox, B. (1975). *My dog Spot: The Cal Worthington story*. Pasadena, CA: Arroyo.

Crary, D. (1990). Antarctic adventurers complete trek. *San Francisco Examiner*, March 4, A4.

Dagnoli, J. (1988). B & H ads to change? *Advertising Age*, April 25, 4.

Dart, B. (1990). House panel looks at TV shows that are hyped commercials. *San Francisco Chronicle*, May 19, A3.

Davies, T. D. (1990). New evidence places Peary at the Pole. *National Geographic*, January, 44–60.

Dexter, P. (1985). A portrait of Evel. *Esquire*, March, 45, 47.

Dobrzynski, J. H., Davies, J. E. (1986). Business celebrities. *Business Week*, June 23, 100–107.

Dobyns, L. (1990). Ed Deming wants big changes, and he wants them fast. *Smithsonian*, August, 74–82.

Dommermuth, W. P. (1989). *Promotion: Analysis, creativity, and strategy*, 2nd ed. Boston: PWS-Kent.

Dos Passos, J. (1969). *The Portugal story: Three centuries of exploration and discovery*. New York: Doubleday.

Drucker, P. F. (1973). *Management: Tasks, responsibilities, practices*. New York: Harper & Row.

Duffy, D. (1990). Charles gets Di to burn fur coats worth 120G. *National Enquirer*, March 27, 15.

Dunheim, D. (1990). Jack LaLanne: Leader of the revolution that shaped Americans. *Pacific Coast*, January, 6–7.

Edwards, B. (1986). Pioneer stuntman Yakima Canutt, 90, dies in California. *Variety*, May 28, 4, 5.

Eichenwald, K. (1990). Drexel Burnham files under bankruptcy law. *San Francisco Chronicle*, February 14, A1, A10.

Elliott, S. (1990). Volvos to take a monster stomping for fun. *USA Today*, November 8, 1.

Elliott, S. J. (1984). Advertorials, straddling a fine line in print. *Advertising Age*, April 30, 3, 36–37.

Endicott, R. C. (1990a). Ad Age 500 grows 9.7%; billings top $85 billion. *Advertising Age*, March 26, S1–S2.

———. (1990b). AT&T pushes past McDonald's. *Advertising Age*, November 19, 27.

Evans, J. R., Berman, B. (1990). *Marketing*, 4th ed. New York: Macmillan.

Fitzgerald, K. (1990a). Card issuers poised to fight AT&T. *Advertising Age*, July 2, 12.

———. (1990b). Cabbage Patch revives. *Advertising Age*, October 29, 10.

Fizdale, R. (1990). Drummed out at Cannes. *Advertising Age*, July 9, 3, 46.

Flanagan, J. (1987). A $1.6-billion credibility gap. *Financial World*, March 24, 134.

Foote, J. (1990). Trying to take back the planet. *Newsweek*, February 5, 24–25.

Forbes Jr., M. S. (1990). The spirit remains. *Forbes*, March 19, 19.

Frank, A. D., Cone, E. (1987). We're a straight business now. *Forbes*, May 18, 43.

Franklin, B. (1955). *The autobiography of Benjamin Franklin*. New York: Pocket Books.

Freeman, L. (1987). P&G has event-ful plans. *Advertising Age*, June 22, 41.

———. (1988). Sponsors flock to local fetes. *Advertising Age*, January 25, S–48.

Fuhrman, C. J. (1989). *Publicity stunt!: Great staged events that made the news*. San Francisco: Chronicle Books.

Fuller, R. B. (1969). *Operating manual for spaceship earth*. New York: Simon & Schuster.

Futrell, C. (1989). *ABC's of selling*, 2nd ed. Homewood, IL: Irwin.

Garchik, L. (1990). Life, liberty and the pursuit of a settlement. *San Francisco Chronicle*, February 22, A10.

Gardner, C. S. (1990). *The Batman Murders*. New York: Warner Books.

Garfield, B. (1990a). Engaging in safe slogans. *Advertising Age*, January 22, S–14.

———. (1990b). Super Bowl: An ad snore. *Advertising Age*, January 22, 1, 56.

Gelman, E., Wang, P., Powell, B., Smith, V. E. (1985). Hey America, Coke are it! *Newsweek*, July 22, 40–42.

Goldman, A. (1970). The Beatles decide to let it be—apart. *Life*, April 24, 38–39.

Goldman, T. (1988). Big spenders develop newspaper strategies. *Marketing Communications*, June, 24–29.

Goldwater, B. (1988). *Goldwater*. New York: Doubleday.

Govoni, N., Eng, R., Galper, M. (1986). *Promotional management*. Englewood Cliffs, NJ: Prentice Hall.

Graves, M. (1987). The coupon gamble: Double or nothing. *Los Angeles Times*, July 29, IV–1.

Green, R. (1984). A boutique in your living room. *Forbes*, May 7, 86–94.

Gresham, W. L. (1959). *Houdini: The man who walked through walls*. New York: Holt, Rinehart and Winston.

Griffith, S. B. (1963). *Sun Tzu on the art of war*. London: Oxford University Press.

Grushkin, P. (1983). *Grateful Dead: The official book of the dead heads*. New York: Morrow.

Guiles, M. G. (1987). Ali, Knievel fight for common cause at K-mart meeting. *Wall Street Journal*, May 27, 43.

Gundersen, E. (1989). Stones tickets are rolling. *USA Today*, July 18, D1.

Habeler, P. (1979). *The lonely victory: Mt. Everest in '78*. New York: Simon & Schuster.

Hagner, J. (1989). Personal interview. Moab, Utah, August 14.

Hall, A. J. (1975). Philosopher of dissent: Benjamin Franklin. *National Geographic*, July, 93–123.

Hall, C. T. (1990). Valentine's Day promo sweetens AT&T coffers. *San Francisco Chronicle*, February 16, C1, C22.

Hammer, J. (1990). Calling Mr. crisis control. *Newsweek*, October 22, 54.

Hartley, R. G. (1985). *Marketing Successes*. New York: Wiley.

————. (1986). *Marketing Mistakes*, 3rd ed. New York: Wiley.

Hastings, H. (1990). Before jumping on environmental bandwagon, be sure it's not drawn by a fading horse. *Marketing News*, August 6, 4.

Hendon, D. W. (1986). *Battling for profits*. Jonesboro, AR: Business Consultants International.

Herold, J. C. (1983). *The Horizon book of the age of Napoleon*. New York: American Heritage.

Hirsch, E. D., Kett, J. F., Trefil, J. (1988). *The dictionary of cultural literacy*. Boston: Houghton Mifflin.

Hodgson, B. (1990). Alaska's big spill: Can the wilderness heal? *National Geographic*, January, 5–43.

Holtman, R. B. (1950). *Napoleonic propaganda*. Baton Rouge, LA: Louisiana State University Press.

Hook, S. (1989). Remember location, location, location? Forget it, now it's image, image, image. *Marketing News*. December 4, 2.

Horovitz, B. (1990). Ad agency helping David-sized clients battle Goliaths. *Los Angeles Times*, May 17, D1, D17.

Horton, C. (1990). Apple's bold "1984" scores on all fronts. *Advertising Age*, January 1, 12, 38.

Howard, H. A. (1941). *The saga of Chief Joseph*. Lincoln, NE: University of Nebraska Press.

Iacocca, L. (1984). *Iacocca: An autobiography*. New York: Bantam.

————. (1988). *Talking straight*. New York: Bantam.

————. (1990). Let's end the "Poltroonery." *Newsweek*, April 16, 10.

Ingrassia, L. (1988). Ice cream makers' rivalry heating up. *Wall Street Journal*, December 21, B1.

Innes, H. (1969). *The conquistadors*. New York: Knopf.

Jacobs, F. (1991). If advertisers made use of old masters. *Mad Super Special*, Summer, 78–81.

Jacobson, G. (1989). Holy bootlegger! What a lot of phony batstuff. *Business Week*, July 17, 70.

Janos, L. (1974). The gathered tribes. *Time*, September 23, 64, 69.

Jennings, D. C. (1969). *Free ice water! The story of Ted and Bill Hustead's Wall Drug*. Aberdeen, SD: North Plains Press.

Johnson, R. (1990). Hollywood hot to make film bio of Andy Warhol. *San Francisco Chronicle*, March 19, F1.

Jones, R. A. (1986). Home-grown airplane is like no other. *Los Angeles Times*, December 24, 1, 6.

Kilian, M. (1990). Philadelphia honors Benjamin Franklin. *San Francisco Examiner*, March 4, T8–T9.

Kershner, V. (1990). Defense cuts promise "golden age." *San Francisco Chronicle*, March 1, A1, A4.

Kessler, F. (1986). The costly coupon craze. *Fortune*, June 9, 83.

Knipe, T. (1990). Mass appeal: Building steel-belted houses. *Calypso Log*, October, 14–17, 22.

Koepp, S. (1988). Do you believe in magic? *Time*, April 25, 66–73.

Kotler, P., Armstrong, G. (1990). *Marketing: An introduction*, 2nd ed. Englewood Cliffs, NJ: Prentice Hall.

Kroll, J. (1987). The most famous artist. *Newsweek*, March 9, 64–66.

LaSalle, M. (1990). A whole lotta lambada goin' on. *San Francisco Chronicle*, March 19, F1.

Lawrence, T. E. (1926). *Seven pillars of wisdom*. New York: Dell.

Lee, D. B. (1989). Tragedy in Alaska waters. *National Geographic*, August, 260–263.

Leerhsen, C. (1989). How Disney does it. *Newsweek*, April 3, 48–54.

Levin, G. (1990). Capitalists warm up to Gorby. *Advertising Age*, June 4, 1, 52.

Levinson, J. C. (1989). *Guerilla marketing attack*. Boston: Houghton Mifflin.

Lidz, F. (1986). Deliver us from Evel. *Sports Illustrated*, March 17, 8–10.

Loder, K. (1987). Andy Warhol: 1928–1987. *Rolling Stone*, April 9, 31–36.

Lord, D. (1990). The truths and myths about Ben Franklin. *The Old Farmer's Almanac*, 44–47.

Loro, L. (1990). Volvo survives "monsters." *Advertising Age*, November 12, 77.

Los Angeles Times (1990). Drexel bonuses create furor. *San Francisco Chronicle*, February 22, C1, C16.

Lowry, J. (1988). Survey finds most powerful brands. *Advertising Age*, July 11, 31.

Mabry, M. (1990). Remembrance of ads past. *Newsweek*, July 30, 42.

Mabry, M., Glick, D., Lewis, S. D. (1990). Fighting ads in the inner city. *Newsweek*, February 5, 46.

Machiavelli, N. (1910). *The prince*. In *Harvard classics*, vol. 36. New York: Collier.

Magiera, M. (1990a). Coming attractions: Movie tie-ins galore. *Advertising Age*, May 28, 1, 58.

————. (1990b). Bo Jackson × 15 = Nike's newest ad, which also includes a solo Sonny Bono. *Advertising Age*, June 25, 4.

Mann, N. R. (1989). *The keys to excellence: The story of the Deming Philosophy*. Los Angeles: Prestwick.

Marbach, W., McAlevey, P. (1986). Around the world in 11 days. *Newsweek*, September 22, 86–88.

Marinucci, C. (1990). Cookie monsters. *Image*, March 11, 10–21.

McMahon, B. (1990). HDTV: Worth all the fuss? *San Francisco Examiner*, April 29, D1, D5.

McMahon, E. (1989). *Ed McMahon's superselling*. Englewood Cliffs, NJ: Prentice Hall.

Melnea, J. K., Enzer, M. J. (1986). Building brand franchises. *Marketing Communications*, April, 42.

Merims, A. M. (1972). Marketing's stepchild: Product publicity. *Harvard Business Review*, November-December, 111–112.

Messner, R. (1979). *Everest*. New York: Oxford University Press.

————. (1981). I climbed Everest alone . . . at my limit. *National Geographic*, October, 552–566.

————, Gogna, A. (1981). *K2: Mountain of mountains*. New York: Oxford University Press.

Meyer, E. (1981). Sum of year's events tip off coming trends. *Advertising Age*, May 4, 66.

Michaels, J. W. (1990). With all thy getting, don't take yourself too seriously. *Forbes*, March 19, 116–121.

Michaelson, G. A. (1987). *Winning the marketing war: A field manual for business leaders*. Lanham, MD: Abt, Madison.

Miller, A., Gleizes, F., Bradburn E. (1990a). Perrier loses its fizz. *Newsweek*, February 26, 53.

————, Gordon, J., Annin, P., Springen, K. (1990b). Advertising goes to war. *Newsweek*, September 24, 66.

————, Smith, V. E. (1990). The soda war fizzes up. *Newsweek*, March 19, 38.

————, Tsiantar, D., Springen, K., Hager, M., Robins, K. (1990c). Oat-bran heartburn. *Newsweek*, January 29, 50–52.

Miller, C. (1989). Cereal maker to kids: Eat breakfast with Barbie. *Marketing News*, September 25, 10.

————. (1990). Consumers ambushed by life-size popcorn bags! *Marketing News*, August 20, 2, 5.

Miller, F. (1986). *Batman: The dark knight returns*. New York: DC Comics.

Miller, M. (1989). A brief spin—and hint of future travel. *Sacramento Bee*, May 11, B1, B4.

Minsky, T. (1989). Batguy. *Premiere*, July, 48–55.

Mordoff, K. F. (1986). Voyager set for world record attempt following five-day evaluation flight. *Aviation Week & Space Technology*, July 21, 26.

Morganthau, T. (1990). Sullivan: Bush's aide makes waves. *Newsweek*, March 5, 19.

Morgenson, G. (1989). Sacrificial brand. *Forbes*, February 6, 41–42.

————, Eisenstodt, G. (1990). Profits are for rape and pillage. *Forbes*, March 5, 94–100.

Mullins, J. (1990). Spunky shopper climbs billboard & clips world's largest coupon. *National Enquirer*, October 16, 5.

Murphy, J. (1986). Hail to the mountain king. *Time*, October 27, 106.

Nickels, W. G. (1984). *Marketing communication and promotion*, 3rd ed. New York: Wiley.

Nolte, C. (1990). Crews, good weather keep oil off beaches. *San Francisco Chronicle*, February 10, A1, A10.

Nussbaum, B. (1988). Smart design: Quality is the new style. *Business Week*, April 11, 102–108.

Ogilvy, D. (1963, 1988). *Confessions of an advertising man*. New York: Atheneum.

———. (1983). *Ogilvy on advertising*. New York: Crown.

Pahwa, A. (1990). Boom generation more receptive to quality TV ads. *Marketing News*, September 17, 8, 18.

Parfit, M. (1990). Earth First!ers wield a mean monkey wrench. *Smithsonian*, April, 184–204.

Parrish, M., Kraul, C. (1990). Three tuna firms vow to save dolphins. *San Francisco Chronicle*, April 13, A1, A20.

Patti, C. H., Moriarty, S. E. (1990). *The making of effective advertising*. Englewood Cliffs, NJ: Prentice Hall.

Pearson, M. M. (1981). Ten distribution myths. *Business Horizons*, May–June, 17–23.

Pelline, J. (1990). Timber company to lay off 195. *San Francisco Chronicle*, March 29, C1.

Perlman, D. (1990). Space telescope being readied for April launch. *San Francisco Chronicle*, March 6, A1, A5.

Peters, T. J., Waterman, R. H. (1982). *In search of excellence: Lessons from America's best run companies*. New York: Harper & Row.

Postman, D. (1989). Exxon's cleanup claims disputed. *Sacramento Bee*, July 3, A6.

Powell, B., Smith, V. E., McAlevey, P. (1987). Turner's windless sails. *Newsweek*, 46–47.

Putnam, J. J. (1982). Napoleon. *National Geographic*, February, 142–189.

Quelch, J. A. (1989). *Sales Promotion Management*. Englewood Cliffs, NJ: Prentice Hall.

Reagan, E. (1990). Examining the moisture managers. *Outside Business*, April, 37–46.

Ressner, J. (1988). Jackson boosting the Beatles. *Rolling Stone*, March 24, 35, 37.

Revett, J. (1983). Marlboro country to main street. *Advertising Age*, August 8, M19–M21.

Reynolds, M. E. (1990). *Earthship: How to build your own*, vol. 1. Taos, NM: Solar Survival Press.

Ries, A., Trout J. (1986). *Marketing warfare*. New York: McGraw-Hill.

Roberts, W. (1985). *Leadership secrets of Attila the Hun*. New York: Warner.

Rosi, O., ed. (1979). *Sales promotion handbook*, 7th ed. Chicago: Dartnell.

Rossabi, M. (1988). *Khubilai Khan: His life and times*. Berkeley: University of California Press.

Rossiter, J. R., Percy, L. (1987). *Advertising and promotion management*. New York: McGraw-Hill.

Russell, D. (1960). *The lives and legends of Buffalo Bill*. Norman, OK: University of Oklahoma Press.

Russell, S. (1990). Companies win environmental awards. *San Francisco Chronicle*, March 30, C1, C4.

Schafer, J. S. (1969). What the editor thinks about publicity. *Public Relations Journal*, January, 22–24.

Schlossberg, H. (1990a). Segmenting becomes constitutional issue. *Marketing News*, April 16, 1–2.

———. (1990b). Pepperidge Farm wins Grand Edison. *Marketing News*, May 14, 12–13.

Sell, H. B., Weybright, V. (1979). *Buffalo Bill and the wild west*. Basin, WY: Big Horn Books.

Serafin, R., Levin, G. (1990). Ad industry suffers crushing blow. *Advertising Age*, November 12, 1, 76–77.

Seymour, D. T., ed. (1989). *The pricing decision: A strategic planner for marketing professionals*. Chicago: Probus.

Shales, T. (1990a). Field day for commercials. *San Francisco Chronicle*, January 30, E1.

———. (1990b). Overblown commercials fill air time. *San Francisco Chronicle*, July 19, E1–E2.

Sherman, S. P. (1987). Ted Turner: TV's boldest gambler bets the plantation. *Fortune*, January 5, 104.

Shimp, T. A. (1990). *Promotion management and marketing communications*. Chicago: Dryden.

Sims, G. (1989). A clot in the heart of the earth. *Outside*, June, 39–42, 95, 100–105.

Singer, H. N., DeBruicker, F. S. (1981). L'eggs Products, Inc. In E. R. Corey, C. H. Lovelock, S. Ward, eds. *Problems in marketing*, 6th ed. New York: McGraw-Hill.

Skenazy, L. (1988). B & H bedtime stories. *Advertising Age*, May 9, 102.

Slutsky, J. (1984). *Streetfighting: Low cost advertising/promotions for your business*. Englewood Cliffs, NJ: Prentice Hall.

Smith, L. (1989). Forbes planning another big party. *San Francisco Chronicle*, E1.

Soares, E. J. (1988). *Cost-effective marketing research: A guide for marketing managers*. New York: Quorum.

———. (1989). Marketing communications in the 90's: The number one professional opportunity for business communicators. Paper presented at the International Convention of the Association for Business Communication, Las Vegas, NV, November 5–9.

Stein, K. J. (1986). Custom systems to aid Voyager in unrefueled record attempt. *Aviation Week and Space Technology*, December 22, 18–21.

Telzer, R. (1987). Rebates challenge coupons' redeeming values. *Advertising Age*, March 23, S18–S20.

Ticer, S., Symonds, W. C., Finch, P., Lieberman, D. (1989). Captain comeback. *Business Week*, July 17, 98–106.

Tompkins, P. (1976). *Mysteries of the Mexican pyramids*. New York: Harper & Row.

Townsend, R. (1970). *Up the organization: How to stop the corporation from stifling people and strangling profits*. Greenwich, CT: Fawcett.

Turner, M. (1990). Turner's gamble proves a dynamite bet. *Peninsula Mid-Week*, April 2, 1, 2.

Vella, C. M., McGonagle, J. J. (1987). *Improved business planning using competitive intelligence*. New York: Quorum.

Von Clausewitz, C. (1966). *On war*. London: Routledge & Kegan Paul.

Walley, W. (1987). Freberg's back on target with non-advertising. *Advertising Age*, April 6, 60.

————. (1989). TV production costs up. *Advertising Age*, July 31, 8.

Washington Post. (1990). All Perrier water in U.S. being recalled. *San Francisco Chronicle*, February 10, A1, A14.

Waters, H. F. (1990). Down to the sea in shtik: MTV's undry humor. *Newsweek*, March 19, 55.

Weinberger, C. W. (1990). Malcolm Forbes. *Forbes*, March 19, 25.

Weinstein, H. (1990). Northrop Corp. pleads guilty in defense fraud—huge fine. *San Francisco Chronicle*, February 28, A9.

Whittemore, H. (1990). Ted Turner stalks his target. *This World*, July 15, 9–12.

Widner, D. (1988). The test of his mettle. *Pursuits*, Spring, 6–8.

Wiggins, K. (1990). Wave of the future. *San Francisco Chronicle*, March 19, E1–E2.

Williams, L. (1990). America paralyzed by choices. *San Francisco Chronicle*, February 14, A1, A10.

Wolfe, T. (1979). *The right stuff*. New York: Bantam.

Worthington, C. (1990). Personal interview. March 16.

Yeager, J., Rutan, D. (1987). *Voyager*. New York: Knopf.

Zaltman, G., Wallendorf, M. (1979). *Consumer behavior: Basic findings and management implications*. New York: Wiley.

Ziglar, Z. (1984). *Zig Ziglar's secrets of closing the sale*. New York: Berkley.

Index

About the Author

ERIC J. SOARES is Chairman of the Marketing Department at California State University, Hayward. He is the author of *Cost-Effective Marketing Research* (Quorum, 1988).